Praise for *The Recipe Hacker Confidential*

"Staying away from harmful foods like gluten, soy, and sugar can seem challenging, but with the help of Diana's recipes this has become a breeze in my home. When my kids ask for a specific food, I know Diana already has the perfect recipe created. If health, fat loss, and ease in the kitchen is your goal, this cookbook is a must-have in your home."

—**ISABEL DE LOS RIOS**, BeyondDiet.com

"Diana's first book, *The Recipe Hacker*, has been an inspiration as a chef and author. With her new book, *The Recipe Hacker Con idential*, she unveils even more secret dishes. On top of that, she also reveals HOW to hack recipes, so that you can 'break the code' and impress your family and friends. One more thing . . . I'm a professional chef, and honestly, I don't know how she comes up with such awesome recipes without grains, gluten, dairy, soy, or cane sugar! Diana really shows the world how easy it is to cook family dishes that are both delicious and super good for you."

—**CHEF GUI ALINAT**

THE
Recipe Hacker
CONFIDENTIAL

Break the Code to Cooking
Mouthwatering & Good-for-You
Meals without Grains, Gluten,
Dairy, Soy, or Cane Sugar

DIANA KEUILIAN

BenBella Books, Inc.
Dallas, TX

BenBella Books, Inc.
10440 N. Central Expy., Suite 800
Dallas, TX 75231
www.benbellabooks.com
Send feedback to feedback@benbellabooks.com

Printed in the United States of America
10 9 8 7 6 5 4 3 2 1

Library of Congress Cataloging-in-Publication Data
Names: Keuilian, Diana, 1981- author.
Title: The recipe hacker confidential : break the code to cooking
    mouthwatering & good-for-you meals without grains, gluten, dairy, soy, or
    cane sugar / Diana Keuilian.
Description: Dallas, TX : BenBella Books, Inc., [2016] | Includes
    bibliographical references and index. | Cooking.
Identifiers: LCCN 2016024952 (print) | LCCN 2016044508 (ebook) | ISBN
    9781942952756 (trade paper : alk. paper) | ISBN 9781942952763 (electronic)
Subjects: LCSH: Health. | LCGFT: Cookbooks.
Classification: LCC TX714 .K494 2016 (print) | LCC TX714 (ebook) | DDC
    641.5—dc23
LC record available at https://lccn.loc.gov/2016024952

Editing by Rachel Holtzman
Copyediting by Karen Levy
Proofreading by Karen Wise and Amy Zarkos
Indexing by Jigsaw Information
Text design and composition by Silver Feather Design
Cover design by Sarah Dombrowsky
Cover photo, top photo on page 3, and author photo by Edmyr Barayang
Photo on page v by Erin Jones Photography
Food photography and other photos by Diana Keuilian
Printed by Versa Press

Distributed by Perseus Distribution
www.perseusdistribution.com
To place orders through Perseus Distribution:
Tel: (800) 343-4499 | Fax: (800) 351-5073
E-mail: orderentry@perseusbooks.com

Special discounts for bulk sales (minimum of 25 copies) are available.
Please contact Aida Herrera at aida@benbellabooks.com.

Before we get started, I'd like to thank the magical people in my life.

My husband, Bedros Keuilian: You inspire me; you teach me; you challenge me; and you make me laugh every single day. I'll be eternally grateful that we walked into the same gym fifteen years ago!

Our babies, Andrew and Chloe: You also inspire me, teach me, challenge me, and make me laugh every single day!

You three fill my life with sweetness and meaning. I love you so, so much.

I'd also like to dedicate this new cookbook to you, reader, and your real-food journey.

You're living in a toxic food culture, where processed and denatured foods are convenient, cheap, and plentiful; where eating healthfully takes focused intention, forethought, and creativity. It's easier to settle for a life lived on packaged foods than to consciously seek out wholesome nourishment; to eat the way of the masses rather than forging your own path. But indifference to nutrition comes at a precious cost, and as obesity and its related diseases become ordinary, sooner or later a reckoning day will arrive, and you will be confronted with the very real, very grim consequences of this modern diet.

I don't want this for you. You deserve better.

And luckily, there is a solution.

It is time to return to a diet that is primarily composed of unadulterated, real food. It is time to stand up for your health. It is time to swim against the current.

My goal with this book is to provide you with recipes, inspiration, tools, and tips to get you moving in the right direction on your real-food journey. Feeling the synergistic power of a real-food diet is only one meal away.

Let's do this!

CONTENTS

THE RECIPES

INTRODUCTION: WELCOME TO
THE RECIPE HACKER CONFIDENTIAL

A FORK IN THE ROAD . . .

Why did you pick up this book and crack it open? Was it the scrumptious-looking food on the cover? Or was it my mischievous smile? (Ha!) Those reasons are fun, but I'm betting you have something bigger on your mind—a real need for change. My guess is that something's got to give. Maybe your weight is higher than ever, you are beginning to dread doctor visits more and more, or you're dealing with food allergies and possible concerns about autoimmune disease. Or maybe your family has recently experienced a health crisis. Or your children are eating the way they see you eat and are headed down a worrisome path. Regardless of what got you this far, the solution hinges on one thing . . . **your diet**. As in the foods that you've cooked and enjoyed for decades, the meals that you've shared with family and friends through the good times and the bad.

You need to change the way you cook and eat.

You are not alone. The current health crisis in our society makes it pretty clear that our modern diet is doing a lot of harm. As obesity and chronic disease become the norm, we have to ask ourselves what we are collectively doing wrong when it comes to the foods that we choose to eat. The facts show us that we live in a toxic food environment, and the future is looking pretty bleak for our children and our children's children if we don't make swift and steady strides to get back on track to a wholesome, healthy way of eating. It sounds daunting, but here's the fact of the matter: If we all started making 80 percent of our meals at home and cut out the grains, dairy, soy, gluten, and cane sugar from our kitchens (which we'll talk about in *much* more detail later on), we could nip obesity and obesity-related diseases in the bud in one generation. So why not start now?

It makes little difference if you are beginning this real journey for your vanity—because you want to lose weight and look amazing for the first time in your life—or if you're making changes because of health concerns. Either way, your results will be spectacular, and you'll be very glad that you began.

That said, I don't blame you for feeling a significant amount of resistance to the idea of changing the foods that you cook and eat. Food is fuel, but it's also so much more than that—it's love. It's comfort. It's tradition. It's fun. It's enjoyment. It's quite literally a part of who you are.

Changing how you cook and eat feels like changing who you are . . . and that's scary.

But guess what? I'm here now! It's you and me, friend. Give me your hand, and let's take the first few steps of your real-food journey together, right here in the pages of this book. I'll let you in on all of my secrets to cooking and eating really healthy and delicious meals, and you'll discover a whole new healthy, slimmed-down you—not to mention a slew of new recipes that will quickly become family favorites.

Why does real food matter? Why invest time and money to swim against the current of the modern diet? It's a laborious pursuit that requires strong motivating forces.

My personal food journey doesn't have a singular incentive; rather, it's a compilation of desired results that have a shared requirement: to eschew industrialized products in favor of real food.

For me, it is about achieving a lean and disease-free body. It's an aspiration to see my children spared from the afflictions of the overfed. It's apprehension over the effects of fake foods on the human race. It's a yearning for honest, uncomplicated food made from a handful of pronounceable ingredients.

All larger motivators aside, I feel my best when partaking in a real-food diet, and that is often incentive enough.

I'm so happy to be here with you as you begin your journey to a diet filled with real, wholesome foods.

SAYING GOODBYE TO GRAINS, GLUTEN, DAIRY, SOY, AND REFINED SUGAR

There are five foods in your diet that are causing you to gain weight, are killing your metabolism, and are keeping you tired. I like to call these the *toxic five*. Once you eliminate these foods from your diet, your body naturally shrinks down to its ideal weight and healthy shape.

GLUTEN

Gluten is a grain protein that often triggers an immune response. In theory, that's not such a bad thing, but over time, this can wear on your body's protective systems and lead to a host of health problems. These can include things like bloating, leaky gut syndrome, and weight gain. Gluten is found in foods containing grains, such as commercial baked goods, breads, pastas, and cereals. (More on grains below.)

GRAINS

Because grains convert to sugars, a diet filled with grains puts stress on your body's insulin regulation mechanism, which leaves you susceptible to weight gain and diabetes. It's also easy to find yourself bloated after eating grains, since these items are also high in calories and carbs and contain "antinutrient" compounds that interfere with your body's digestion and absorption of nutrients.

DAIRY

According to *USA Today*, 75 percent of adults have a decrease in lactase activity. Why does this matter? Because without lactase, your body can't properly digest calorie-rich dairy products, and this means painful, bloated belly syndrome that adds inches to your waistline.

SOY

Soy has a high concentration of goitrogens, which block the production of thyroid hormones. When your thyroid hormone production is low, your energy gets zapped, your metabolism crashes, and weight gain becomes automatic.

REFINED SUGAR

Research continues to prove that sugar is making AND keeping you fat, in addition to making your body bloated and puffy. And then, of course, there's diabetes, which now affects more and more people worldwide, including children. Refined sugar comes in many forms, such as white sugar, brown sugar, brown rice syrup, cane sugar, evaporated cane juice, raw cane sugar, corn syrup, corn syrup solids, and high-fructose corn syrup.

FIVE THINGS YOU SHOULD KNOW ABOUT ME

I suppose I should introduce myself, seeing as how we just committed to spending more than 250 pages together, but I'll stick with the CliffsNotes version so that we can get on to the tasty stuff!

1) I'M A HACKER . . . OF RECIPES. What is recipe hacking? It's the art of taking a traditional recipe that's made with processed ingredients and replicating it using only wholesome ingredients. A successfully hacked recipe will have the same look, feel, and flavor of the original. It's a way to stack the nutritional benefits in your favor, while enjoying essentially the same beloved food item.

I've been hacking recipes since 2009 and have conquered enchiladas, pizza, muffins, cakes, cookies, and much more. To this day I have yet to find a recipe that I couldn't hack, though some recipes are certainly more challenging than others!

2) I STARTED COOKING AT A VERY YOUNG AGE BUT NEVER HAD ANY FORMAL TRAINING. Unless you count high school Home Ec, from which I was kicked out of class multiple times for not following recipes correctly (my way was going to be better) and repeatedly eating raw cookie dough (salmonella who?). You'll find my recipes to be quick and simple enough for anyone to make—no chef's training needed here. Because some nights you need to make dinner on the fly while helping the kids with their homework at the kitchen table!

Hi, I'm Diana, and they call me The Recipe Hacker!

3) I'M NOT TECHNICAL, AND I USE THE LEAST AMOUNT OF PRECISION NECESSARY. If you read my first book, *The Recipe Hacker*, then you'll remember my self-given nickname of The Lazy Chef. Until I started recipe blogging, I didn't even own measuring cups. I think it's so much more fun to rely on instincts and to throw in what feels right, but don't worry—I have since invested in measuring instruments and will supply all the measurements for you. But if you start to feel confident with the new ingredients, then get crazy, let your hair down, and throw in a handful instead of a cupful.

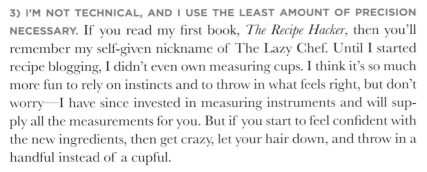

My baking debut back in the eighties!

4) I'M NOT PERFECT—NOT AT EATING HEALTHY OR AT ANYTHING ELSE! The bookstore shelves are filled with books written by idealized health gurus, but I'm not one of them. I'm a busy mom and business owner, a real human just like you, doing what I can to make healthy eating fun for my two kids. A "real-food journey" is just that, a journey, and one that I'm still on. I still have cheat days. I love going to fancy restaurants and ordering the tasting menu with zero concern about the ingredients that the chef dazzles us with. What I focus on is the day-to-day cooking and eating at home with the family and on creating high-fiber, high-protein, low-carb, and low-sugar versions of our

Chloe, my little Recipe Hacker Jr!

Making healthy eating eating fun for my babies: Andrew and Chloe

favorite traditional recipes so that everyday meals feel satisfying, healthy, delicious, and exciting.

5) I HAVE A PURPOSE—TO HELP YOU LEARN TO COOK, EAT, AND LOVE HEALTHIER FOODS. I earned my nickname of "Recipe Hacker" because I have a burning passion for tweaking recipes to make them healthier and more delicious. I want to see our society get fitter, leaner, and stronger. So let's remember what real food tastes like. Let's stand up to big businesses and their subpar food products. Let's give our families the best nutrition that will then translate into the best health. We only get to live once, so let's make it count!

RealHealthyRecipes.com

Like my Facebook page for new recipes, tips, and motivation!

GETTING STARTED:
SECRETS FROM THE RECIPE HACKER

When making lifestyle changes, there's a tendency to focus on the negative of losing. Yes, many of the foods that you currently love to eat—pasta, burgers, milkshakes—are on the do-not-fly list. But instead of focusing on the empty space that was once filled with something beloved, I prefer to start by talking about all of the NEW and amazing things that your diet is going to include.

For every packaged, processed, and refined food that you give the boot to, a wholesome, fresh, and vibrant food will take its place. That's why this way of eating works—because there are no gaps. If you want a chocolate-glazed doughnut, you can darn well eat a CHOCOLATE-GLAZED DOUGHNUT (page 50). If Thursday was Hamburger Helper night, well, Thursday is now HAMBURGER CASSEROLE night (page 120). If packaged peanut butter cups are your nightly indulgence, well, HOMEMADE PEANUT BUTTER CUPS (page 226) are now your nightly indulgence.

You don't have to be deprived. You shouldn't be deprived. But you do need to begin to expect more from your food. Expect that it should taste great while providing you with superb nutrition.

If your relationship with food is currently adversarial (it is for most people), then get ready for a group hug, because you and food are about to become besties with a mutual interest in your long-term health as well as your short-term satisfaction. You *should* and *can* have it all when it comes to food. And I'm going to show you how.

A big piece of the puzzle is simply being prepared. Once you've filled your fridge and pantry with delicious ingredients, gotten some useful tools, and picked out some tasty recipes from this book, there's not much keeping you from a new way of eating. When you switch over to eating only real food, your eating habits won't fundamentally change; rather, the change will be in the specifics. You'll still have go-to fast meals, favorite quick snacks, basic meal recipes, and even favorite indulgences. The only difference is that your new "same foods" don't promote weight gain and are better for your health. It's really cool when you begin to love the new, real-food options more than your old unhealthy ones!

Eating real food is not boring. If I want a piece of bread, I simply make some ALMOND BREAD (page 43) and enjoy one small slice. If I want a brownie, I make it with a bit of raw honey and nuts. Real-food dishes are spectacular! Sure, these new recipes will taste a little different than your old favorites, but soon your palate grows accustomed to the new flavors.

Before we jump into the more than 120 new and scrumptious recipes in this book, I'm going to spill all of my secrets to eating healthy, hacking recipes, and making strides on your real-food journey.

Let's take healthy eating by storm! Let's clear all the junk out of your cupboards! Let's stock your fridge with wholesome eats! Do you feel me? Are you pumped?! Alright, friend, let's do this thing!

RECIPE HACKER SECRET #1: START WITH A CLEAN SLATE

Making a massive, life-altering improvement to your diet is no joke. It requires courage. It requires strength. It requires commitment. It requires burning your ships, giving you no choice but to press forward into the unknown.

How do you burn your ships? By clearing out all of the toxic foods from your home, kitchen, car, pantry, and secret stash (you know the one).

Take a big garbage bag or a box and round up the following:

> › Packaged and processed foods: snack items, candy bars, chips, crackers, etc.
> › Grains and gluten: all-purpose flour, bread, rolls, noodles, rice, cereals, etc.
> › Dairy: milk, cheese, yogurt, cream, ice cream, etc.
> › Soy: soy sauce, dressings, tofu, packaged foods, etc.
> › Cane sugar: cookies, cakes, candy, packaged foods, etc.

Now stand back and admire the environment that you have just created. When was the last time your home was free of all packaged and processed foods? For many, the answer to that question is *never*!

Sure, processed and packaged foods deliver in taste, convenience, and inexpensive cost—but by ripping open that bag of Cheetos or M&M's, you're putting your body on a crash course toward obesity, diabetes, heart disease, and more.

If we truly desire to change our eating habits from the inside out, then the first step is to clear the toxic food items out of our immediate environment. It must be done!

And now to fill the blank spaces back up with food worth getting excited about.

RECIPE HACKER SECRET #2: FILL YOUR PANTRY WITH THESE NEW INGREDIENTS

I am not in favor of deprivation as a means of losing weight. This is partly because I simply love food way too much to rob myself of it. But it's mainly due to the fact that when we eat real, wholesome foods, it is very possible to do so in an enjoyable way. All it takes is becoming familiar with a few new and exciting ingredients that will help you create your favorite dishes in a way that is grain-free, gluten-free, dairy-free, soy-free, and cane sugar–free. You'll see these ingredients pop up throughout the recipes in this book, and they include:

BLANCHED ALMOND FLOUR Blanched almonds are ground to create a fine powder that's high in protein and low in carbohydrates, while containing healthy servings of manganese, monounsaturated fats, and vitamin E.

ALMOND MEAL Raw almonds (with skins) are ground to create a fine powder. This is darker in color and heavier in consistency than blanched almond flour, but it can still be subbed 1:1. Just be careful when subbing either form of almond flour for wheat flour. It's always best to use recipes specifically designed for almond flour in order to ensure success!

COCONUT FLOUR Dried and defatted coconut meat is ground to create this fine powder that's high in fiber and low in digestible carbohydrates. Coconut flour requires an equal ratio of flour to liquid, because it absorbs so much more liquid than traditional flours. There isn't a simple equation to use when replacing wheat flour with coconut flour, so it's best to use recipes that are specifically designed to use coconut flour. Most recipes will use a percentage of coconut flour in conjunction with another flour on this list to create pleasing moisture and texture.

ARROWROOT STARCH I like using this grain-free flour in conjunction with almond flour to lighten the texture of baked goods. You can also use it to thicken sauces, and it can be subbed 1:1 for cornstarch.

FLAXSEED MEAL Composed of ground flaxseeds, flaxseed meal is full of nutritional benefits, including omega-3 essential fatty acids and both soluble and insoluble fiber. I often use flaxseed meal as a grain-free flour, though never for more than 25 percent of a recipe's flour to prevent it from becoming too grainy. Flaxseed meal is also fantastic for replacing eggs in baking. To replace one egg, simply whisk 1 tablespoon flaxseed meal with 3 tablespoons water.

NUTRITIONAL YEAST These big, tasty, yellow flakes are fantastic for adding savory, nutty, cheesy flavor to dairy-free dishes. It also contains a nice serving of vitamin B$_{12}$.

COCONUT PALM SUGAR Also sold as "coconut crystals" and "coconut sugar," this is made from the nectar of coconut tree blossoms. It's a wholesome, 1:1 replacement for refined cane sugar that retains many nutrients, such as iron, zinc, potassium, and calcium, and is known to be a low-glycemic sweetener (meaning it won't raise blood sugar levels as high as refined sugar does). However, coconut sugar still contains calories and fructose, so we will use it sparingly.

RAW HONEY A wholesome sweetener that is unrefined, pure, and natural, raw honey contains live enzymes, vitamins, minerals, and antioxidants. When used in baking recipes, I nearly always melt it gently in a lazy man's double boiler (see page 221). As with coconut palm sugar, it's important to watch how much raw honey you use, because it is calorie-rich and filled with fructose.

PURE MAPLE SYRUP This healthy sweetener is filled with nutrients and minerals. However, beware of the many maple-*flavored* syrups that are simply corn syrup in disguise—avoid at all costs! Pure maple syrup is better for you than corn syrup or refined cane sugar, but it still needs to be used sparingly.

STEVIA I have found stevia to be one of the most misunderstood sweeteners on the market today, with many people assuming that it is artificial and therefore unhealthy. Yes, there are brands that combine stevia with artificial sweeteners, so be sure to select organic, pure stevia. Stevia comes from a simple plant, one that you could grow in your garden. Place one of the leaves from the stevia plant on your tongue and you'll instantly understand where the sweet flavor of stevia comes from! It has zero calories, is potently sweet, and comes in both liquid and powdered form. Some people complain that stevia has an aftertaste; however, I have found that by combining it with another sweetener such as coconut palm sugar or raw honey, much of the aftertaste is removed.

DARK AND UNSWEETENED CHOCOLATE You probably already know this, but chocolate—when it's not loaded up with sugar—does contain some health benefits! My dessert recipes call for very dark chocolate, or even unsweetened chocolate, and then add in wholesome sweeteners and stevia to taste. This way, the benefits of the chocolate are preserved while keeping sugars and calories low. Oh, you're welcome!

CANNED COCONUT MILK I use quite a bit of canned coconut milk in my recipes because it's an ideal dairy replacement. I prefer Thai Kitchen, organic and full-fat. When chilled overnight, the cream and liquid separate easily. I make it a habit to keep three or four cans of coconut milk in the fridge at all times so that whenever I need cream in a recipe, I simply grab one, turn it over to open from the bottom, then pour out the liquid and scoop out the cream. So handy!

COCONUT AMINOS Made from the sap of a coconut tree, coconut aminos are my go-to replacement for soy sauce in savory dishes.

COCONUT OIL Coconut oil is widely acknowledged as a superfood, and its health benefits from a unique blend of fatty acids continue to impress researchers. From its helpfulness with weight loss, better brain functioning, and improved cholesterol levels, organic unrefined coconut oil deserves to be a staple in your kitchen. You'll find it as the most widely used ingredient in this book, from CRAB CAKE EGGS BENEDICT (page 26) to GINGERSNAPS (page 216).

QUINOA Often mistaken for a grain, quinoa is actually a nutrient-rich, gluten-free seed. It's a complete protein, containing all nine essential amino acids in addition to being filled with healthy fiber. I like to occasionally serve quinoa as you would rice, sometimes combined with cauliflower rice. It's also really fun to bake with quinoa! In the upcoming pages, you'll find quinoa in everything from muffins, to energy bars, to meatballs.

APPLE CIDER VINEGAR What makes apple cider vinegar healthier than regular vinegar? For starters, it contains amino acids, antioxidants, and potassium. It's also said to promote healthy immune and digestive function and help maintain a healthy weight. Choose organic, unpasteurized, unfiltered apple cider vinegar for the highest quality and most nutritional benefits.

NATURAL SALT (SEA SALT OR PINK HIMALAYAN SALT) All salt is not created equal. Whereas table salt contains chemicals and artificial iodine, natural salts like sea salt and pink Himalayan salt offer up trace natural elements that work synergistically with your body in promoting good health. To save space I list "sea salt" in my recipes, but pink Himalayan salt is equally welcomed—it just takes so much longer to type!

HERBS AND SPICES Is your spice rack stocked with a variety of fresh and organic herbs and spices? If not, you're missing out on another opportunity to pack delicious flavor into your food. The only rule: replace your dried herbs and spices every year to ensure the highest quality of flavor. Here are the herbs and spices used in this book:

Allspice	Cumin	Oregano
Basil	Fennel Seed	Red Pepper
Black Pepper	Garlic Powder	Rosemary
Cajun Seasoning	Ginger	Saffron Strands
Cardamom	Italian Seasoning	Smoked Paprika
Chili Powder	Marjoram	Sweet Paprika
Chinese Five-Spice	Mint	Thyme
Cinnamon	Mustard Powder	Turmeric
Cloves	Nutmeg	Unsweetened Cocoa
Coriander	Onion	White Pepper

FRESH PRODUCE Throughout this cookbook you will find many new and exciting ways to serve fresh produce. We will turn zucchini, butternut squash, and sweet potatoes into low-carb, high-fiber noodles. We will shred cauliflower into rice. We will press fresh produce into juice. We will sauté, bake, broil, chop, slice, and puree fresh, organic veggies and fruits into tantalizing dishes filled with rich, crave-worthy flavors. Stick with me and you'll see how to promote veggies from simple side dishes to the stars of your meals. As a rule of thumb, use local produce that is in season, and always choose fresh over canned in order to get the most nutritional benefit.

NUTS AND SEEDS To help us fill in the gap left by removing grains, we will often turn to nuts and seeds. Their nutritional benefits are plentiful, their flavors are deeply rich, and the recipe possibilities are endless. We will grind them into flour. We will soak them and blend them into cream. We will toast and chop and sprinkle. If you have an allergy to almonds (I'm sorry, that stinks), feel free to sub unsalted sunflower seeds. You can even grind them into an almond flour replacement.

LEAN PROTEINS Organic, hormone-free chicken, turkey, pork, fish, beef, lamb, bison, duck, shellfish, and eggs are all hearty, filling additions to a meal. Avoid processed meats, like lunchmeats, as these contain potentially harmful additives and lots of refined salt. Also just say no to highly processed fake meats made with soy.

. . . . **A WORD ON QUALITY** . . . .

I'm a big believer in purchasing the highest quality ingredients and in reading the fine print on all food labels. When it comes to meat and vegetables, which should make up the bulk of your diet, it's worth the extra expense to select local, organic, hormone-free, grass-fed, and free-range. You won't see those words in front of all the ingredients in the upcoming pages, but know that whenever they're an option, that's what I'm using. Your food will always come out tasting better while being more wholesome.

RECIPE HACKER SECRET #3: INVEST IN A FEW HANDY TOOLS

Creating recipes that are innovative and nontraditional requires some new tools. Here are the ones that I simply couldn't live without:

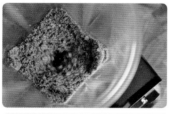

FOOD PROCESSOR A quality food processor is a must for shredding cauliflower, chopping nuts, creaming cashews, and combining dough.

SLOW COOKER Slow cooker recipes are a phenomenal way to spend less time in the kitchen while still getting a hot, home-cooked meal on the table each night. And slow cooker meals typically freeze well, so you can portion out leftovers for another day. I recommend getting a large one so that you're able to make a good amount of food with each recipe.

SPIRAL SLICER This magical contraption takes a regular vegetable and turns it into long, spaghetti-like noodles.

JUICE PRESS Daily green juice is an important part of my life, and a cold juice press is a household must.

MANDOLINE SLICER This gadget safely, quickly, and evenly slices produce into thin strips.

HIGH-SPEED BLENDER This is one investment that you'll be glad you made, especially when you're blending up a KAHLÚA SHAKE (page 248). A high-speed blender is necessary for creating smoothies, sauces, and soups.

DEHYDRATOR Dried fruits and veggies make nutritious on-the-go snacks, and making these at home is easy with the use of a dehydrator.

MINI MUFFIN PAN Baking mini muffins makes portion control a no-brainer. Plus, regular muffin pans have twelve tins while mini muffin pans have eighteen—so more bang for your buck!.

HIGH-QUALITY SKILLETS, CASSEROLE PANS, BAKING SHEETS Don't skimp here because the quality of your equipment can make or break the success of many dishes, mainly because of how heat conducts through cheaper materials. Look for nonstick skillets, glass casserole pans, and heavy, rimmed baking sheets.

HIGH-QUALITY KNIVES Any chef will tell you that a good, sharp knife is essential for efficient chopping, so go ahead and splurge here. Choose a non-stainless steel knife with a comfortable grip that feels nice and balanced in your hand. Use good knife-skill safety by keeping your fingers tucked away from the blade, and keep your knives sharpened for easier (and safer) chopping.

RECIPE HACKER SECRET #4: BUILD A BETTER MEAL

Traditional meals—those built around grains, gluten, and dairy and flavored with soy and cane sugar—are simply too rich, too filled with carbohydrates (not to mention various chemicals, allergens, and other not-good-for you things), and too high in calories to eat on a regular basis. When you do eat this way, it quickly adds up around your waist and makes you feel sluggish and drained of energy.

In the past, I would center my meals around grains, which would result in a heavier, starchier meal. Now my cooking is all about fresh vegetables, meats, fruits, nuts, and seeds. The end results are delicious yet light, and I'm not left with a bloated, full feeling.

The great news is that it is very possible to create delicious, good-for-you meals that aren't too rich, carb filled, or calorie dense. All it takes is a simple shift in how you compose your meals, and as a result you'll effortlessly shed pounds, enjoy the natural and steady energy produced by real food, and be delighted to discover that your new meals taste even better than the old ones.

There's only four steps to remember:

1) START WITH VEGGIES. Most people start with meat when it comes to menu planning, but a truly wholesome meal is planned around a pile of fresh veggies in some form or another. If your experience with veggies is limited to the grayish, lifeless ones from a can, then you're in for a treat—I have some fun, innovative ways to incorporate flavorful vegetable preparations into your regular rotation.

188

2) ADD A PROTEIN. For a hearty element on the plate, think about including some lean, organic, hormone-free protein such as chicken, turkey, pork, fish, beef, lamb, bison, duck, shellfish, or eggs. Lunchmeat and fake soy meats need not apply.

96

3) SKIP THE GRAINS AND THE DAIRY. Instead of turning to noodles, pasta, potatoes, rice, or food that has been breaded or is served with bread, tortillas, chips, or buns—which have way more carbs than we need and end up being stored as fat—think about kicking grains off your plate. In addition, it's time that we lay off the cheese, butter, and cream that so often goes into our meals, causing them to balloon in calories and us to balloon with bloating and inflammation. I promise you, it's possible to create grain-free dinners that satisfy even the hungriest, pizza- and taco-addicted member of your family.

156

208

4) HAVE FRUIT FOR DESSERT. When was the last time that you took a bite of fresh, organic, perfectly ripe fruit? Delicious, wasn't it? As a society, we often overlook fruit as the perfect dessert that it is, and instead turn to artificially flavored, cane sugar–sweetened, processed desserts that encourage rapid weight gain and declining health. Let's bring fruit back to its rightful place as an after-dinner sweet.

Yes, there's a time and a place for the healthy and fun desserts, which you'll find toward the end of this book—like holidays, birthdays, and special occasions. These desserts contain a fraction of the health consequences of desserts made with refined sugars, while still delighting your taste buds and wowing your friends and family.

230

RECIPE HACKER SECRET #5: DEVELOP THE HABIT OF PLANNING

Eating healthy meals on a daily basis is very possible, but it does require some planning on your part. Quick meals from fast-food restaurants or convenience stores are not an option if you want to avoid toxic foodstuffs, so it's up to you to have your meals and snacks planned and at the ready for each new week of wholesome eating. Here's how to do it.

SMART GROCERY SHOPPING

These days when I shop, my cart looks a lot different than it used to. Gone are the bags of snack foods, cereals and grains, soda pops, packaged sweets, and yogurts and milk. Instead my cart is filled with:

 › Lots and lots of fresh, organic produce, including beautiful, colorful fruits and veggies

 › Fresh organic meat, seafood, and eggs

 › Nuts and seeds

 › Spices, healthy oils, and some wholesome sweeteners

When roaming the aisles, consider all the ingredients that you can use to make endless combinations of delicious meals and easy-to-grab snacks (more on this in a bit). Here's what I'm thinking about when stocking up:

STOCK YOUR FRIDGE WITH organic brown eggs (raw); organic brown eggs (hard-boiled); seasonal fruit; seasonal veggies; whole nuts; a homemade sauce for eggs and meat such as PICKLE PESTO (page 91); cooked chicken to add to omelets, salads, and soups; a container of QUINOA EGG MUFFINS (page 34); and a loaf of ALMOND BREAD (page 43)

STOCK YOUR PANTRY WITH coconut oil, coconut milk, flaked unsweetened coconut, stevia in the raw, unsweetened cocoa, almond meal, raw honey, onions, sweet potatoes, and spices

LINE YOUR COUNTER WITH avocados, grapefruit, bananas, and oranges

ON-THE-GO SNACKS

Having grab-and-go snacks is a must, since temptation hits hardest when you're feeling hungry with no immediate options. Have these handy in your house, at the office, in the car, and/or in your purse. Some ideas include raw nuts, a piece of travel-friendly seasonal fruit, a small amount of dried fruit, sliced veggies, hard-boiled eggs, a few GINGERSNAPS (page 216), a QUINOA EGG MUFFIN (page 34), and a large container of spring water (since thirst is often mistaken for hunger).

SEVEN WAYS TO SAVE TIME IN THE KITCHEN

One of the biggest obstacles that will stand between you and a home-cooked meal each night is the time-crunch factor. Between work, children, hobbies, exercise, and a multitude of other obligations, spending time in the kitchen is often not a high priority. So here are seven ways that you can cut corners and save time in the kitchen.

1) BATCH PROCESS YOUR WEEKLY DINNERS. Doing all of your grocery shopping and meal prep on one day—typically Sunday or Saturday—is a fantastic way to stay on track all week and save time by getting

all of your cooking out of the way. You can cook everything ahead of time and store it in the fridge or freezer. Or can you simply do most of the prep, such as chopping, measuring out, etc.—everything right up to the cooking portion. This method can be time-consuming, but it is worth the effort.

2) GET A SLOW COOKER. Slow cooker recipes are a phenomenal way to spend less time in the kitchen while still getting a hot, home-cooked meal on the table each night. When you shop for your slow cooker, I'd recommend getting a large one so that you're able to make a good amount of food with each recipe. Slow cooker meals typically freeze well, so you can portion out leftovers to freeze for another day.

3) CHOP AND GRATE VEGETABLES FOR THE WHOLE WEEK. Even if you don't take it as far as cooking all of your meals on the weekend, take an hour or so to chop all of the vegetables that you'll need for the week to save time. This is especially awesome to do with cauliflower for rice—get that food processor out once, shred a few heads of cauliflower, and then save the riced cauliflower in large zip-top bags for a quick side dish during the week.

4) SALAD FOR DAYS. Refrigerate a big salad with hardy veggies such as romaine, carrots, and celery. Each night, portion out what you'll eat and mix in dressing along with other more perishable ingredients, such as tomatoes, cucumbers, and peppers.

5) BREAKFASTS ON-THE-GO. Make a big batch of QUINOA EGG MUFFINS (page 34), APPLE SPICE MUFFINS (page 40), HAM AND CHIVE QUICHE (page 30), or HARVEST NUT PANCAKES (page 54), and store them in the fridge or freezer for on-the-go healthy breakfasts.

6) COOK CHICKEN BREAST IN A SLOW COOKER WHILE YOU'RE AT WORK. Rub a couple of boneless, skinless chicken breasts with fajita seasoning, sea salt, and black pepper. Place them in your slow cooker and cover them with chicken broth. Cover and cook on low for 6 hours. The chicken comes out moist, easy to shred, and ready to serve over cauliflower rice or a big salad when you get home.

7) MAKE YOUR BREAD ON THE WEEKEND: Crank out a batch of COCONUT FLOUR TORTILLAS (page 89), ALMOND BREAD (page 43), NAAN BREAD (page 156), or WALNUT RAISIN ROLLS (page 158)—enough to accompany your meals for the week. Store them in the fridge or freezer, then put them in the oven for a quick warm-up before serving.

To make my own weekly meal planning easier, I created online software complete with new monthly recipes, menus, shopping lists, and how-to videos. Visit www.RealHealthyRecipes.com to take a look and give it a try.

RECIPE HACKER SECRET #6:
MAKE A COMMITMENT; REAP THE REWARDS

I recently read a quote that really angered me.

So I read it again. And again. And again.

By the fourth read, my anger subsided and the weight of the quote settled in. There was no denying it . . . it was the truth. The harsh truth.

I'll share the quote with you now (from *Conscious Living* by Gay Hendricks), and you'll see what I mean:

"You always get what you're committed to getting."

If you're broke and not liking it, you're committed to being broke and not liking it. If you're out of -shape and unsatisfied, you're committed to being out of shape and unsatisfied. If you're eating processed foods and feeling uncomfortable, you're committed to eating processed foods and feeling uncomfortable.

It stings a little, right? To accept full responsibility for your lot in life is no small undertaking. It's huge. It's uncomfortable. It's the truth. #TheHarshTruth.

By understanding this truth deep in your bones, you gain a better understanding of how life truly works. And you realize that you have the ability to turn the dial in the direction that you want to go, simply by fully committing yourself.

What are you committed to?

To eating a healthy, real-food diet. To maintaining a disease-free body. To teaching your kids good habits.

You will achieve whatever it is you fully commit yourself to . . . and if it doesn't happen, then you weren't truly committed.

I'm committed to creating and sharing healthy, real-food recipes. I made this commitment because it supports another one of my commitments: to ensure that my children eat wholesome, nutritious foods and learn healthy eating habits to sustain them for life.

What are you committed to?

OVERCOME SELF-SABOTAGE

You may have the best intentions in the world for beginning this journey. You feel like you're finally ready to change your body and transform your health. But if you're prone to self-sabotage, then that's where you need to begin.

I know self-sabotage.

For years I had all the knowledge and tools to lose weight and improve my health, but time and time again I would cut my progress short and revert back to my old eating habits. Something inside of me didn't want to succeed, and it wasn't until I confronted these issues head-on that I was able to break the cycle.

Self-sabotage comes from within you. It whispers in your ear that you NEED to eat that burrito. It urges that you DESERVE to have a slice of cake. It laughs at your ambition to eat only real food.

But it's really just you.

So that little dark voice inside of you can only be shut up by YOU.

The cool thing is that once you become aware of your brain's dirty little tricks and get your footing, self-sabotage loses 99 percent of its power.

When you say, "I'm done with processed foods," and you haven't had a bite of bread or pasta for forty days, it's much easier to walk past the sample of free pizza than if you had just eaten a huge muffin for breakfast that morning. Very much like an addict who counts the number of days that he's been clean, you will begin to feel much pride over each day that you avoid those self-sabotaging foods. And, also like the addict, if you take one bite, that could be all it takes to send you spiraling downward, back under the suppression of self-sabotage.

Don't let it win. Stay on top.

C o n g r a t u l a t i o n s for putting in the time and effort to improve your diet—what a wonderful gift to give yourself and your family!

Now let's have some fun, find some motivation, learn some healthy cooking hacks, and dive right in . . .

THE
Recipes

BREAKFAST

At 5:30 A.M. every morning I go outside for a dawn trail run through the rolling hills near my house. It's peaceful and still; the noise of the day hasn't yet begun. It's time to choose a beverage. My urge is to reach for a natural, caffeinated, flavored energy drink—but the message my body is sending is one single word: hydrate. Water. I need to recalibrate with plenty of water before taking a sip of caffeine.

Your body gives you messages like this throughout your day, all designed to keep you on track for optimal health. The more practiced you get in slowing down to listen, the more wisdom your body will continue to give you. Should you eat that breakfast pastry? Or is your body asking for protein? How will you feel after that bowl of frosty flakes? How would you feel after eating a plate of BACON BRUSSELS SPROUT HASH WITH FRIED EGG (page 25)? Who cares that big food companies have told us that muffins and cereal and pancakes are what we should eat for breakfast? So what?! What is your body telling you to eat? A pile of greens for breakfast? Some sweet potato and egg? Maybe a few hours of fasting are in order. There's no wrong answer if it's coming from a true place.

If you've been filling your body with processed foods and refined sugars, though, then right now there's a lot of food noise happening. It's hard to decipher what it is your body wants because it's too busy trying to clean out the toxic stuff. But as you start to fill your diet with only real, wholesome foods, you'll learn to eat what your body actually wants. And sometimes your body wants a wholesome, filling breakfast that includes things like vegetables!

At a deep, essential level, your body knows what's good for you.

Take the time now to listen.

YOUR DAILY GREEN JUICE

prep time: 15 minutes ● *serves:* 2

Let's get things started off in this new cookbook the same way that I begin each new day . . . with a tall jar of home-pressed green juice. Now, before you go turning the page to find my new Chocolate-Glazed Doughnuts and Real Healthy Snickers Bars recipes (yes, those are coming up!), hear me out for a minute as I impress upon you the importance and power of freshly pressed, organic greens.

No one thinks they're going to get cancer, not really. Sure, you know one or two poor souls who have faced it: the diagnosis, the surgeries, the chemo. Some made it through and came out on the other side grateful and enlightened. Some didn't make it through at all.

You frown and shake your head at such sad news. You shed tears and then you soldier on with the comforting thought that it won't happen to you. I certainly didn't believe it would ever happen to me. Not me, with my passion for nutrition and exercise. Not me, with my love of healthy cooking and my mission to spread my hacked recipes across the globe. Not me, in my early thirties with two young children to raise. Someone else, sure, but it wouldn't happen to me.

Until the day it did.

On July 2, 2015, I received a phone call that turned my life upside down. My dermatologist had found malignant melanoma in a mole on my back, during a routine skin check, and just like that I became a cancer patient. Me?! A cancer patient?! Up until that point I had spent most of my thirty-four years eating well and exercising often. To say I was blindsided would be an understatement.

My time as a cancer patient was (thankfully) short-lived. Due to the early diagnosis, the melanoma was small enough to be removed with an outpatient surgery. The frightening experience left me changed, though. While I was always excited about healthy foods, post-cancer I became *intent* on eating for health. I never wanted to face down another serious diagnosis. I asked my doctor for direction. *What should I eat to prevent the cancer from coming back?*

Her answer didn't surprise me: **freshly pressed green juice**.

The concentration of nutrients found in fresh-pressed juice helps strengthen immunity, and its natural vitamins and minerals are easily, and completely, absorbed by the body.

Ingredients

6 cups mixed spinach, kale, and chard

1 large cucumber

1 orange, peeled and quartered

1 green apple, cored and quartered

½ bunch parsley

½ bunch cilantro

2-inch knob fresh ginger

Steps

Run all of the ingredients through your juicer. Drink immediately. Enjoy!

(Per serving) Calories: 204 | Fat: 1g | Sodium: 142mg
Carbs: 37g | Fiber: 9g | Sugar: 9g | Protein: 6g

QUICK TIP

It's important to limit the amount of fruit and carrots in your juice because these add natural sugars, and too much sugar of any kind can lead to weight gain. The best way to do this is by gradually reducing the sweet produce over time, while increasing the green produce. It's a process to develop a taste and appreciation for pressed greens, but one that is very worthwhile.

BREAKFAST SALAD WITH POACHED EGG

prep time: 15 minutes ● *cooking time:* 6 minutes ● *serves:* 2

Whenever I eat salad for breakfast, I can't help but feel a little smug. A goofy voice in my head starts singing my own praises to the tune of "Stayin' Alive" . . . *Look at me, starting my day out with a big ol' pile of greens. Such discipline, I'm a machine! I'm looking pretty spectacular today! Passed by that pastry display like it wasn't even there, oh . . . stayin' alive, stayin' alive, mm hmm mm hmm, staying alive . . .*

What the be-bopping voice in my head doesn't realize is that my breakfast salad was just as tasty as a sinful breakfast, so nothing was actually sacrificed—save for the bloating and energy crash that follows a breakfast pastry.

In addition to a hearty dose of natural fiber, this salad delivers healthy fat (from the avocado) and a nice serving of protein (from the egg) as well as fantastic, tangy flavor (from the dressing). Don't feel pressed to eat it before noon. I have it on good authority that it'll make you feel just as smug when eaten for lunch or dinner.

Ingredients

FOR THE LEMON VINAIGRETTE:

1 packet powdered stevia

⅛ teaspoon sea salt

pinch of black pepper

2 tablespoons lemon juice

2 tablespoons extra-virgin olive oil

1 teaspoon Dijon mustard

½ teaspoon grated lemon zest

FOR THE SALAD:

1 tablespoon white wine vinegar

2 eggs

1 head frisée lettuce, chopped

1 avocado, pitted, peeled, and sliced

2 tablespoons chopped fresh chives

2 teaspoons toasted sesame seeds

Steps

FOR THE LEMON VINAIGRETTE:

Combine all of the vinaigrette ingredients in a small bowl. Set aside.

FOR THE SALAD:

1. Bring a large pot of water to a simmer. Add the vinegar to the simmering water. Crack the eggs carefully into individual ramekins. Use a large, slotted spoon to create a whirlpool in the simmering water, then remove the spoon and carefully slip one of the eggs into the water. Use the slotted spoon to remove the egg after 3 minutes. Transfer the egg to a plate lined with paper towels. Repeat with the remaining egg.

2. Arrange the lettuce, avocado, chives, and sesame seeds on 2 serving plates. Top each with a poached egg and serve with the Lemon Vinaigrette. Enjoy!

(Per serving) Calories: 394 | Fat: 33g | Sodium: 246mg
Carbs: 7g | Fiber: 10g | Sugar: 2g | Protein: 19g

QUICK TIP

If this is your first time poaching an egg, have no fear because it's actually a very simple process. To poach an egg is to cook it in boiling water without its shell until the white is firm and the yolk is still soft. Here are three key factors that will ensure that your poached eggs turn out perfectly plump instead of stringy and soggy:

1. **Use very fresh eggs.** The quickest way to find out if an egg is fresh is to place it whole in a bowl of water and watch if it sinks or floats. The sinkers are fresh; the floaters are old. Since eggshells are porous, older eggs have a looser seal, hence the floating act.

2. **Use a little vinegar.** A splash of vinegar in the poaching water increases the rate at which the egg whites firm and reduces the chances of feathering.

3. **Use a ramekin.** First crack your fresh egg into a ramekin (or small bowl) and then slip the egg into the simmering water from the ramekin.

KALE AND BUTTERNUT SQUASH HASH

prep time: 15 minutes ● *cooking time:* 25 minutes ● *serves:* 4

Sure, we are only three recipes in to our 120+ recipe journey, but I'm feeling really comfortable with you. Comfortable enough to let you in on a little secret . . .

I hate leftovers! And while eating the same thing for dinner two nights in a row makes my nose wrinkle, I'm also not a fan of wasting perfectly good food. Which is why recipes like hash—where you can transform parts of last night's dinner into something new and exciting—are so awesome.

Leftover roasted veggies, leftover meat, bits and pieces of onions, and a handful of kale are all you need for a stellar hash. Throw it all together into a hot skillet; season with garlic, fresh herbs, sea salt, and black pepper; and then top it off with some over-easy eggs. Just like that, leftovers become a whole new meal.

Use leftovers from these recipes to create your own flavorful hash recipe:

> › FAUX FRIED CAULIFLOWER (page 70): Dice the breaded cauliflower pieces.
> › ROASTED VEGGIE POCKETS (page 86): Use the leftover roasted veggies.

> › BALSAMIC MUSHROOMS (page 166): A handful of these tangy mushrooms would really liven up a hash.

> › MASSAGED KALE AND APPLE SALAD (page 178) and KALE SALAD WITH POPPY SEED DRESSING (page 180): Use leftovers from either of these salads to supply the chopped greens in a quick hash.

> › Leftovers from ROASTED CARROTS (page 190), SHAVED AND ROASTED ASPARAGUS (page 192), BACON BRUSSELS SPROUTS (page 194), and MOROCCAN-SPICED BUTTER-NUT SQUASH (page 198) would all make ideal hash ingredients.

Ingredients

1 tablespoon extra-virgin olive oil, divided

1 butternut squash, peeled, seeded, and cubed

1 white onion, chopped

2 teaspoons minced garlic

2 tablespoons minced fresh rosemary

1 bunch kale, chopped

sea salt and black pepper, to taste

4 eggs

Steps

1. Heat half of the oil in a large skillet over medium-high heat. Add the butternut squash, onion, garlic, and rosemary. Cook until tender, about 15 minutes. Mix in the kale and cover for 5 minutes, until wilted. Season generously with salt and pepper. Remove from the heat.

2. Grease a clean large skillet with the remaining half of the olive oil and place over medium-high heat. Individually, crack the 4 eggs into the hot skillet and do not stir. Season with salt and pepper and cook, untouched, for 2 minutes. The whites should be crispy and the yolks runny. Place on top of the hash and serve hot.

(Per serving) Calories: 180 | Fat: 11g | Sodium: 128mg
Carbs: 13g | Fiber: 3g | Sugar: 3g | Protein: 18g

QUICK TIP

To increase the protein factor of this dish, feel free to add any cooked and diced meat that you have on hand. Ham, roast, chicken breast, brisket, sausage, or steak would all work wonderfully.

EGGS IN CLOUDS

prep time: 15 minutes ☁ *cooking time:* 6 minutes
serves: 4

My kids love it when I make Eggs in Clouds. These flavor-rich, fluffed, and baked eggs are great for delivering big nutrition in a fun package. The nutritional yeast adds nutty, cheesy flavor, making it the perfect substitute for dairy cheese.

Ingredients

4 eggs

2 tablespoons nutritional yeast

¼ cup minced scallion

¼ cup minced cooked bacon (about 2 strips)

sea salt and black pepper, to taste

Steps

1. Preheat the oven to 450°F. Line a baking sheet with parchment paper and set aside.

2. Separate the egg whites from the egg yolks, placing the whites in the bowl of an electric mixer fitted with the whisk attachment and the yolks in individual ramekins, being careful not to break the yolks.

3. Whip the egg whites until stiff peaks form, about 3 minutes. Gently fold in the nutritional yeast, scallion, and bacon.

4. Spoon the egg white mixture onto the prepared baking sheet in 4 mounds. Use the spoon to create a well in the center of each mound, then bake for 3 minutes. Remove the pan from the oven and add a yolk to the center of each mound. Return to the oven for 3 minutes, until the yolk has set. Season with salt and pepper.

(Per cloud) Calories: 101 | Fat: 7g | Sodium: 229mg
Carbs: 1g | Fiber: 1g | Sugar: 0g | Protein: 9g

BACON BRUSSELS SPROUT HASH WITH FRIED EGG

prep time: 15 minutes 🍳 *cooking time:* 20 minutes
serves: 4

Brussels sprouts for breakfast? *Fo sho!* Not only will you love the salty-savory-satisfying flavor of this dish, but you'll also love watching the kids scarf it down. This dish makes a flavorful and exciting dinner as well. Or lunch. Or late morning snack. Or late afternoon snack. Or midnight snack . . .

Ingredients

- **4 strips bacon**
- **1 parsnip, peeled and finely chopped**
- **1 yellow onion, finely chopped**
- **2 cloves garlic, finely chopped**
- **4 cups shredded Brussels sprouts**
- **½ cup chicken broth**
- **2 tablespoons balsamic vinegar**
- **sea salt and black pepper, to taste**
- **1 teaspoon extra-virgin olive oil**
- **4 eggs**

Steps

1. Cook the bacon in a skillet over medium-high heat until crispy. Transfer the bacon to a paper towel–lined plate. Once cooled, chop and set aside. Reserve the bacon drippings in the pan.

2. Put the skillet and bacon drippings over medium-high heat and add the parsnip, onion, and garlic. Cook for 3 minutes. Add the Brussels sprouts, broth, and balsamic vinegar to the skillet, mix well, and continue to cook until tender, about 8 minutes. Mix in the chopped bacon and remove the pan from the heat. Season to taste with salt and pepper.

3. Grease a clean large skillet with the olive oil and place it over medium-high heat. Individually, crack the 4 eggs into the hot skillet and do not stir. Season with salt and pepper and cook the eggs, untouched, for 2 minutes. The whites should be crispy and the yolks runny. Place on top of the hash and serve hot.

(Per serving) Calories: 272 | Fat: 11g | Sodium: 252mg
Carbs: 22g | Fiber: 7g | Sugar: 7g | Protein: 17g

HEALTHY EATING TIP

It takes just as much effort to eat unhealthy foods as it does to eat healthy ones, but the outcome is very different. A body that's lean, healthy, strong, and free of disease comes as the result of eating wholesome, real foods—like a plate of Bacon Brussels Sprout Hash with Fried Egg for breakfast.

CRAB CAKE EGGS BENEDICT

prep time: 20 minutes ⁐ *cooking time:* 15 minutes ⁐ *serves:* 4

While on a weekend trip to Las Vegas a couple of months ago, I had crab cake eggs Benedict for breakfast at the Bellagio. *Wowsa.* It was so delicious and such a fun idea to use a crab cake instead of a slice of bread! I quickly made this version of the dish when I returned home. The recipe needed some hacking—to remove the grains and gluten from the crab cake and the dairy from the sauce—but the new version turned out better than I could have hoped.

Ingredients

FOR THE MOCK HOLLANDAISE SAUCE:

1 teaspoon ground turmeric

1 teaspoon arrowroot starch

½ cup canned full-fat coconut milk

1 tablespoon Dijon or yellow mustard

2 teaspoons lemon juice

sea salt and black pepper, to taste

FOR THE EGGS BENEDICT:

1 large sweet potato

1 tablespoon coconut oil

1 tablespoon apple cider vinegar

4 eggs

sea salt and black pepper, to taste

4 CRAB CAKES (page 69)

2 tablespoons minced parsley

Steps

FOR THE MOCK HOLLANDAISE SAUCE:

Combine all of the sauce ingredients in a small saucepan. Cook and stir over medium-low heat until warm and thickened, about 10 minutes, then season to taste with salt and pepper.

FOR THE EGGS BENEDICT:

1. Peel the sweet potato and shred in the food processor using the grating attachment.

2. Heat the coconut oil in a medium skillet over medium-high heat. Add the shredded sweet potato and cook until golden, about 12 minutes.

3. Add 4 cups water and the vinegar to a clean large skillet and bring to a boil. Reduce to a simmer. Use a large slotted spoon to create a whirlpool in the simmering water. Remove the spoon and carefully slip one of the eggs into the water. Use the spoon to remove the egg after 3 minutes and transfer it to a plate lined with paper towels. Repeat with the remaining eggs and season them with salt and pepper.

ASSEMBLING THE BENEDICT:

1. Preheat the broiler.

2. Arrange Crab Cakes on a baking sheet and broil for 4 minutes, or until browned.

3. Plate the shredded sweet potato. Top with the crab cakes. Top with a poached egg, and spoon sauce over the egg. Sprinkle with the minced parsley and serve.

(Per Benedict) Calories: 349 | Fat: 21g | Sodium: 708mg
Carbs: 17g | Fiber: 4g | Sugar: 2g | Protein: 24g

QUICK TIP

If crab cakes aren't your thing, then feel free to serve your eggs Benedict over **NAAN BREAD** (page 156), a slice of **ALMOND BREAD** (page 43), or a **WALNUT RAISIN ROLL** (page 158). Or simply replace the crab cake with a thick slice of roasted ham.

SAUSAGE AND SWEET POTATO SKILLET

prep time: 15 minutes *cooking time:* 30 minutes
serves: 6

Here's a dish that is so incredibly simple to throw together that it always shocks me when I take that first bite and the savory flavors collide on my tongue. It really should be more difficult than this to create breakfast skillet magic . . . I cook the Cajun sweet potato cubes in a separate skillet to ensure that they come out crispy on the outside and creamy on the inside. If you're in a hurry, then cook the sweet potato together with the rest of the hash, but know that it will result in soft cubes. These Cajun sweet potatoes are an amazing dish all on their own—I like to serve them alongside a nice steak dinner. Enjoy!

Ingredients

FOR THE POTATOES:

3 tablespoons extra-virgin olive oil

3 sweet potatoes, peeled and cut into ½-inch cubes

1½ tablespoons Cajun seasoning blend

1 teaspoon sea salt

2 tablespoons coconut palm sugar

FOR THE SAUSAGE:

1 tablespoon extra-virgin olive oil

4 bell peppers, any color combination, seeded, and chopped

1 yellow onion, chopped

6 links chicken sausage, casings removed and sliced

Steps

FOR THE POTATOES:

Heat the olive oil in a large skillet over medium-high heat. Add the sweet potato cubes and sprinkle with the Cajun seasoning, salt, and palm sugar. Mix and cook for 15 minutes, or until crispy on the outside and creamy on the inside. Remove from the heat and set aside.

FOR THE SAUSAGE:

Heat the olive oil in the same skillet over medium-high heat. Add the bell peppers and onion and cook until tender, about 12 minutes. Add the chicken sausage and cook for 5 minutes. Add the Cajun sweet potatoes, mix well, and remove from the heat. Serve hot.

*(Per serving) Calories: 264 | Fat: 12g | Sodium: 542mg
Carbs: 23g | Fiber: 4g | Sugar: 11g | Protein: 17g*

HEALTHY EATING TIP

Healthy eating is simple: Avoid processed and packaged foods. Cook and eat meals at home. Drink water. Eat fresh veggies, fruits, meat, eggs, nuts, and seeds. Stop eating sugar. It's not always *easy*, but it's simple.

HERB-CRUSTED TOMATO

prep time: 15 minutes ☕ *cooking time:* 10 minutes
serves: 8

It's pretty rare that I go out to a restaurant for breakfast, since most of my mornings are spent running the kids to school and then myself to my local Fit Body Bootcamp for an invigorating 30-minute workout. Then there's coffee and either something grabbed from the fridge or a quick protein shake before settling down with my computer. When I do have the time to enjoy a restaurant breakfast, it's usually when I'm traveling. What I've noticed is that over the past year or so, trendy breakfast spots have started to serve herb-crusted tomato halves with their egg dishes. But, alas, nowhere have I found a restaurant with a grain-free, gluten-free version of this tasty side dish. So, naturally, I spent some time in the RHR (Real Healthy Recipes!) Kitchen and came up with this quick and easy preparation. Serve it up with your favorite egg-based breakfast or even just as a snack. This is a fantastic way to enjoy garden-fresh tomatoes during those summer months when tomatoes abound.

Ingredients

¼ **cup blanched almond flour**

2 **teaspoons Italian seasoning blend**

½ **teaspoon sea salt**

⅛ **teaspoon black pepper**

¼ **teaspoon garlic powder**

4 **vine-ripened tomatoes, halved widthwise**

Steps

1. Preheat the broiler to high and position a rack 4 inches from the heat source. Lightly grease a casserole pan with olive oil and set aside.

2. In a small bowl, combine the flour, Italian seasoning, salt, pepper, and garlic powder.

3. Arrange the halved tomatoes on the prepared pan, cut side up. Sprinkle the tops of each tomato with the seasoning blend. Place under the broiler for 10 minutes, or until golden and tender.

(Per half tomato) Calories: 32 | Fat: 2g | Sodium: 146mg
Carbs: 3g | Fiber: 1g | Sugar: 1g | Protein: 1g

QUICK TIP

This recipe was written to be very simple and quick to throw together, using almond flour rather than grain-free bread crumbs. However, if you have some **ALMOND BREAD** (page 43), **NAAN BREAD** (page 156), or **WALNUT RAISIN ROLLS** (page 158), then feel free to crumble up ¼ cup and use that in place of the almond flour. It'll result in a more flavorful dish.

HAM AND CHIVE QUICHE

prep time: 20 minutes ● *cooking time:* 40 minutes ● *makes:* 10 quiches

As you've probably already figured out (because you're quick like that), nearly all of my recipe inspirations come from naughty, fattening foods that I've either tasted or really wanted to taste. I go into the kitchen with that naughty item in my mind, and I don't come out until I have created a new version of that item—sans the grains, gluten, dairy, soy, and cane sugar. To this day I have yet to find a food item that couldn't be enhanced and recreated using wholesome ingredients.

Take this recipe for Ham and Chive Quiche, for example. B, the kids, and I were in Del Mar, California, spending New Year's weekend in vacation mode. The sun was out, the sky was blue, and we sat down to a leisurely outdoor brunch. I ordered an omelet and B (always the adventurous one) got the special . . . ham quiche.

One of my favorite perks of marriage is getting to taste everything he orders. One bite of that quiche and I knew that it had to be hacked!

The crust in this quiche is made with a combination of almond flour and coconut flour, to keep it nice and light. I also adapted these as mini quiches using a mini muffin tin, to help us all with portion control. Oh, you're welcome.

Ingredients

FOR THE CRUST:

1½ cups blanched almond flour

3 tablespoons coconut flour

¼ teaspoon sea salt

2 tablespoons coconut oil

1 egg

FOR THE FILLING:

1 teaspoon extra-virgin olive oil

¼ cup diced yellow onion

½ cup diced ham

4 eggs

2 tablespoons coconut cream

¼ teaspoon sea salt

pinch of black pepper

FOR THE GARNISH:

2 tablespoons minced chives

Steps

FOR THE CRUST:

1. Preheat the oven to 350°F. Generously grease 10 mini muffin cups with coconut oil.

2. Pulse the crust ingredients in a food processor until fully combined. Divide the crust among the 10 cups and press firmly, creating a raised crust around the sides like mini pie crusts. Bake for 8–12 minutes, until golden.

FOR THE FILLING:

1. In a small skillet, warm the olive oil over medium heat and sauté the diced onion until soft, about 10 minutes.

2. In a large bowl, combine the soft onion and the remainder of the filling ingredients. Whisk until fully combined. Fill each of the pie crusts with the filling. Loosely cover the pan with foil and bake for 15–20 minutes, until the eggs are set.

FOR THE GARNISH:

Top with the minced chives and serve. Store leftovers in an airtight container in the fridge for up to 3 days.

(Per quiche) Calories: 214 | Fat: 17g | Sodium: 116mg
Carbs: 16g | Fiber: 4g | Sugar: 3g | Protein: 11g

QUICK TIP

There are tons of ways that you could modify this recipe to make it your own. Try any combination of cooked, diced meat and herbs. Also, if you prefer to forgo the crust, and you have every right to do so, then follow these three steps to make Ham and Chive Egg Muffins:

1. Preheat the oven to 350°F. Disregard the crust ingredients and steps.

2. Add 2 eggs to the filling ingredients. Line a full-sized muffin pan with paper liners. Fill 6 muffin tins with the filling ingredients.

3. Bake for 20–22 minutes, until fully set.

BREAKFAST PIZZA

prep time: 20 minutes ❧ *cooking time:* 20 minutes ❧ *serves:* 4

Pizza for breakfast? Why not! This is one of the tastiest ways that I know to conflate the flavors of bacon, tomato, and egg. The crust is crispy with a hint of sweetness and an undercurrent of rosemary, plus it's gluten- and grain-free. It's the perfect base for breakfast-flavored toppings that are completely dairy-free, though the egg whites may fool you into thinking there's melted cheese. I love making this for a weekend brunch.

It's not a speedy recipe (you'll need to take your time forming the dough and arranging the toppings), so save this one for a leisurely Saturday morning.

Ingredients

FOR THE PIZZA CRUST:

1 tablespoon raw honey

1 packet (2 teaspoons)
active dry yeast

1/4 cup warm water

3/4 cup blanched almond
flour

3 tablespoons coconut
flour

1/2 cup arrowroot
starch

1/4 teaspoon sea salt

1 teaspoon dried
rosemary, crushed

1 egg

1 tablespoon extra-
virgin olive oil

1 teaspoon apple cider
vinegar

FOR THE TOPPINGS:

1 cup organic marinara
sauce

1 tomato, chopped

4 strips bacon, cooked
and crumbled

4 eggs

3 tablespoons minced
fresh chives

3 tablespoons minced
fresh parsley

Steps

FOR THE PIZZA CRUST:

1. Preheat the oven to 425°F. Line a rimmed baking sheet with parchment paper. Set aside.

2. In a small bowl, combine the honey, yeast, and warm water. Mix gently with a fork. Set aside for 5 minutes, until foamy.

3. In a medium bowl, combine the almond flour, coconut flour, arrowroot starch, salt, and rosemary. Work out the lumps with a fork. Add the egg, olive oil, and vinegar to the yeast mixture and stir to combine.

4. Add the wet ingredients to the dry. Mix well with a large wooden spoon and form a ball of dough. Work the dough for about 30 seconds in the bowl with your hands, smoothing out any lumps.

5. Place the dough ball in the middle of your prepared pan. Dip your fingers in a little olive oil and use them to flatten the dough into a 12-inch circle. Be sure to pinch the dough up around the edges to make a crust. Transfer the dough to the oven and cook for 5–7 minutes, until golden. (You're not cooking all the way through yet.)

FOR THE TOPPINGS:

1. Spread the marinara sauce over the pizza crust. Arrange the tomatoes and bacon over the sauce, leaving four 2-inch round openings for the eggs. Crack the eggs onto the crust, and sprinkle with the chives and parsley.

2. Return to the oven and bake for 12–15 minutes, until the egg whites are set but the yolks are still soft.

(Per serving) Calories: 421 | Fat: 24g | Sodium: 506mg
Carbs: 35g | Fiber: 12g | Sugar: 10g | Protein: 23g

QUICK TIP

To save time, make the dough the night before, cover it with plastic wrap, and store it in the fridge. You can also cook the bacon the night before and chop the tomato, chives, and parsley. In the morning, simply assemble and bake. There's nothing quite like waking up to the aroma of this bacon and egg pizza baking in the oven—yum!

QUINOA EGG MUFFINS

prep time: 10 minutes ● *cooking time:* 20 minutes ● *makes:* 10 muffins

Are your actions congruent with your dreams and desires?

This is a question that my dear friend Craig Ballantyne asked that really stuck with me.

If you say you want to lose the weight—once and for all—then why are you still giving in to those unhealthy food cravings? Your actions aren't lining up with what you say you want . . . and your actions always dictate your results.

Having quick, wholesome breakfast options that are readily available is one of the biggest challenges of real-food eating. Most traditional breakfast foods like cereals and pastries are quick to grab, but then they set you up for a full day of unhealthy eating. Not to mention the sugar crash that quickly ensues.

Egg muffins are one of my favorite ways to serve a quick, nutritious breakfast. I whip up a batch and keep it in the fridge for a three-day supply. It's easy to eat on the run and provides delicious protein and veggies to get the day started right.

Keeping a supply of quick and nutritious breakfast items like this in your fridge is a great way to take positive action that is congruent with your desire to lose the weight and regain your health—yippee!

This recipe is extra-hearty due to the quinoa and ham. It's one of the few breakfasts that will satisfy my eleven-year-old son, Andrew, until lunchtime. (He's in the middle of a major growth spurt!) However, if you are aiming to lose weight and want to make these protein-packed little muffins a bit lighter and lower in calories, then feel free to reduce the amount of quinoa or simply leave it out.

Ingredients

1 cup cooked red quinoa

4 eggs

2 cups shredded zucchini

1 cup diced ham

¼ cup chopped fresh parsley

2 scallions, whites and greens, sliced

sea salt and black pepper, to taste

Steps

1. Preheat the oven to 350°F. Grease 10 muffin cups with coconut oil and set aside.

2. Combine all the ingredients in a large bowl and mix well. Spoon the mixture to the top of each cup. Bake for 15–20 minutes, or until the edges of the cups are golden brown.

3. Let the muffins cool for at least 5 minutes before removing from the muffin tin.

(Per muffin) Calories: 91 | Fat: 5g | Sodium: 156mg
Carbs: 7g | Fiber: 3g | Sugar: 1g | Protein: 9g

QUICK TIP

You may have noticed that quinoa comes in different colors. There's basic white quinoa, which is the most common, and there's also the more exotic red and black quinoa. Bags of quinoa that are labeled as rainbow are actually a combination of all three colors. Aside from the obvious difference in appearance, these three types of quinoa are basically the same in both flavor and nutrition. The only slight variation that I've found is that the white quinoa tends to cook slightly faster than the darker varieties. It's perfectly fine to choose your quinoa based on which color you think will look the best in the recipe at hand. I think the rainbow quinoa is pretty, so you'll see me use that one often.

ZUCCHINI MUFFINS

prep time: 15 minutes ● *cooking time:* 20 minutes ● *makes:* 12 muffins

I lost it in a doctor's waiting room a few years ago. Flat. Out. Lost. It. The kids and I were there to take Chloe for her pre-kindergarten checkup. As we sat in the waiting room, a flat-screen TV on the wall broadcast a wellness channel to the captive patients. It was the normal stuff—a profile on a forty-four-year-old man who had had a heart attack and then started living a healthier lifestyle, a piece on consulting your pharmacist when any changes occur with your medications, and then came the segment on healthy cooking.

That's when I lost it.

A sweet, slender woman on the screen told us that regular muffins are bad for us and are basically doughnuts. Sure, I definitely agreed with her on that. Then she went on to share a "HEALTHY" muffin recipe that made my head spin. These muffins called for white flour, wheat flour, brown sugar, canola oil, and low-fat milk. And as the lady next to me scribbled the recipe down on a piece of paper, all I could think about is how doomed we are. Our society isn't getting healthier anytime soon. Not when the doctor's office tells us that muffins filled with grains, gluten, cane sugar, dairy, and GMO-filled canola oil are healthy.

And it makes my otherwise healthy blood pressure rise.

So, before I get too fired up again, I'm going to share my ACTUALLY HEALTHY muffin recipe with you. It has zero grains, zero gluten, zero cane sugar, zero canola oil, and zero dairy. Instead, it's filled with nutrient-dense almond flour, eggs, banana, raw honey, coconut oil (good fat!), zucchini, pecans, and raisins. Wholesome, nutritious, real-food ingredients. That's where health begins.

Pass this recipe along to people you know who still think that gluten, sugar, canola oil, and dairy are good for them. Let's do what we can to make a dent in the sad state of our society's health. Oh, and p.s., these muffins taste awesome! They're the perfect way to enjoy fresh-from-the-garden zucchini!

Ingredients

1½ cups almond flour

1½ teaspoons baking soda

½ teaspoon sea salt

1 teaspoon ground cinnamon

pinch of ground nutmeg

3 eggs

3 tablespoons raw honey

1 teaspoon vanilla extract

1 banana, mashed

1 tablespoon coconut oil, melted

1 cup grated zucchini, drained

¼ cup golden raisins

½ cup chopped pecans

Steps

1. Preheat the oven to 350°F and lightly grease 12 muffin cups with coconut oil. Set aside.

2. Combine the almond flour, baking soda, salt, cinnamon, and nutmeg in a medium bowl and set aside. Combine the eggs, honey, vanilla, banana, and melted oil in a large bowl. Mix well, then add the dry ingredients. Mix until fully combined. Fold in the zucchini, raisins, and pecans.

3. Pour the batter into the muffin cups and bake for 20 minutes, or until golden and set.

4. Let the pan cool for 5 minutes, then transfer the muffins to a wire rack.

(Per muffin) Calories: 142 | Fat: 7g | Sodium: 275mg
Carbs: 14g | Fiber: 3g | Sugar: 9g | Protein: 5g

QUICK TIP

Whenever you use shredded zucchini while baking, it's a good idea to drain off the excess liquid before mixing it into the batter. This helps prevent your muffins from being too moist or even soggy after baking. The method I use is to place the shredded zucchini in the center of a clean dish towel, wrap it up tight, and squeeze over the sink. Some greenish liquid will drip out. Yeah, not too cute, but the muffins turn out great.

DOUBLE CHOCOLATE ZUCCHINI MUFFINS

prep time: 30 minutes ⬥ *cooking time:* 20 minutes ⬥ *makes:* 16 muffins

There's a war raging within you.

The enlightened side wants you to turn over a new leaf. To stop falling into the temptation of processed foods and sugary treats. To get up earlier. To exercise more often and with greater intensity. To crave and seek out wholesome, real foods. To fill your diet with colorful fruits and veggies, dark leafy greens, lean meats, and fresh nuts and seeds. To lose the weight and feel confident and energized—once and for all. To have others notice your inspiring transformation. To be the best version of yourself.

Then there's the dark side . . .

The dark side is happy with your bad habits and doesn't see a problem with your daily indulgences. It whispers to you to reset your alarm for some extra sleep. It grants you permission to take a break from exercise. *You're so tired*, it comforts; *there's always tomorrow.* It tells you that wholesome foods are boring, take too much time to prepare, and are much too expensive to be practical. It wants you to stay the same, to fade into the background, and to keep quiet. It's afraid of you becoming the best version of yourself.

All day long battles between these two sides are fought, won, and lost, leaving you to wonder . . . who will win the war?

The answer is simple. The side that wins is the side that you feed with your thoughts and attention. It's the side that you most identify with. It's the side that you decide is most comfortable.

But alliances can change. The battle isn't truly lost unless you give up. If your dark side has been on a winning streak, then maybe it's time for that to change.

Never give up on what you truly want. Strive toward it with laserlike focus. Get up and dust yourself off. Decide who you want to be and don't stop working for it. Imagine yourself at the finish line.

You. Can. Do. It.

If there's one recipe that can help you change course—and convince you that veggies can indeed be dangerously decadent—it's this one. These muffins are hiding nutritious and fiber-filled zucchini in their chocolaty depths. What a delightful secret! The best part is that most people don't even notice the little specs of veggie—children and adults alike. Another vegetable that I love to hide in chocolate treats is beets. Turn to page 232 for MINI CHOCOLATE LAYER CAKES that are stuffed with beets.

Ingredients

⅓ cup unsweetened chocolate pieces

½ cup raw honey

½ cup coconut oil

¼ cup coconut cream

3 eggs

1 teaspoon vanilla extract

2 cups blanched almond flour

¼ cup unsweetened cocoa powder

1 teaspoon baking soda

1 teaspoon sea salt

1 teaspoon ground cinnamon

2 cups grated zucchini, drained

¾ cup stevia-sweetened dark chocolate chips

Steps

1. Preheat the oven to 350°F. Line 16 muffin cups with paper liners. Set aside.

2. In a lazy man's double boiler (see page 221), combine the chocolate pieces, honey, oil, and cream. Stir often until smooth. Remove from the heat and let cool.

3. In a large bowl, combine the eggs, vanilla, and melted chocolate mixture and mix well.

4. In a separate bowl, combine the flour, cocoa powder, baking soda, salt, and cinnamon. Add the wet ingredients and mix until full combined. Fold in the grated zucchini and chocolate chips.

5. Fill the muffin cups and bake for 20 minutes, until set.

(Per muffin) Calories: 234 | Fat: 19g | Sodium: 220mg
Carbs: 16g | Fiber: 4g | Sugar: 10g | Protein: 6g

APPLE SPICE MUFFINS

prep time: 15 minutes ● *cooking time:* 20 minutes ● *makes:* 12 muffins

Have you ever fallen into the droopy-sleepy-yawny-have-no-energy trap? When both the middle of the morning and the middle of the afternoon feel like bedtime? Ugh. I have. Back when my breakfast consisted of mainly grain-based cereals or processed and refined breakfast pastries. Add to that a cup or two of sugar-sweetened coffee in the morning and a couple of corn syrup–sweetened caffeinated beverages in the afternoon, and I was left with a roller coaster of inconsistent energy levels.

All of that changed when I started avoiding refined sugars and processed and packaged breakfast foods. The dips in my energy evened out into one steady stream of reliable energy. What a difference a consistent pep in your step makes!

I contemplated naming these "All-Day Energy Muffins," because these moist morsels give you wings—more so than any energy drink I've ever tried. Check out the ingredients and you'll see what I mean: flax, almonds, eggs, banana, apple, pecans—I double-dog dare you to find a muffin recipe with more goodness crammed into it than this.

No really, don't waste your time looking—just make these and enjoy!

Ingredients

⅓ cup flax meal

½ cup almond meal or blanched almond flour

2 teaspoons baking powder

1 teaspoon baking soda

½ teaspoon sea salt

½ teaspoon ground cinnamon

2 eggs

2 tablespoons raw honey

2 ripe bananas, mashed

1 cup finely chopped Fuji apple

1 cup chopped pecans

12 slices Fuji apple, for garnish

12 whole pecans, for garnish

Steps

1. Preheat the oven to 400°F. Line 12 muffin cups with paper liners and set aside.

2. In a large mixing bowl, combine the flax meal, almond meal, baking powder, baking soda, salt, and cinnamon. Mix well.

3. In another large mixing bowl, combine the eggs, raw honey, and mashed banana. Mix well until no large lumps of banana remain.

4. Add the dry ingredients to the wet and mix until fully combined. Fold in the chopped apples and pecans.

5. Fill each muffin cup three-fourths full. Top with an apple slice and a pecan. Bake for 18–20 minutes, or until golden and set.

6. Let the pan cool for 5 minutes, then transfer the muffins to a wire rack to cool.

(Per muffin) Calories: 145 | Fat: 10g | Sodium: 318mg
Carbs: 11g | Fiber: 3g | Sugar: 6g | Protein: 4g

QUICK TIP

As you progress in your real-food journey, you'll go from the beginning stages of eliminating refined sugar to a diet that includes only the wholesome sweeteners that we talked about earlier. And then you'll begin to lighten your use of these wholesome sweeteners. Really! As you eat less and less of the sweet stuff, your palate begins to change and your desire and need for it lessens. Take these muffins, for example. I wrote the recipe to include 2 tablespoons of raw honey in addition to 2 ripe bananas. This is where the wholesome sweetness for the recipe comes from, rather than the refined sugars that other muffins contain. It's perfectly fine to reduce the sweetness by reducing or eliminating the honey, or by subbing in a pinch or two of stevia for the honey, or in conjunction with a reduced amount of the honey. Keep on evolving, my friend!

CHUNKY MONKEY BREAD

prep time: 10 minutes ☙ *cooking time:* 45 minutes ☙ *makes:* 16 slices

Do you remember those old commercials for Nestlé Toll House Chocolate Chips where the sweet, smiling mother pulls a tray of warm chocolate chips cookies from the oven, stylishly arranges them on a plate, and then happily serves them to her beautiful children?

She has this look on her face like she's got this mom thing down . . . and she feels good about what she just fed to her kids.

I guess if I didn't know the harm that gluten, refined grains, dairy, and cane sugar do, then I'd look that way when feeding my kids cookies, too. Sorry, kids, no Toll House cookies being pulled out of this oven anytime soon.

Since I do know the harm caused by the obscene amounts of sugar that kids today are eating, I'm always coming up with new, cane sugar–free treat recipes that the kids will love.

This Chunky Monkey Bread is my new favorite sweet indulgence to bake for a delicious after-school snack or a quick, on-the-go tasty breakfast. The dark chocolate and minimal amount of coconut sugar make this bread very mildly sweet, with the comforting flavors of banana and walnut shining through.

Oh, and don't forget to wear that "I've got this mom thing down!" look when you serve this delicious, wholesome, yummy bread.

Ingredients

½ cup coconut flour

½ cup arrowroot starch

1 teaspoon baking soda

½ cup coconut oil, melted

⅓ cup coconut sugar

3 bananas, mashed

1 teaspoon vanilla extract

4 eggs

½ cup roughly chopped dark chocolate (73% cacao content)

½ cup walnuts, chopped

Steps

1. Preheat the oven to 350°F. Lightly grease a $4\frac{1}{2} \times 8\frac{1}{2}$-inch loaf pan with coconut oil and set aside.

2. In a medium mixing bowl, combine the coconut flour, arrowroot starch, and baking soda. In another medium bowl, combine the melted coconut oil, coconut sugar, mashed bananas, vanilla, and eggs. Mix well.

3. Add the dry ingredients to the wet, then fold in the chocolate and walnuts. Pour the batter into the prepared loaf pan and smooth out the top. Bake for 35–45 minutes, until golden on top and a toothpick inserted into the center comes out clean. Store leftovers in an airtight container in the fridge for up to 1 week.

(Per slice) Calories: 167 | Fat: 11g | Sodium: 105mg
Carbs: 15g | Fiber: 2g | Sugar: 7g | Protein: 3g

QUICK TIP

Here's the ingredient list for plain Almond Bread, which you could use with the same baking instructions as this Chunky Monkey Bread: 5 cups blanched almond flour, 1 teaspoon baking soda, ½ teaspoon sea salt, 6 eggs, 2 tablespoons raw honey, and 2 teaspoons apple cider vinegar.

PUMPKIN BREAD

prep time: 15 minutes ⬤ *cooking time:* 1 hour 20 minutes ⬤ *makes:* 16 slices

What is it about spiced treats around the holidays that encourage us to make regrettable decisions? I had a showdown with a slice of pumpkin bread this winter while in line at my local coffee shop. The thick, moist bread (or cake, let's be honest) was topped with pepitas and dotted with spices. I knew it would taste amazing. I could smell it being warmed up in the toaster oven, all sugar and spice and everything tasty . . .

Well, you know how this story ends. I snapped a picture with my phone (paparazzi style), ordered my black coffee, and raced home to get baking. A couple of hours later, the RHR Kitchen was filled with the swirling aroma of cinnamon, nutmeg, cloves, ginger, and, of course, pumpkin.

Why is it worth our time and effort to make real-food versions of the pastries in the glass display? One slice of pumpkin bread at the coffee shop for breakfast seems like a pretty small thing in the grand scheme of your day, but it's the same as throwing a small stone into a tranquil pond—the ripple effect is far-reaching.

Ingredients

½ cup raw honey

½ cup coconut oil

¼ cup coconut cream

1 (15-ounce) can pumpkin puree

4 eggs

2 cups blanched almond flour

2 teaspoons baking soda

1 teaspoon sea salt

1 teaspoon ground cinnamon

1 teaspoon ground nutmeg

½ teaspoon ground cloves

¼ teaspoon ground ginger

¼ cup pepitas

Steps

1. Preheat the oven to 350°F with a rack in the center position. Grease a 5 × 9-inch glass loaf pan with coconut oil.

2. In a lazy man's double boiler (see page 221), combine the raw honey, coconut oil, and coconut cream. Stir over medium-low heat until smooth. Remove from the heat and let cool.

3. In a large bowl, combine the honey mixture with the pumpkin puree and eggs and mix well. In a medium bowl, combine the flour, baking soda, salt, cinnamon, nutmeg, cloves, and ginger. Stir the dry ingredients into the pumpkin mixture until just blended. Pour into the prepared pan and top with the pepitas.

4. Bake for 50 minutes. Remove the pan from oven and tent (loosely cover) the loaf with a piece of foil to prevent the pepitas from getting too toasted. Continue to bake with the tented top for an additional 30 minutes, or until a knife inserted into the center comes out clean.

5. Serve with coconut butter, a shmear of honey, and a piping hot cup of coffee. Store leftovers in an airtight container in the fridge for up to 1 week.

(Per slice) Calories: 222 | Fat: 17g | Sodium: 227mg
Carbs: 14g | Fiber: 5g | Sugar: 10g | Protein: 6g

QUICK TIP

Grain-free bread loaves tend to be extra-moist, compared to traditional grain-filled breads, and they require a slightly different approach to baking until they're perfectly baked through. At the end of the bake time, give your loaf a little shake (be sure to use an oven mitt!). If the batter still wiggles in the middle, but the top and edges of the bread are looking done, then cover the top lightly with foil and add another 5–10 minutes of baking time. Continue to add a few minutes of baking time until the jiggle is gone and the bread is cooked through.

QUINOA ENERGY BARS

prep time: 30 minutes ● *cooking time:* 40 minutes ● *makes:* 12 bars

The idea of an energy bar is so appealing. Something you can throw into your bag to fish out when hunger strikes. The prepackaged energy bars that you find at your local market have the right idea—most are made with a lot of great ingredients like nuts, shredded coconut, and dried fruit. However, it's the extra ingredients added in that go and ruin the whole thing. The biggest culprit is sugar. So I don't purchase energy bars at the store. I simply bake them myself.

Now you too can create homemade, wholesome, no-suspicious-ingredients energy bars with this simple recipe. These Quinoa Energy Bars are made with energizing ingredients like quinoa, almond meal, walnuts, and raisins. You can also transform them into a dessert by simply warming them up and spreading them with coconut butter and raw honey—yum!

Ingredients

1 cup uncooked quinoa

2 tablespoons raw honey, divided

2¼ cups water, divided

2 eggs

½ cup coconut oil, melted

1 teaspoon apple cider vinegar

1 cup almond meal

1 tablespoon coconut flour

¼ cup arrowroot starch

½ teaspoon baking soda

½ teaspoon sea salt

½ cup raw walnuts, chopped

½ cup black raisins

Steps

1. In a small pot, combine the quinoa, 1 tablespoon of the honey, and 2 cups of the water. Place over medium heat to reach a low boil, then decrease the heat to low, cover, and simmer for 20 minutes. Remove from the heat, fluff the quinoa with a fork, and set aside.

2. Preheat the oven to 350°F. Generously grease 12 mini loaf pans with coconut oil. If you are using pans that aren't nonstick, then it's a good idea to line the bottoms with parchment paper in addition to greasing with coconut oil.

3. In a medium bowl, combine the eggs, melted coconut oil, remaining ¼ cup water, remaining 1 tablespoon honey, and vinegar. Mix until fully combined.

4. In another bowl, combine the almond meal, coconut flour, arrowroot starch, baking soda, and salt. Mix until fully combined.

5. Add the almond meal mixture to the egg mixture and mix until fully incorporated. Mix in the cooked quinoa, walnuts, and raisins. Reserve a handful of walnuts and raisins to sprinkle over the tops of the bars.

6. Divide the batter among the 12 mini loaf pans, filling them just about halfway and smoothing out the tops. Sprinkle the tops with the reserved walnuts and raisins.

7. Bake for 15–20 minutes, until golden and set. Let the bars cool for 15 minutes before removing them from the pans. Store them in an airtight container in the fridge and enjoy as a nutritious, energy-packed, on-the-go snack.

(Per bar) Calories: 288 | Fat: 19g | Sodium: 128mg
Carbs: 23g | Fiber: 3g | Sugar: 7g | Protein: 6g

QUICK TIP

I make these Quinoa Energy Bars in a mini loaf pan, which is like a muffin pan but with little loaf shapes instead of circles, filling the loaves about halfway. If you don't have one of these nifty loaf pans, then line a large, rimmed baking sheet with parchment paper and arrange the batter in little ¼-cup plops. Watch the baking time—start checking the bars at 10 or 12 minutes.

APPLE FRITTERS

prep time: 15 minutes ☀ *cooking time:* 18 minutes ☀ *makes:* 8 fritters

I can't hear you over the volume of your actions.

Now that's a line worth reading over a few times to really let it sink in. What we do is so much more important than what we say. Actions thunder, words whisper.

I have found this especially true when it comes to encouraging my kids to develop healthy eating habits. I can (and do) talk until I'm blue in the face about the harm of processed foods versus the synergistic power of wholesome foods, but the kiddos are really just waiting for me to stop talking to see what I serve for dinner.

What you do matters so much more than what you say.

Making grain-free and refined-sugar-free versions of treats like these Apple Fritters is a great way to practice what you preach. I was raised on sugary, greasy doughnuts, and apple fritters were my absolute favorite. This version takes wholesome ingredients to create a sweet, light, apple-y treat that will put a smile on your face without giving you a tummy ache.

Ingredients

1½ cups blanched almond flour

½ cup coconut palm sugar

2 teaspoons baking powder

½ teaspoon sea salt

2 teaspoons ground cinnamon

¼ teaspoon ground nutmeg

4 tablespoons coconut oil

2 eggs, separated

½ teaspoon vanilla extract

½ cup coconut cream

1¼ cups chopped Fuji apple

1 cup shredded Fuji apple

Steps

1. Preheat the oven to 350°F. Generously grease a doughnut twist pan with coconut oil. Alternatively, you could use a circular doughnut mold pan, muffin pan, or doughnut-hole pan—simply decrease the baking time for smaller pans.

2. In a large mixing bowl, combine the blanched almond flour, coconut palm sugar, baking powder, salt, cinnamon, and nutmeg. Use 2 knives to cut in the coconut oil until coarse crumbs form.

3. In a small bowl, combine the egg yolks, vanilla extract, and coconut cream. Add the yolk mixture to the flour mixture and mix until well combined.

4. In a stand mixer fitted with the whisk attachment or in a large bowl with a whisk, beat the egg whites until soft peaks form. Carefully fold the whites into the batter, then carefully fold in the chopped and shredded apples.

5. Fill the prepared doughnut molds. Bake for 15–18 minutes, until golden and baked through. Allow the fritters to cool slightly before removing them from the pan. Store leftovers in an airtight container in the fridge for up to 1 week.

(Per fritter) Calories: 303 | Fat: 20g | Sodium: 364mg
Carbs: 24g | Fiber: 4g | Sugar: 16g | Protein: 7g

QUICK TIP

I have another recipe for getting an apple fritter fix. I call it Apple Fritter Muffins, and it's a version of **QUINOA EGG MUFFINS** (page 34) that incorporates tender, cinnamon-y apples. Preheat the oven to 350°F and line 12 muffin cups with paper liners. Sauté 2 diced apples with 1 tablespoon coconut oil, 1 tablespoon ground cinnamon, and a handful of both golden raisins and chopped pecans. Then whisk together 9 eggs, 3 tablespoons coconut milk, 1½ tablespoons coconut flour, ¼ teaspoon baking soda, and a pinch of sea salt. Fold in half of the apple mixture, then fill the muffin cups, and sprinkle the remaining apple mixture over the tops. Bake for 35 minutes, until fully set. A protein-filled apple treat!

CHOCOLATE-GLAZED DOUGHNUTS

prep time: 20 minutes ☙ *cooking time:* 15 minutes ☙ *makes:* 6 doughnuts

Do you have an open mind?

An open mind hasn't been calcified in its idea of how the world works. An open mind is willing to consider that a new way of doing something could be a better way.

An open mind is a gift.

Children naturally have open minds. Their idea of the world is delightfully pliable. Isn't this why you love spending time with the children in your life? The magic of possibility and wonder dances in their eyes.

This recipe for Chocolate-Glazed Doughnuts requires that you have an open mind. Forget your idea of what a doughnut is and open up to the possibility that maybe, just maybe, these baked, grain-free, lightly sweetened doughnuts are exactly what a doughnut should be.

Open your mind, my friend, open your mind . . .

Ingredients

FOR THE DOUGHNUTS:

1¼ cups blanched almond flour

¼ teaspoon baking soda

2 tablespoons coconut oil, melted

1 tablespoon pure maple syrup

10 drops liquid stevia

¼ teaspoon almond extract

½ teaspoon vanilla extract

1 teaspoon apple cider vinegar

2 eggs, at room temperature, separated

FOR THE CHOCOLATE GLAZE:

¾ cup unsweetened chocolate pieces

2 tablespoons raw honey

1 tablespoon coconut oil

20 drops liquid stevia

FOR THE GARNISH:

RAINBOW COCONUT SPRINKLES (page 240)

Steps

FOR THE DOUGHNUTS:

1. Preheat the oven to 350°F. Generously grease a 6-mold doughnut pan with coconut oil and set aside.

2. Combine the flour and baking soda in a medium bowl. In another medium bowl, combine the coconut oil, maple syrup, liquid stevia, almond extract, vanilla extract, vinegar, and egg yolks. Mix the dry ingredients into the wet and set aside.

3. In a stand mixer fitted with the whisk attachment or in a large bowl with a whisk, beat the egg whites until peaks form. Gently fold the egg whites into the batter.

4. Equally distribute the batter among the 6 doughnut molds. Smooth out the tops of each doughnut. Bake for 12–15 minutes, until lightly golden. Allow the doughnuts to cool before removing them from the pan and transferring to the fridge to chill.

FOR THE CHOCOLATE GLAZE:

In a lazy man's double boiler (see page 221), combine the glaze ingredients. Mix until smooth. Pour the melted chocolate into a shallow dish and dip each chilled doughnut into the mixture. Place the glazed doughnuts on a plate and chill in the fridge until the chocolate has set.

FOR THE GARNISH:

Sprinkle with Rainbow Coconut Sprinkles.

(Per doughnut) Calories: 336 | Fat: 24g | Sodium: 101mg
Carbs: 17g | Fiber: 3g | Sugar: 9g | Protein: 9g

QUICK TIP

When stevia is used in conjunction with another wholesome sweetener, it's possible to reduce calories while keeping a pleasant, sweet flavor—sans the stevia aftertaste. If you aren't quite there yet and are still getting used to switching from refined sugars to wholesome sweeteners, then feel free to use my original recipe: 3 tablespoons maple syrup in lieu of the stevia for the doughnuts, and ¼ cup raw honey in lieu of the stevia for the glaze. But next time I know you'll give the stevia a try . . . with an open mind.

THREE-INGREDIENT PANCAKES

prep time: 10 minutes 🍂 *cooking time:* 10 minutes 🍂 *serves:* 4

I love simplifying—like going through my clothes and giving away everything I no longer wear, so that my closet only holds things I really like. Organizing the pantry and throwing out anything expired, so that the kitchen only holds usable ingredients. Filtering my inbox, so that I only see relevant emails.

And the simplification doesn't stop there.

Lately I've been making recipes that are simpler and contain fewer ingredients, and it doesn't get any simpler than these Three-Ingredient Pancakes. So many pancake recipes out there contain loads of ingredients (I've been guilty of this!), and while they probably taste fantastic, there is an elegance to making something as simply as possible.

The three ingredients used here are banana + egg + almond butter (you can also add some vanilla extract or cinnamon for enhanced flavor). It sounds crazy that these three ingredients can come together to form delicious, wholesome pancakes, but trust me on this one—it works!

(For a refresher on having an open mind, flip back one page.)

Ingredients

3 ripe bananas

2 eggs

3 tablespoons almond butter

½ teaspoon vanilla extract or ground cinnamon (optional)

Steps

1. Blend the bananas in a food processor. Add the eggs, almond butter, and any flavor additions, if using. Blend until smooth.

2. Preheat a griddle or skillet and lightly grease it with coconut oil. Scoop the batter ¼ cup at a time onto the griddle.

3. Once you see bubbles form, about 4 minutes, flip and cook the other side until golden, about another 4 minutes. Serve with fresh fruit.

(Per serving) Calories: 193 | Fat: 9g | Sodium: 36mg
Carbs: 20g | Fiber: 3g | Sugar: 10g | Protein: 6g

· · · · · · · · · **I'LL SHOW YOU HOW** · · · · · · · · ·

Click over to https://youtu.be/B9_-SjaEVEk
and I'll walk you through this easy pancake recipe!

QUICK TIP

The blending process is key to making this recipe work. It's only three ingredients, but they need to be thoroughly blended together until they become one cohesive batter for your pancakes to turn out perfectly. Blend, blend, blend. Also, don't forget to generously grease that skillet before pouring in the batter. And cook the pancakes until bubbles appear before flipping to cook the other side. Oh, and have fun with this!

HARVEST NUT PANCAKES

prep time: 15 minutes ☕ *cooking time:* 8 minutes per batch ☕ *serves:* 6

Have you ever had one of those days where your eating just spirals out of control? Don't be embarrassed; it's just me here, and I don't judge.

I've had those days before—and for me it would usually start with a big stack of grain-filled pancakes. There's just something about the weekends that makes me crave pancakes. One bad decision begets the next bad decision and the next . . . After one of these days, I need a hard reset. A hard reset is just like turning off your computer or phone, completely powering it down so that it can regroup, reshuffle, reorganize, and power back on at full capacity. You sometimes need a hard reset, too.

The key to a truly effective hard reset is to completely let go of the mistakes you made so that you can start again, clean and fresh. If you're holding on to those mistakes, then it will cloud your mind and will bring you crashing back down again.

Breathe. Release the past. Make like Elsa and *let it go*.

Ingredients

- 1 cup pecans
- ¼ cup coconut flour
- 4 eggs
- 1 tablespoon coconut cream
- ¼ teaspoon baking soda
- 1 tablespoon pure maple syrup, plus more for serving
- ½ teaspoon vanilla extract
- 1 tablespoon coconut oil
- 2 bananas, sliced in half lengthwise and widthwise

Steps

1. Toast the pecans in a large dry skillet over medium heat until golden, about 8 minutes. Remove the pan from the heat and set a few tablespoons of nuts aside. Cool the remaining pecans and pulse them in a food processor until they're finely ground.

2. Add the coconut flour, eggs, coconut cream, baking soda, syrup, and vanilla to the food processor and mix until fully combined.

3. Lightly grease a griddle and place it over medium-high heat. Scoop the batter ¼ cup at a time onto the griddle and cook for 4 minutes, until golden, then flip and cook the other side. Repeat with the remainder of the batter and more coconut oil as needed.

4. Heat the coconut oil in a skillet over medium-high heat. Add the banana pieces and cook until they're golden and caramelized, about 5 minutes. Serve the caramelized bananas with the pancakes and sprinkle with the reserved toasted pecans and maple syrup.

(Per serving) Calories: 266 | Fat: 20g | Sodium: 109mg
Carbs: 16g | Fiber: 4g | Sugar: 8g | Protein: 7g

QUICK TIP

When I experience a craving for pancakes (like, pretty much every Saturday), I love whipping up a batch of these Harvest Nut Pancakes. There are lots of fun ways to modify pancakes to fit your mood: Mash some bananas and add them to the batter. Mix in a scoop or two of vanilla protein powder. Throw in a handful of stevia-sweetened dark chocolate chips (like Lily's brand). Sprinkle in some ground cinnamon. Add shredded apple. Ooooh, or how about some crumbled bacon?

CHOCOLATE CHIP PANCAKE SANDWICHES

prep time: 15 minutes ☙ *cooking time:* 8 minutes ☙ *serves:* 8

Back in my early twenties, when I was a junk food vegetarian and blissfully unaware of the massive nutritional voids in my diet, I would eat purely for taste. (Gasp!)

Yep, if it tasted good and was fairly quick and cost-effective, then I would dip it in ketchup and eat it. Looking back, I'm sure that the only reason that I wasn't 600 pounds and counting was my love of exercise. (Phew!)

My favorite breakfast, at the time, was a toasted chocolate chip bagel (bought at the supermarket in bulk on Sundays) slathered in cream cheese, mounded with scrambled eggs, and smothered in cheddar cheese. I'd cut it into four pieces and dip it in ketchup. (Oh how far I've come . . .)

These days, I'll occasionally make an egg sandwich out of chocolate chip pancakes with a scrambled egg and crispy bacon—and dip it in natural ketchup. Ahhh, a delicious walk down memory lane—without the grains, gluten, dairy, and refined sugar!

Ingredients

FOR THE CHOCOLATE CHIP PANCAKES:

1 ripe banana, mashed

2 eggs

¼ cup coconut milk

¼ cup coconut palm sugar

1 tablespoon vanilla extract

¼ teaspoon almond extract

1½ cups blanched almond flour

½ teaspoon baking soda

½ teaspoon sea salt

½ cup stevia-sweetened dark chocolate chips

FOR THE BREAKFAST SANDWICH:

4 eggs, scrambled

4 strips bacon, cooked and halved lengthwise and widthwise

Steps

FOR THE CHOCOLATE CHIP PANCAKES:

1. In a large mixing bowl, combine the banana, eggs, coconut milk, coconut palm sugar, and vanilla and almond extracts. Mix until the big banana lumps have disappeared.

2. In a medium bowl, combine the almond flour, baking soda, and salt. Mix well. Add the dry ingredients to the wet and mix until fully combined. Stir in the chocolate chips.

3. Place a pancake griddle over medium heat and generously grease with coconut oil. Scoop the batter ¼ cup at a time onto the griddle. (If you want your pancake sandwiches to be perfectly symmetrical, then use a metal cookie cutter or pancake shaper—otherwise, appreciate the beauty of asymmetry.) Once you see bubbles form, about 4 minutes, flip and cook the other side until golden, about another 4 minutes.

FOR THE BREAKFAST SANDWICH:

Assemble the sandwiches with a pancake on the bottom, a scrambled egg and strip of bacon, and a pancake on top. If you want the full experience, then cut your sandwich into 4 pieces and dip into some (all-natural) ketchup.

(Per sandwich) Calories: 307 | Fat: 21g | Sodium: 313mg
Carbs: 21g | Fiber: 4g | Sugar: 8g | Protein: 12g

HEALTHY EATING TIP

If you look really closely at my coffee (feel free to admire Chloe's bright smile on the mug), you'll notice a shine—that's a spoonful of coconut oil. Really! Being surrounded by a lot of fitness experts—starting with B (who is the personal trainer who went on to create the franchise Fit Body Bootcamp)—I get the inside scoop on the latest and greatest fat-burning breakthroughs. Most recently, everyone's talking about medium-chain triglycerides, MCTs (which are found in coconut oil), and their amazing fat-burning properties.

Now, I start to tune out right around the "C" in "MCT," but I'm always game for trying something new, especially when people I respect are benefitting from it. So, rather than taking a spoonful of coconut oil by itself, like the hard-core guys do, I started adding it to my coffee in the morning. Turns out that it's the perfect replacement for half-and-half, as it gives a creamy, yummy texture to the coffee. Add a packet of stevia and a pinch of coconut palm sugar and you've just made the perfect cup of coffee.

COCONUT FLOUR CREPES

prep time: 10 minutes ⬤ *cooking time:* 4 minutes per crepe ⬤ *serves:* 6

Um, have you heard? Healthy living is a journey, not a destination.

You'll never wake up one day to find that you've arrived. Instead, you'll wake up to each and every new day with choices and opportunities to make and take.

Make small, conscious decisions in the right direction for years and eventually you'll find yourself in a place where it's second nature and you're authentically, organically living in health, wellness, and fitness.

But make no mistake about it—you'll still be actively living the journey.

Don't expect permanent change to happen overnight. Change happens in fits and starts, and that's okay. You are rewriting habits, taste preferences, and a hardwired lifestyle—this will take careful, gradual rewiring to truly, permanently alter.

But make no mistake about it—you *can* and *will* win in this process—and it's easier than you might think. Especially with recipes like this one. These crepes are so crazy delish that B actually accused me of using refined white flour when he first tried them!

Ingredients

¼ **cup coconut flour**

½ **cup arrowroot starch**

½ **teaspoon sea salt**

1 **(13.7-ounce) can full-fat coconut milk**

6 **eggs**

Steps

1. Combine all of the ingredients in a high-speed blender and blend until completely smooth.

2. Heat a lightly oiled griddle or frying pan over medium-high heat. Scoop the batter ¼ cup at a time onto the griddle. Tilt the pan in a circular motion so that the batter evenly coats the pan.

3. Cook the crepe for about 2 minutes, until the bottom is light brown. Loosen with a spatula, flip, and cook the other side for 2 minutes or until golden. Repeat with the remaining batter and more coconut oil as needed. Serve hot.

(Per serving) Calories: 284 | Fat: 15g | Sodium: 293mg
Carbs: 24g | Fiber: 7g | Sugar: 7g | Protein: 10g

· · · · · · · **SUPER APPLE PANCAKES** · · · · · · ·

Click over to https://youtu.be/hVcCVYfC0bM and I'll show you how to make these tasty Apple Ring Pancakes!

QUICK TIP

If you have fresh or frozen berries on hand, then whip up a little berry sauce. In a saucepan, combine 1 cup berries with 1 teaspoon arrowroot starch, a pinch of sea salt, ¼ cup water, the juice and zest from a small lemon, and raw honey or stevia to taste. Bring to a boil, stirring constantly, then cook for another 2–3 minutes, until thickened.

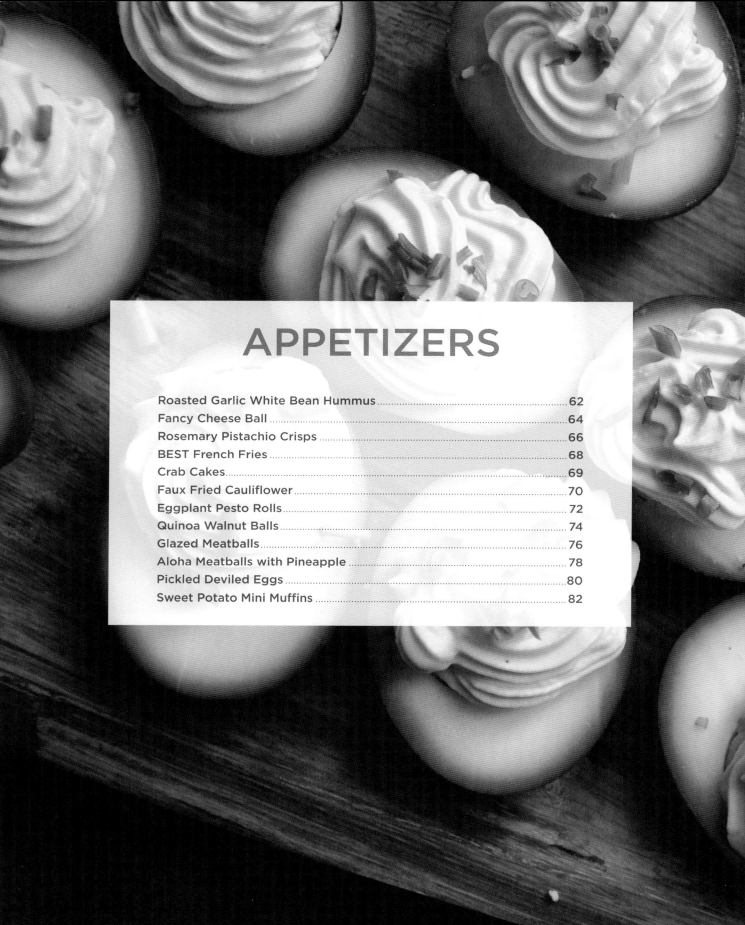

APPETIZERS

When you realize that it's time to start paying more attention to nutrition, one of the first things that usually happens is you cut out the delicious things that you put out when guests come to visit—chips, crusty bread, creamy dips, and cheese platters.

And then you wonder, *What's left?*

What will you serve when friends and family come to call? Sliced veggies? Again? And how exactly are you going to explain the change?

My approach—and what I aim to share with you in this chapter—is to fill the void with tantalizing dishes that are reminiscent of your old favorites but made with 100 percent wholesome ingredients. These recipes will wow your guests with exciting bites that you'll proudly serve!

ROASTED GARLIC WHITE BEAN HUMMUS

prep time: 10 minutes ● *cooking time:* 1 hour ● *makes:* 2 cups

Do you pay attention to how food makes you feel when you eat it? Some foods will make you feel lethargic. Some foods will make you feel bloated. Some foods will make you feel heavy.

Other foods will make you feel energetic. Other foods will make you feel svelte. Other foods will make you feel light and airy.

Judge food based on the way it makes you feel rather than anything else. Eat the foods that help you operate at your highest level.

It's not often that I cook with beans, as you'll see with my bean-less chili coming up (page 128), which is mainly because of how I feel after eating them. Not my best!

However, since white bean hummus is the base for my favorite chicken soup recipe (CHICKEN SOUP WITH QUINOA AND ROASTED RED PEPPERS, page 162), I wanted to have a quick, homemade version to use rather than the store-bought kind.

Also, hummus is a much better option when it comes to party dips, because it's rich and creamy but isn't filled with calorie-laden dairy products. So it's nice to have this recipe on hand to fill that little bowl in the center of the cut veggies.

Ingredients

2 heads garlic

¼ cup plus 2 teaspoons extra-virgin olive oil, divided

2 (15-ounce) cans white kidney beans, drained and rinsed

juice of 1 lemon

2 tablespoons tahini

1 teaspoon Dijon mustard

1 teaspoon ground cumin

1 teaspoon sea salt

pinch of black pepper

4 sun-dried tomatoes, minced

¼ cup chopped fresh basil

Steps

1. Preheat the oven to 350°F. Cut a ½-inch slice off the top of each garlic head. Drizzle a teaspoon of olive oil over each bulb, and then wrap them each in foil. Bake for 1 hour.

2. Once the garlic has cooled a bit, gently squeeze out the cloves and transfer them to the bowl of a food processor.

3. Add the beans to the food processor along with the lemon juice, tahini, Dijon, remaining ¼ cup olive oil, cumin, salt, and pepper. Blend until the mixture is smooth and thick. Add the tomatoes and basil and pulse until incorporated into the hummus. Store leftovers in an airtight container in the fridge for up to 1 week.

(Per 2 tablespoons) Calories: 126 | Fat: 6g | Sodium: 256mg
Carbs: 13g | Fiber: 3g | Sugar: 1g | Protein: 5g

QUICK TIP

I fancied up this recipe with roasted garlic, sun-dried tomatoes, and fresh basil, which is awesome for dipping. However, if you're simply making the hummus to use as the base for the soup on page 162, then feel free to leave out these extra ingredients. The soup already has phenomenal flavor from the roasted red peppers, so it doesn't need the fancy stuff.

FANCY CHEESE BALL

prep time: 15 minutes
chilling time: 4 hours
serves: 24

I had a conversation with a man named Dan recently about his struggle with type 2 diabetes. Dan told me that losing 50 pounds would likely get him off his daily medication, an accomplishment that would greatly improve the quality of his life.

Dan *needed* to change. His health hinged on it, and he had a wife and young daughter who depended on him. He wiped tears from his eyes at the thought of not being there for them.

Dan *wanted* to change. His life hadn't turned out the way he thought it would, and the state of his weight and health were largely to blame. Losing weight and regaining his health would open up a host of new possibilities and opportunities for him.

And yet . . . the chasm between where he currently sits and where he wants to go gapes wide and deep. He teeters on the edge of this frighteningly dark abyss, and doubt and impossibility seep into his mind.

Dan is no different than you and me. We all have our chasms to traverse. Any time that you want to instill change and improvement into your life, it requires crossing over from one way of doing things to a new way.

But *how* do you make it across?

How do you go from 50 pounds overweight to a healthy body mass index (BMI)?

How do you go from a junk food lover to a health food lover?

How do you go from a snooze-hitter to an early riser?

How do you go from a couch potato to active and fit?

How do you go from someone who *talks* about his goals to someone who *accomplishes* his goals?

Lucky for us there's a formula to follow that will get you from point A to point B every single time without fail. And all you have to do is stick with it.

Small Degree of Change + Time = A New You

Commit to making one small degree of change each and every day, and over time you will arrive on the other side of that chasm, a brand-new you.

Did you eat white rice with dinner yesterday? Today choose brown rice. Next week choose cauliflower rice.

Did you eat a doughnut for breakfast yesterday? Today eat half of a doughnut and a piece of fruit. Next week choose a CHOCOLATE-GLAZED DOUGHNUT (page 50).

Did you wake up at 7 A.M. today? Tomorrow wake up at 6:45. Next week wake up at 6:30.

Did you sit all day today? Tomorrow walk for 15 minutes. Next week walk for 30 minutes.

And the end result, the reward, comes after you've made that new way of doing things a part of who you are.

We are all capable of great change and great improvement—just not all at once.

Permanent change takes place one degree at a time, so don't look at this recipe as simply a dairy-free cheese ball, but rather as a degree of (delicious) change in the right direction.

Ingredients

- 3 cups cashews, soaked in hot water for 2 hours
- 1 teaspoon sweet paprika
- 1 teaspoon ground turmeric
- 2 teaspoons sea salt
- 2 teaspoons onion powder
- ¼ cup minced sun-dried tomatoes
- ½ cup nutritional yeast
- 1 teaspoon yellow mustard
- 2 tablespoons dry white wine
- 2 tablespoons apple cider vinegar
- 1 cup coconut oil, melted
- ½ cup sliced almonds

Steps

1. Drain the cashew soaking water and add the nuts to the bowl of a food processor. Add the remaining ingredients except for the almonds and blend until smooth. Transfer the mixture to the fridge to chill for 4 hours.

2. Divide the mixture in half and form each half into a ball. Roll both balls in the sliced almonds, wrap them each in plastic wrap, and return them to the fridge to chill until you're ready to serve.

(Per serving) Calories: 125 | Fat: 10g | Sodium: 129mg
Carbs: 6g | Fiber: 2g | Sugar: 1g | Protein: 4g

QUICK TIP

Before making this cheese ball. be sure to first soak the cashews in hot water for a couple of hours. This will ensure that your cheese is really creamy.

ROSEMARY PISTACHIO CRISPS

prep time: 30 minutes ● *chilling time:* overnight ● *cooking time:* 30 + 30 minutes
makes: 36 crisps

This is one of the tastiest snack foods that I've ever made. B and I destroyed a bag of these yummy crisps on a drive to Mammoth, California, for a weekend of snowboarding last month. De-stroyed it. If you're feeling generous, then package some of your crisps in pretty holiday bags to give away to friends and family as scrumptious edible gifts. Or hide them in the back of your freezer and secretly eat them when the kids are at school. Your choice.

Ingredients

1 cup golden raisins

1 cup pistachios, shelled

1 (13.7-ounce) can full-fat coconut milk

2 tablespoons lemon juice

1 cup blanched almond flour

3/4 cup raw pecans, ground

2 tablespoons flax meal

2 tablespoons minced fresh rosemary

2 teaspoons baking soda

1 teaspoon sea salt

1/3 cup coconut palm sugar

1/2 cup raw unsalted pepitas

1/4 cup raw unsalted sunflower seeds

Steps

1. Preheat the oven to 350°F. Generously grease 6 mini loaf pans (4 × 2½ inches) with coconut oil.

2. Soak the raisins in a small bowl of hot water for 15 minutes, until plumped. Drain and set aside.

3. Spread the pistachios over a rimmed baking sheet and toast in the oven for 8–10 minutes, until golden. Set aside.

4. In a small bowl, combine the coconut milk and lemon juice. Stir and allow to sit for 10 minutes.

5. In a large mixing bowl, combine the blanched almond flour, ground pecans, flax meal, rosemary, baking soda, salt, and coconut palm sugar. Add the coconut milk mixture and stir until well combined. Stir in the toasted pistachios, raisins, pepitas, and sunflower seeds.

6. Divide the mixture among the prepared mini loaf pans. Bake for 30–35 minutes, until golden on the top and fully set. Once cooled, remove the loaves from the pans, place in an airtight container, and transfer to the freezer to chill overnight.

7. Preheat the oven to 350°F. Line two 18 × 26-inch rimmed baking sheets with parchment paper. Thinly slice the frozen loaves into ¼-inch-thick slices and arrange them in a single layer on the baking sheets. Bake for 30 minutes, or until crisp and golden. Keep in mind that the slices will continue to crisp up as they cool.

(Per 3 crisps) Calories: 191 | Fat: 12g | Sodium: 179mg
Carbs: 17g | Fiber: 4g | Sugar: 12g | Protein: 5g

HEALTHY EATING TIP

If you continue to eat the way that you've always eaten, then you'll continue to have the body that you've always had.

BEST FRENCH FRIES

prep time: 10 minutes ● *cooking time:* 25 minutes
serves: 6

Yes, this is happening! Real healthy fries that taste AMAZING and are made with BAKED PARSNIPS!

I have always been very open and honest about my love for French fries. Regular, curly, seasoned, sweet potato—I don't discriminate!

However, regular fries really are so bad for us. All that unhealthy fat and all of those calories are hard to justify eating very often. And having a belly full of greasy fries never feels too awesome.

In the past I have baked sweet potato fries, which are amazing, and I've even baked carrot fries, which are also quite good. But *nothing* has come as close to tasting like real, authentic fries than these baked parsnip fries.

If you are a fry lover, please, please, please try this recipe and let me know what you think!

Ingredients

2 large parsnips

1 tablespoon minced fresh rosemary

2 cloves garlic, chopped

3 tablespoons extra-virgin olive oil

pinch of sea salt and black pepper

½ teaspoon sweet paprika

natural ketchup, for serving

Steps

1. Preheat the oven to 450°F. Line an 18 × 26-inch rimmed baking sheet with parchment paper.

2. Peel the parsnips and trim the ends. Cut each parsnip in half horizontally, then make 2 cuts in each direction to create 9 sticks out of each half. In a large bowl, toss the parsnip sticks with the rosemary, garlic, olive oil, salt, pepper, and paprika.

3. Spread the fries over the prepared baking sheet. Roast for 10 minutes, flip, and then roast for another 10–15 minutes, until browned and crispy. Serve with the ketchup.

(Per serving) Calories: 128 | Fat: 8g | Sodium: 37mg
Carbs: 15g | Fiber: 5g | Sugar: 3g | Protein: 1g

QUICK TIP

Feeling spicy? To make Cajun Fries, season the fries before baking with a spice blend of ¼ teaspoon each of sea salt, garlic powder, and smoked paprika and ⅛ teaspoon each of onion powder, cayenne pepper, dried oregano, and dried thyme.

CRAB CAKES

prep time: 15 minutes ● *cooking time:* 15 minutes
serves: 6

If you were hoping to change your eating habits with good old-fashioned willpower, then I'm about to let you off the hook: Willpower is a myth.

There's no universal bucket of willpower that someone forgot to grant you access to. You don't need willpower to succeed at living a healthy life. You don't need willpower to succeed at anything.

All you need is the ability to commit to a habit.

It's really that simple. Our daily habits quite literally make us—day after day, week after week, month after month, year after year. Your past failures did not come as the result of failed willpower, but simply as a failure to instill the daily habit required to achieve the outcome that you desired. Decide the outcome you want and then set the daily habits needed to systematically achieve the outcome.

Ingredients

1 pound crabmeat, picked over for shells

1 cup cauliflower florets, steamed and mashed

3 scallions, whites and greens, minced

1/2 cup minced red bell pepper

1 tablespoon flax meal

1 teaspoon mustard powder

1 teaspoon sea salt

pinch of ground cayenne pepper

2 eggs

3 tablespoons coconut cream

2 tablespoons coconut flour

TARTAR SAUCE **(page 201), for serving**

Steps

1. Preheat the broiler to high. Lightly grease a 10 × 15-inch rimmed baking sheet with olive oil.

2. In a large bowl, combine all of the ingredients. Use your hands to shape the mixture into 6 patties and place them on the prepared pan.

3. Broil the crab cakes for 10–15 minutes, until golden. Serve with Tartar Sauce.

(Per crab cake) Calories: 125 | Fat: 4g | Sodium: 708mg Carbs: 4g | Fiber: 2g | Sugar: 1g | Protein: 17g

QUICK TIP

This recipe uses the broiler as the cooking method, but it's also possible to pan-fry your crab cakes. To do so, heat a few tablespoons of olive oil or coconut oil in a large skillet and cook each side for 4–5 minutes, until golden.

FAUX FRIED CAULIFLOWER

prep time: 15 minutes ● *cooking time:* 24 minutes ● *serves:* 8

Oh em gee! A cauliflower recipe from the Recipe Hacker that doesn't involve the grating attachment of a food processor? What in the world . . . ?

If you haven't ever tried fried cauliflower, then this recipe will very likely rock your world. No exaggerating, this stuff is legit.

My love affair (yes, it's gotten that serious) with fried cauliflower started at one of our favorite local restaurants, a cozy Lebanese-Mediterranean eatery. Sammy, the owner and resident food genius, fries his simply seasoned cauliflower and then drizzles it with two flavor-intensive sauces. While I've enjoyed this dish for years, I was doubtful that I'd be able to give it a proper Real Healthy Recipes makeover.

Recently, while hanging out with friends in Santa Monica, I experienced another fried cauliflower dish that rivaled Sammy's. This one had the flavor built into the breading on the cauliflower and was dotted with pickled veggies. *Wowsa!* The combo of seasoned, crispy cauliflower and tangy, crunchy pickled veggies was phenomenal.

And I was pretty sure I could recreate it without the oil and with grain-free breading.

The process of "breading" the cauliflower does take a little time and finesse, and there are lower-calorie ways to serve up cauliflower, but for a special treat, this recipe is out of this world. Serve it up hot and don't be stingy with the pickled veggies.

Ingredients

1 head cauliflower

2 tablespoons coconut flour

1/4 teaspoon garlic powder

2 eggs, beaten

1/4 cup coconut milk

1/2 teaspoon sea salt

1/2 cup blanched almond flour

1/3 cup nutritional yeast

1 teaspoon sweet paprika

pinch of ground cayenne pepper

1/2 teaspoon dried oregano

1 (16-ounce) jar pickled carrots, cauliflower, celery, pearl onions, and red peppers, chopped (pickled in vinegar and found in the olive section in most markets)

Steps

1. Preheat the oven to 425°F. Lightly grease an 18 × 26-inch rimmed baking sheet with olive oil.

2. Bring a large pot of water to a boil over high heat. Wash the cauliflower, discard the leaves, and trim the stem. Add the whole head of cauliflower to the boiling water. Cover the pot and allow it to boil for 5 minutes. Remove the cauliflower from the water (careful—it's hot!) and rinse it with cold water. When it's cool enough to handle, quarter the cauliflower head, then separate each section into individual florets. Set aside.

3. In one medium bowl, combine the coconut flour and garlic powder. In a second medium bowl, combine the eggs, coconut milk, and salt. In a third bowl, combine the almond flour, nutritional yeast, paprika, cayenne, and oregano.

4. In batches, coat the florets first in bowl #1, then in bowl #2, and finally in bowl #3. Arrange them, spaced 1/2 inch apart, on the prepared baking sheet. Bake for 12 minutes, then turn each piece using tongs. Bake for another 12 minutes, until golden. Sprinkle with the pickled veggies and serve hot.

(Per serving) Calories: 105 | Fat: 7g | Sodium: 178mg
Carbs: 7g | Fiber: 4g | Sugar: 2g | Protein: 6g

QUICK TIP

You could pan-fry these bad boys instead of baking them, if you wanted to. I've done it before, in a little olive oil, and it comes out beautifully. Keep in mind, though, that this method does increase the calorie and fat content of the recipe, and it does make the kitchen a wee bit messier.

EGGPLANT PESTO ROLLS

prep time: 40 minutes
cooking time: 30 minutes
serves: 8

When it comes to cooking eggplant, the results can be rather hit or miss. All too often eggplant is undercooked and underseasoned. You know what I'm talking about—we've all taken a bite of spongy, tasteless eggplant. Ick! On the other hand, when eggplant is properly cooked until it's perfectly tender and seasoned courageously, it becomes one of the most delicious vegetables on the planet.

In this recipe we are going to salt and drain the sliced eggplant—one way to ensure it'll be tender and not spongy; coat it with olive oil, lemon juice, and garlic; roast it; then slather it with homemade pesto. Add a simple strip of roasted bell pepper rolled up in the middle, and you've got yourself one amazingly flavorful, nutritious appetizer.

Ingredients

FOR THE PESTO:

½ cup walnuts

2–3 cups basil leaves

4 cloves garlic

sea salt

¼ cup extra-virgin olive oil

½ cup nutritional yeast

1 tablespoon lemon juice

FOR THE EGGPLANT ROLLS:

4 large eggplants

sea salt

3 tablespoons extra-virgin olive oil, divided

1 heaping tablespoon minced garlic (about 3 cloves)

juice of 1 lemon

2 red bell peppers

chopped fresh basil, for garnish

Steps

FOR THE PESTO:

1. Toast the walnuts in a toaster oven, regular oven, or dry skillet for a few minutes—watch closely, as they go from browned to black very quickly.

2. Combine the walnuts, basil, garlic, and a generous pinch of salt in the bowl of a food processor and blend until combined. Add the olive oil, then the nutritional yeast, and then the lemon juice, blending after each addition. Combine until your pesto has the consistency of paste—don't overblend.

FOR THE EGGPLANT ROLLS:

1. Trim the ends from the eggplants. Slice the eggplants lengthwise into $1/4$-inch-thick pieces. Arrange the pieces on parchment paper–lined baking sheets and generously sprinkle with salt. Allow the eggplant to sit for 20 minutes, until some liquid is drawn out. Preheat the oven to 400°F.

2. Use a paper towel to blot any moisture that's been drawn out of the eggplant, as well as most of the salt. Set aside.

3. In a small bowl, combine 2 tablespoons of the olive oil, the garlic, and the lemon juice. Generously coat the tops of the eggplant with the mixture. Transfer the eggplant to the oven and roast for about 20 minutes, until it's tender and very soft. If the eggplant feels firm, then continue to roast until it's soft. Allow the eggplant to cool slightly before topping it with pesto.

4. Rub the red bell peppers with the remaining 1 tablespoon olive oil and place them in a grill pan over high heat. Use tongs to turn the bell peppers until the skin is black on all sides. Transfer the peppers to a paper bag with the top folded and let them steam for 10 minutes. Remove the peppers from the bag, rub off all of the skin, and remove the stems and seeds. Slice the tender, roasted peppers into thin strips and set aside.

5. Spread 1 tablespoon pesto down the center, crosswise, of each slice of roasted eggplant. Top with a strip of bell pepper, then roll and secure with a toothpick. Repeat with the remaining eggplant, pesto, and bell pepper. Arrange the rolls on a serving platter and top with the chopped fresh basil. Store in the fridge until serving. Store leftovers in an airtight container in the fridge for up to 5 days.

(Per serving) Calories: 175 | Fat: 6g | Sodium: 296mg | Carbs: 20g | Fiber: 11g | Sugar: 10g | Protein: 11g

QUICK TIP

If you have leftover pesto, keep it wrapped in plastic in the fridge and use it when you make scrambled eggs or omelets throughout the week. Nothing jazzes up eggs like some fresh pesto.

QUINOA WALNUT BALLS

prep time: 15 minutes ● *cooking time:* 1 hour ● *makes:* 60 balls

When I was twelve years old, I decided on a whim to stop eating meat, and then spent the next eighteen years nibbling on veggie burgers and cheese sandwiches. It wasn't until a particularly fragrant plate of bacon proved to be irresistible that I returned to the land of chicken breast, grilled fish, and savory short ribs. (Vegetarians be warned: Bacon is a gateway meat!) I still do love homemade, savory vegetarian food, though!

I made this recipe for the vegan and vegetarians in my life . . . yes, Pete, Betsy, and Cara, I'm talking about y'all! Share this recipe with the veggie lovers in your life.

Ingredients

- 1¼ **cups uncooked quinoa**
- 2½ **cups vegetable broth**
- ¼ **cup flax meal**
- ³⁄₄ **cup filtered water**
- 1 **teaspoon extra-virgin olive oil**
- 1 **yellow onion, finely chopped**
- 3 **large carrots, finely chopped**
- 1 **teaspoon dried oregano**
- ½ **teaspoon dried thyme**
- ½ **teaspoon dried basil**
- 1 **cup walnuts**
- 2 **tablespoons coconut aminos**
- 1 **tablespoon** BALSAMIC GLAZE **(page 200 or store-bought)**
- 2 **teaspoons molasses**
- ½ **teaspoon sea salt**
- ¼ **cup minced fresh chives**

Steps

1. Preheat the oven to 350°F and lightly grease an 18 × 26-inch rimmed baking sheet with olive oil.

2. In a medium saucepan, combine the quinoa and broth over medium heat. Bring it to a boil, then decrease to a simmer and cover. Cook for 20 more minutes and set aside.

3. In a small bowl, combine the flax meal and water. Whisk them together with a fork and set aside.

4. In a medium skillet over medium heat, add the olive oil, onion, carrots, oregano, thyme, and basil. Sauté for 10 minutes, until tender. Transfer the mixture to a bowl and wipe out the skillet.

5. Return the skillet to the stove over medium-low heat. Add the walnuts and toast, stirring often, until golden, about 8 minutes. Remove from the heat and cool.

6. Combine the walnuts, coconut aminos, Balsamic Glaze, molasses, salt, cooked onion and carrot mixture, and flax mixture in the bowl of a food processor. Pulse until fully pureed.

7. Transfer the mixture to a large bowl and stir in the cooked quinoa and chives. Use your hands to form 60 Ping-Pong-size balls. Place the balls on the prepared baking sheet spaced 1 inch apart. Bake for 20–25 minutes, until cooked through. To test for doneness, cut one of the balls in half—if it holds its shape, then it's done.

8. *Optional: After baking you could brown the balls further in a skillet over medium heat with a bit of olive oil. This will make the balls a little more savory, but it's not a necessary step.

*(Per ball) Calories: 32 | Fat: 2g | Sodium: 56mg
Carbs: 4g | Fiber: 1g | Sugar: 1g | Protein: 1g*

HEALTHY LIVING TIP

Can you think back to a day when you chose to eat healthy and then later regretted it? Ya, I didn't think so.

GLAZED MEATBALLS

prep time: 20 minutes • *cooking time:* 30 minutes • *makes:* 30 meatballs

Thanksgiving is my holiday to host each year, and I have so much fun planning the menu and preparing the feast. Appetizers are as important as the main course, in my opinion. The small, savory pre-dinner dishes are often the most delicious bites of the evening.

Holiday appetizers are particularly awesome because, unlike with holiday dinner mainstays, you can be creative, inventive, and nontraditional without ruffling anyone's feathers!

This recipe for Glazed Meatballs is, quite possibly, the perfect appetizer (and snack and lunch). Serve them with toothpicks on a bed of fresh baby arugula or make them a main dish by pairing them with a bigger salad.

However and whenever you serve up these sweet-tangy meatballs, I hope that you and your taste buds enjoy them as much as I do.

Ingredients

Steps

FOR THE MEATBALLS:

1 tablespoon extra-virgin olive oil

2 cloves garlic, minced

1 yellow onion, finely chopped

1 pound ground turkey

1 green apple, shredded

1 egg, beaten

1 cup spinach, chopped

½ teaspoon sea salt

¼ teaspoon black pepper

1 teaspoon ground marjoram

1 teaspoon fennel seed

FOR THE GLAZE:

1 cup apple cider vinegar

½ cup pure maple syrup

2 tablespoons balsamic vinegar

FOR THE MEATBALLS:

1. Preheat the oven to 350°F. Lightly grease a 13 × 11-inch casserole pan with olive oil and set aside.

2. In a large skillet over medium heat, add the olive oil, garlic, and onion. Sauté for 4 minutes, until soft. Remove from the heat and allow to cool. Transfer the mixture to a large bowl.

3. Add the remaining meatball ingredients to the bowl and mix well. Form golf ball–size meatballs with your hands and place them in a single layer in the prepared casserole pan. Bake for 25 minutes.

FOR THE GLAZE:

1. Meanwhile, wipe out the skillet, add the glaze ingredients, and bring to a boil over medium heat. Decrease to a simmer and cook for 10 minutes. Remove from the heat and set aside.

2. Place the cooked meatballs in a single layer in the skillet with the glaze. Cook over low heat for 5 minutes, making sure to completely coat the meatballs with the glaze. Serve warm.

(Per 5 meatballs) Calories: 252 | Fat: 9g | Sodium: 264mg
Carbs: 25g | Fiber: 1g | Sugar: 20g | Protein: 21g

QUICK TIP

While this recipe is fantastic as an appetizer for a fancy meal, it's also really great to have on hand for quick on-the-go protein snacks. There's nothing better than opening the fridge to find a container of these savory meatballs. Throw a few on top of fresh greens and you've got yourself a phenomenal meal!

ALOHA MEATBALLS WITH PINEAPPLE

prep time: 20 minutes ● *cooking time:* 1–4 hours ● *makes:* 36 meatballs

Hawaii is one of those rare places where I'm able to really, truly relax.

Stepping off the plane, being embraced by the warm tropical air, filling my lungs with the heady fragrance of blooming plumeria, and feasting my eyes on a pink candy sunset over the Pacific puts my work brain right to sleep.

I'm sure that if I lived on the islands, I'd never lift a finger again. I'd sleep on the beach, warm waves lapping at my toes and mangoes hanging over my head. Hey, a girl can dream . . .

In the meantime (back on planet Earth), these moist meatballs deliver a generous serving of aloha with every savory bite. They're baked in the oven and then infused with flavor by simmering in a sweet and savory glaze in the slow cooker. If your party, or dinner, is still a few hours away, set the slow cooker on low heat for 3–4 hours. If you're in a hurry, then cook on high for 1–1½ hours.

Ingredients

FOR THE MEATBALLS:

2 eggs, beaten

⅓ cup blanched almond flour

½ cup finely chopped yellow onion

¼ cup full-fat coconut milk

½ teaspoon sea salt

¼ teaspoon black pepper

1 pound loose pork sausage

1 pound ground beef

FOR THE GLAZE:

1 cup APRICOT PRESERVES (make your own with the recipe on page 204 or purchase a fruit-only brand from the store)

⅓ cup coconut aminos

¼ cup apple cider vinegar

4 teaspoons grated fresh ginger

1 teaspoon chili paste

FOR ASSEMBLY:

36 thin slices cucumber (a mandoline is great for this)

36 pieces fresh pineapple

36 toothpicks

Steps

FOR THE MEATBALLS:

1. Preheat the oven to 375°F. Lightly grease an 18 × 26-inch rimmed baking sheet with olive oil.

2. Combine all of the meatball ingredients in a large bowl and mix well with your hands until fully incorporated. Form into 36 meatballs, each slightly smaller than a golf ball. Place them on the baking sheet and bake for 30 minutes.

FOR THE GLAZE:

Combine all of the glaze ingredients in a slow cooker. Transfer the cooked meatballs from the baking sheet to the slow cooker. Cover and cook on low for 3–4 hours or on high for 1–1½ hours.

FOR ASSEMBLY:

When you're ready to serve, assemble the meatball skewers. Fold a piece of cucumber in half, top with a piece of pineapple, then pierce the garnish with a toothpick. Insert the toothpick into a meatball. Arrange the finished skewers on a platter and serve.

(Per meatball) Calories: 135 | Fat: 7g | Sodium: 197mg
Carbs: 12g | Fiber: 1g | Sugar: 7g | Protein: 17g

QUICK TIP

I've served these sweet-'n'-spicy meatballs all fancied up with garnish as an appetizer as well as straight out of the slow cooker for a comforting family meal—and have loved it both ways. To complete it as a family meal, serve the meatballs over zucchini or butternut squash noodles or a big pile of leafy greens.

PICKLED DEVILED EGGS

prep time: 30 minutes ● *chilling time:* overnight ● *makes:* 24 deviled eggs

You wouldn't judge a book by its cover, would you?

No, dear reader, you wouldn't do such a thing.

Would you judge a recipe by its name? Of course not! You're far too evolved to rush to conclusions without doing your homework first.

Pickled Deviled Eggs? Have I lost my mind on this one? I know, it sounds weird. Really weird. But once you take that first sweet and tangy, bite you'll totally get it . . .

Ingredients

FOR THE PICKLED EGGS:

1 dozen eggs

1 cup coconut palm sugar

1 cup white vinegar

1 (15-ounce) can sliced beets

FOR THE DEVILED EGGS:

³/₄ cup coconut cream

2 teaspoons apple cider vinegar

2 teaspoons yellow mustard

¹/₄ teaspoon sea salt

pinch of black pepper

¹/₄ cup finely chopped fresh chives

Steps

FOR THE PICKLED EGGS:

1. First, hard-boil the eggs: If using older eggs (2 weeks or more after purchase), place them in a pot and cover with cold water by 1 inch. Bring the water to a boil, cover the pot, then remove the pot from the heat. Let the eggs sit in the hot water for 8 minutes. Drain, cool in ice water, and peel. If using fresh eggs, see the tip. Place the peeled eggs in a large glass container with a lid.

2. Combine the coconut palm sugar, vinegar, and juice from the can of beets in a medium saucepan and bring to a boil. Immediately decrease the heat to medium and add the sliced beets. Simmer for 2 minutes. Remove the pot from the heat and cool for 15 minutes.

3. Pour the beet mixture into the container holding the eggs. Cover and chill in the fridge overnight.

FOR THE DEVILED EGGS:

1. Slice the eggs in half lengthwise and carefully scoop out the yolks, keeping the whites intact. Arrange the egg whites, cup side up, on a platter.

2. In a large bowl, combine the yolks, coconut cream, apple cider vinegar, mustard, salt, and pepper. Cream the yolks with a large fork until smooth. Cut the end off of a piping bag and fill with the yolk mixture. Pipe the yolk mixture into the egg whites and sprinkle with the fresh chives. Store the eggs in the fridge until right before serving.

(Per deviled egg) Calories: 63 | Fat: 2g | Sodium: 116mg Carbs: 11g | Fiber: 1g | Sugar: 8g | Protein: 3g

QUICK TIP

One of my big pet peeves is difficult-to-peel hard-boiled eggs. Hard-boiling eggs the traditional way—by bringing them to a boil and letting them sit in the hot water—is a great method to use when your eggs aren't fresh. However, when you are using fresh eggs, this method often results in eggs that are difficult and frustrating to peel (ugh!).

The technique that works well is to steam the eggs, rather than boil them. Heat water to boiling in a steamer. Place the eggs on top of the steamer, cover, and steam for 12 minutes. Immediately plunge the eggs into a bowl of ice water. Once they're cool enough to handle, roll the eggs on the counter to quickly and painlessly peel them.

SWEET POTATO MINI MUFFINS

prep time: 20 minutes ● *cooking time:* 1 hour ● *makes:* 36 mini muffins

These are annoyingly addicting.

This could be due to the creamy consistency of the sweet potato or the savory crumbled bacon. Hard to say.

My intention behind the recipe was to hack the popular muffin recipe that's made with whipped white potato and shredded cheese. It sounded like such a fun little appetizer to serve with a holiday meal or to enjoy as a straight-from-the-fridge snack.

And, boy, are they ever! I was pleasantly shocked when thirty of these tasty little morsels disappeared from my fridge in a matter of days.

Keep in mind that these are a fun, unique way to serve mashed sweet potato, so it's not like a typical muffin. Make no mistake, they are moist, creamy, and awesome—but they won't crumble or feel like regular muffins. (If you still need a muffin fix, turn to page 36 for ZUCCHINI MUFFINS, page 38 for DOUBLE CHOCOLATE ZUCCHINI MUFFINS, and page 40 for APPLE SPICE MUFFINS.)

Serve up these creamy, dreamy sweet potato muffins with COCONUT SOUR CREAM (page 201) and garnish with chives for a fancy-shmancy party, or simply make a batch to throw into a big container and keep in the fridge for up to a week for on-the-go snacks.

Ingredients

2 medium sweet potatoes

1 tablespoon coconut oil

sea salt and black pepper, to taste

1 (13.7-ounce) can full-fat coconut milk

2 tablespoons raw honey

3 eggs

$^1/_4$ cup nutritional yeast

4 strips bacon, cooked and crumbled

$^1/_4$ cup finely chopped fresh chives, for garnish (optional)

Steps

1. Preheat the oven to 400°F. Rinse and scrub the sweet potatoes, then dry them and poke them all over with a fork. Put the potatoes in a 10 × 15-inch casserole dish, grease them with coconut oil, and season with salt and pepper. Bake for 30–40 minutes, until fork-tender. Cool and peel.

2. Blend the sweet potatoes in a food processor until smooth. Measure out 2 cups of the puree and blend with the coconut milk, honey, eggs, nutritional yeast, and $^1/_4$ teaspoon salt until smooth. Fold in the crumbled bacon with a spoon.

3. Generously grease 36 mini muffin cups with coconut oil. Fill each cup with the sweet potato batter and bake for 20–25 minutes, until the muffins are set and lightly browned on top. Ganish with the chives if desired. Allow muffins to cool before serving.

(Per muffin) Calories: 51 | Fat: 3g | Sodium: 32mg
Carbs: 3g | Fiber: 1g | Sugar: 2g | Protein: 6g

HEALTHY EATING TIP

When in doubt, eat less sugar. (You're sweet enough already!)

MAIN DISHES

Who cooks your food? Is it a human or a corporation?

According to Michael Pollan, the well-known food author and journalist, how you answer this question determines your health more than any other factor. More than economic status. More than race. More than family history.

Eating a diet filled with food that has been prepared by humans is the key to good health.

This revelation is both exciting and ominous.

It's exciting for those of us whose favorite moments of the day involve fresh ingredients, a good knife, and our favorite stack of pans. It's ominous for those of us who consider pulling the plastic off a TV dinner the same as making dinner.

For most of history, humans have been sustained by meals prepared and consumed at home. Cooking was an essential part of life—if you didn't know how to cook or didn't live with someone who did, then you'd go hungry. However, since the mid-1960s, home cooking has been steadily on the decline. We've turned our pots and pans in for TV dinners and takeout menus.

As home cooking declines, the rates for obesity and diet-related diseases such as diabetes, heart disease, and cancer steadily rise. And these trends don't show signs of slowing down.

I shudder to think of where we, collectively as humans, will find ourselves in another ten, twenty, or thirty years. What will our quality of life look like? And what does this mean for our kids and our grandkids?

All because as a society we have decided to let corporations industrialize our meals. Because we have decided to believe that home cooking is something we don't have time for or simply aren't trained to do. Because we choose convenience over quality.

What if we took a stand, in the face of our industrialized food culture, by making our own real-food meals at home? How quickly would we begin to see a difference, both in our own weight and health and also in our status as a society? Let's restore home cooking to its rightful place in our homes. Let's change the world, one home-cooked meal at a time!

The satisfaction of cooking a wholesome, real-food meal is something to be treasured—it's a gift.

Give it and receive it freely.

ROASTED VEGGIE POCKETS

prep time: 30 minutes ● *cooking time:* 50 minutes ● *makes:* 8 pockets

These Roasted Veggie Pockets are like a cross between a savory, veggie-stuffed pastry and a veggie pizza. They're a fantastic way to enjoy bountiful fall and winter vegetables. If you prefer, feel free to shape the dough into one large pocket, rather than the individual pockets, and then slice it into pieces like a pizza once cooked.

Ingredients

FOR THE ROASTED VEGGIES:

1½ cups cubed butternut squash (about 1 medium squash)

½ cup diced carrot

1 cup diced parsnip

1½ cups diced leek

1 red bell pepper, cored, seeded, and diced

1 orange bell pepper, cored, seeded, and diced

1 tablespoon minced fresh rosemary

1 tablespoon fresh thyme leaves

½ teaspoon sea salt

¼ teaspoon black pepper

1 tablespoon lemon juice

1 teaspoon extra-virgin olive oil

FOR THE DOUGH:

1½ cups blanched almond flour

¼ cup plus 2 tablespoons coconut flour

1 cup arrowroot starch

½ teaspoon sea salt

3 eggs, divided

½ cup warm water

2 tablespoons extra-virgin olive oil

2 teaspoons apple cider vinegar

Steps

FOR THE ROASTED VEGGIES:

1. Preheat the oven to 400°F. Line an 18 × 26-inch rimmed baking sheet with parchment paper and set aside.

2. Combine all of the roasted veggie ingredients in a large bowl. Mix well and spread the veggies over the prepared pan. Roast for 25 minutes, until the vegetables are tender. Keep the oven on.

FOR THE DOUGH:

1. Combine the flours, starch, and salt in a large bowl. In a medium bowl, beat together 2 of the eggs and the water, olive oil, and vinegar. Add the wet ingredients to the dry and mix to form a dough. Knead the dough in the bowl into a ball. Cover it with plastic wrap and chill in the fridge for 10 minutes.

2. Line a clean 18 × 26-inch rimmed baking sheet with parchment paper. Lightly oil the parchment paper with olive oil. Pour a few teaspoons of oil into a small bowl.

3. Divide the dough ball into 8 equal pieces on the pan. Dip your fingers in olive oil and gently press the dough pieces out from the center to create roughly 4-inch squares. Continue to dip your fingers in olive oil as you press out the dough.

4. Transfer the roasted veggies to the center of each square of dough, leaving a little room around the edges. Carefully bring the edges of the dough up over 1 inch of the veggies on all sides of the square, pressing the dough together with your fingers where it breaks and leaving an opening in the center. Whisk the remaining egg in a small bowl and brush it over the dough.

5. Bake for 25 minutes, until the dough is golden. Cool, slice, and enjoy.

(Per pocket) Calories: 323 | Fat: 28g | Sodium: 339mg
Carbs: 32g | Fiber: 9g | Sugar: 4g | Protein: 9g

QUICK TIP

When it comes to shaping the dough for these Roasted Veggie Pockets, I've found that dipping my fingertips in olive oil and pressing the dough out by hand is easier than trying to roll it between two pieces of parchment.

STUFFED PITAS WITH TAHINI SAUCE

prep time: 20 minutes
cooking time: 25 minutes
serves: 12

Emotional eating is a part of our food culture, and it's hard to escape.

As emotional beings, it's no wonder that our eating habits occasionally get tangled with the highs and lows of our feelings. The problem sets in when emotional eating takes precedence over thoughtful, healthful eating.

Remember this: Emotional eating temporarily relieves distress and then makes it impossible to attain what you really want.

Ingredients

FOR THE ROASTED VEGGIE RICE:

1 parsnip, diced

1 zucchini, diced

1 red bell pepper, cored, seeded, and chopped

2 tablespoons extra-virgin olive oil, divided

sea salt and black pepper, to taste

1 butternut squash, peeled, seeded and diced

pinch of ground nutmeg

1 head cauliflower

1 tablespoon coconut oil

juice of 2 lemons

2 cloves garlic, minced

½ cup pomegranate seeds

½ red onion, finely minced

1 cup chopped fresh parsley

FOR THE TAHINI DRESSING:

½ cup tahini

2 tablespoons water, or more as needed

½ cup full-fat coconut milk

juice of 1 lemon

1 clove garlic, minced

½ teaspoon ground cumin

pinch of sea salt and white pepper

FOR THE STUFFED PITAS:

12 COCONUT FLOUR TORTILLAS (**see Quick Tip**)

1 (16-ounce) jar pickled carrots, cauliflower, celery, pearl onions, and red pepper (pickled in vinegar and found in the olive section in most markets)

FOR THE ROASTED VEGGIE RICE:

1. Preheat the oven to 425°F and line two 18 × 26-inch rimmed baking sheets with parchment paper. In a large bowl, toss the parsnip, zucchini, and bell pepper with 1 tablespoon of the olive oil and a pinch of salt and pepper, then spread the veggies over one of the pans so they sit in a single layer.

2. In the same bowl, toss the butternut squash with the nutmeg, a pinch of salt, and the remaining 1 tablespoon olive oil. Spread the squash over the second baking sheet. Transfer both pans to the oven and roast for 17–20 minutes, until the vegetables are tender.

3. Wash the cauliflower, discard the leaves, trim and discard the stem, and chop into small pieces. Grate the pieces using the grater attachment of a food processor. In a large skillet, heat the coconut oil over medium heat. Add the shredded cauliflower and sauté for about 5 minutes, until tender. Season with salt and pepper. Remove from the heat.

4. Add the roasted veggies to the skillet and mix well. Stir in the lemon juice, garlic, pomegranate seeds, onion, and parsley. Mix until well combined. Set aside.

FOR THE TAHINI DRESSING:

In a medium bowl, combine the tahini with the water and whisk until well combined. Add the remaining ingredients and mix well. Add more water, as needed, to reach a pourable consistency. Set aside.

FOR THE STUFFED PITAS:

1. Place a grill pan over medium-high heat and grease with olive oil. Grill each tortilla for a minute or two, just long enough to make pretty grill marks.

2. Fill each tortilla with the roasted veggie rice and drizzle with the tahini dressing. Serve with the pickled vegetables.

(Per serving) Calories: 346 | Fat: 21g | Sodium: 632mg | Carbs: 22g | Fiber: 9g | Sugar: 3g | Protein: 11g

QUICK TIP

You'll need my go-to recipe for Coconut Flour Tortillas for this dish. It's a classic grain-free staple in my kitchen and super-easy to make: In a high-speed blender, combine 6 eggs, 1 (13.7-ounce) can full-fat coconut milk, 1/4 cup coconut flour, 1/4 cup flax meal, 1/2 teaspoon baking powder, and 1/2 teaspoon sea salt. Blend until smooth, then let the batter sit at room temperature for 10 minutes. Cook on a heated grill or skillet greased with coconut oil as you would crepes or pancakes.

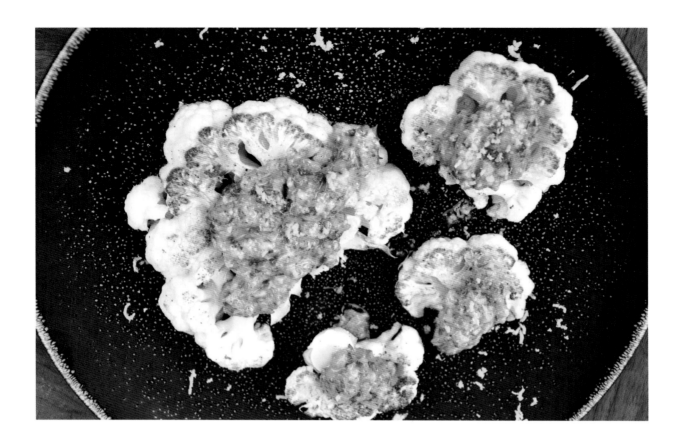

CAULIFLOWER STEAKS WITH PICKLE PESTO

prep time: 20 minutes ● *cooking time:* 15 minutes ● *serves:* 4

Is your food *real?*

That might sound like a funny question because isn't all food *real?* Well, yes and no.

All food is real in the sense that you can eat it, digest it, and derive calories from it. But there's a huge variance in the quality and nutritional density of different food items. Food that has been processed and packaged in a factory is less *real* than food that we find in nature.

Real food will go bad if left sitting out for a few days. (With the exception of honey.)

Real food is something your great-grandma would be able to recognize. (If Gran-Gran were around today.)

Real food is grown and flavored by Mother Nature. (Not produced in a factory and flavored with artificial chemical compounds.)

Eating a diet that is primarily made up of real food is where you'll find your best body, your best health, and your most vibrant energy levels.

It doesn't get more real than steaks made from big slabs of fresh cauliflower topped with homemade pickle pesto.

Having spent eighteen years as a vegetarian, I know how lovely it feels when someone takes the time to make a meat-free main dish when you visit, rather than leaving you to survive on side dishes. These Cauliflower Steaks are wonderful served alongside real steaks—and will please both the meat eaters and the herbivores among you. The Pickle Pesto will keep for up to a week in the fridge and is fantastic on eggs or chicken or mixed into a salad.

Ingredients

FOR THE PICKLE PESTO:

¼ cup fresh parsley, chopped

2 tablespoons fresh cilantro, chopped

1½ tablespoons drained capers

½ cup chopped sweet pickles

1 clove garlic, minced

1 tablespoon Dijon mustard

1 tablespoon whole grain mustard

1 tablespoon extra-virgin olive oil

1 tablespoon lemon juice

1 teaspoon white wine vinegar

FOR THE CAULIFLOWER STEAKS:

2 heads cauliflower

sea salt and black pepper, to taste

2 tablespoons coconut oil

½ cup dry white wine

½ teaspoon lemon zest

Steps

FOR THE PICKLE PESTO:

Combine all of the Pickle Pesto ingredients, except the lemon juice and vinegar, in a food processor and pulse until a paste forms. Stir in the lemon juice and vinegar, transfer the mixture to a bowl, cover with plastic wrap, and place in the fridge for 15 minutes. Store leftovers in an airtight container in the fridge for up to 1 week.

FOR THE CAULIFLOWER STEAKS:

1. Wash the cauliflower and remove the stalk and leaves. Using a large knife, carefully slice the cauliflower into 1-inch-thick pieces, cutting straight down from the top of the head through to the stalk. Some of the slices will crumble into smaller pieces, and that's okay. The key is that each piece of cauliflower has two flat sides and is about 1 inch thick.

2. Generously season both sides of each cauliflower slice with salt and pepper. Heat the coconut oil in a large skillet over medium-high heat. Add the cauliflower slices and sear each side, 4–5 minutes per side.

3. Decrease the heat to medium and add the white wine to the skillet. Cook until the wine has evaporated and the cauliflower is tender, about 5 minutes.

4. Serve the cauliflower steaks with a dollop of Pickle Pesto and a sprinkling of lemon zest.

(Per serving) Calories: 224 | Fat: 11g | Sodium: 674mg
Carbs: 14g | Fiber: 11g | Sugar: 5g | Protein: 9g

HEALTHY EATING TIP

It's time we stop asking why real food is so expensive and start asking why processed food is so cheap.

FRENCH ONION PIZZA

prep time: 15 minutes
cooking time: 45 minutes
serves: 6

You've probably heard of IQ (intelligence quotient) and EQ (emotional quotient), but did you know that there's another quotient that's equally vital to your life journey? It's called adversity quotient (AQ).

Your AQ is a measure of your ability to deal with the adversities that life throws your way. It's the science of your resilience, the strength with which you weather the storm.

The more frequent and intense the challenges that you are faced with, the greater your AQ grows. Like a muscle being put under the stress and strain of a workout, your ability to handle and quickly move through stressful situations improves with experience.

I used to think that I had a pretty high AQ, having been through my share of adversity in childhood and young adulthood . . . and then I was diagnosed with cancer. That experience brought me to my knees, quite literally, and through the experience I felt my AQ grow.

It's funny to look back at the things that used to stress me out before cancer—writing deadlines, dirty dishes, Christmas shopping, squabbles between the kids—all things that now make me smile and feel grateful to be alive.

I've also made up another quotient. I call it your cooking quotient (CQ). If you're new to cooking or if you're just out of practice, then your CQ is low, and making a grain-free pizza from scratch probably feels like climbing Everest.

Have no fear, and hang in there. With each recipe you make, your CQ increases, and before you know it, you'll be whipping up real-food dinners like this one in 30 minutes or less.

Oftentimes dairy-free pizza feels incomplete—naked, almost. But when cheese isn't part of your diet, what other option do you have? While DAIRY-FREE CHEESE SPREAD (page 99) made from cashews is a fantastic creamy sub for cheese on pizza, the gooeyness factor is missing. Enter this ahhh-mazing French Onion Pizza! The soft and creamy onions have fantastic flavor and authentic cheesy texture. Enjoy it on your next pizza night!

Ingredients

FOR THE FRENCH ONIONS:

1 tablespoon extra-virgin olive oil

2 large white onions, sliced

3 cloves garlic, minced

sea salt and black pepper, to taste

1 (13.7-ounce) can full-fat coconut milk, cream separated from the liquid (save the liquid to use in other recipes)

fresh thyme leaves

FOR THE PIZZA CRUST:

³/4 cup blanched almond flour

3 tablespoons coconut flour

¹/2 cup arrowroot starch

¹/4 teaspoon sea salt

1 egg, beaten

1 tablespoon extra-virgin olive oil, plus more for brushing crust

1 teaspoon apple cider vinegar

¹/4 cup water

Steps

FOR THE FRENCH ONIONS:

Heat the olive oil in a large skillet. Add the sliced onions and cook for about 15 minutes, until golden. Stir in the garlic and cook for another 10 minutes. Season with salt and pepper and stir in the coconut cream. Cook for another 5 minutes, then remove from the heat.

FOR THE PIZZA CRUST:

1. Preheat the oven to 425°F.

2. In a large bowl, combine the almond flour, coconut flour, arrowroot starch, and salt. Mix well.

3. In a medium bowl, combine the egg, olive oil, vinegar, and water. Add the wet ingredients to the dry and mix until a dough forms; shape into a ball. Wrap the dough in plastic wrap and chill for 15 minutes in the fridge.

4. Place the dough on a piece of parchment paper. Cover it with another piece of parchment paper and use a rolling pin to flatten the dough into a pizza crust shape, about ¹/2 inch thick. Pinch the edges of the dough to form a crust. Brush the crust with olive oil and transfer it and the parchment paper to a large baking sheet. Bake for 8 minutes, until golden.

5. Spread the creamy onion mixture over the crust, then sprinkle with the fresh thyme. Bake for another 8 minutes. Slice and enjoy!

(Per serving) Calories: 275 | Fat: 21g | Sodium: 156mg Carbs: 20g | Fiber: 5g | Sugar: 2g | Protein: 7g

HEALTHY EATING TIP

You are capable of amazing things! Stop doubting yourself and live with faith—faith that you *can* eat a real-food diet. Faith that you're meant to do something extraordinary. I believe in you! (But it's more important that *you* believe in you.)

GARLIC HERB CHICKEN TENDERS

prep time: 30 minutes ● *cooking time:* 20 minutes ● *serves:* 8

Chicken tenders are a staple of childhood—a quick, kid-approved meal that every mom has resorted to on occasion. I had my fair share of fast-food chicken nuggets before turning twelve and swearing off meat forever . . . er, well, until I turned thirty and wanted to introduce more protein back into my diet . . .

Andrew and Chloe, like most kids, also love chicken nuggets. The problem is that processed chicken nuggets are filled with lots of nasty stuff—MSG, sugar, gluten, sodium phosphates, and TBHQ (a petroleum derivative used as a stabilizer in perfumes, resins, varnishes, and oil field chemicals that has been linked to stomach tumors).

No thanks.

These Garlic Herb Chicken Tenders are made with only wholesome, real ingredients, so you can rest assured that your family is eating only the best. And we've added some fun extra flavors and balsamic ketchup to elevate this dish from kid food to gourmet.

Ingredients

FOR THE CHICKEN TENDERS:

$^1/_2$ **cup coconut flour**

sea salt and black pepper, to taste

3 eggs

1 cup almond meal

1 cup nutritional yeast

$^1/_2$ **cup flax meal**

$^1/_3$ **cup minced fresh parsley**

2 teaspoons garlic powder

2 teaspoons dried oregano

4 pounds chicken tenders

FOR THE BALSAMIC KETCHUP:

1 cup natural ketchup

3 tablespoons BALSAMIC GLAZE **(page 200)**

Steps

FOR THE CHICKEN TENDERS:

1. Preheat the oven to 425°F. Line a baking sheet with parchment paper and set aside.

2. Fill one medium bowl with the coconut flour and a sprinkle of salt and pepper. Mix well. Fill a second bowl with the eggs and whisk to combine. Fill a third bowl with the almond meal, nutritional yeast, flax meal, parsley, garlic powder, and oregano and mix well.

3. Rinse the chicken tenders and pat dry with a paper towel. One by one, dip each tender in bowl #1, then bowl #2, and then bowl #3, completely coating the chicken in each bowl. Arrange the coated tenders on the prepared baking sheet.

4. Bake for 15–20 minutes, until golden on the outside and cooked through.

FOR THE BALSAMIC KETCHUP:

Combine the ketchup and Balsamic Glaze in a small bowl. Serve with the chicken.

(Per serving) Calories: 370 | Fat: 10g | Sodium: 440mg
Carbs: 12g | Fiber: 3g | Sugar: 4g | Protein: 40g

QUICK TIP

This is the perfect dish to make extras and stock in the freezer for those crazy I-don't-have-time-to-cook weeknights when soccer practice, guitar lessons, and homework eat up all of your time. Once the tenders have cooled completely, pack them into freezer-safe zip-top bags in meal-sized portions (depending on how much your family will eat). Store them in the freezer for up to 3 months. To reheat, simply place them in the oven at 350°F for 10–12 minutes, until heated all the way through.

EASY TERIYAKI CHICKEN

prep time: 8 minutes ● *cooking time:* 45 minutes ● *serves:* 4

Should you order teriyaki chicken from your local Chinese takeout place or should you make your own?

If you go with the takeout option, the meal will come with traditional white rice, refined sugar–sweetened sauce, fortune cookies, and very likely another dish or two that either are fried or contain noodles or other starches.

If you were to make your teriyaki chicken at home, then your meal would be served with cauliflower rice, wholesome homemade sauce, and possibly a side of vegetables or salad.

The difference between the two meals is easily a few hundred calories, and the nutritional compositions couldn't be more different.

Then there is the disruption in your momentum that also occurs.

When you're eating right, exercising daily, drinking plenty of water, and generally being on point with your health, those habits begin to carry themselves with the momentum of inertia. As soon as you disrupt this flow or jump off the wagon, you're faced with the difficult task of getting back into the swing of things.

Unfortunately, it often takes days to regain your momentum, days where precious progress is lost. And in some cases, the momentum is lost for good.

So, will you make your own teriyaki chicken at home tonight, or will you order it from your local Chinese takeout place?

Ingredients

1 cup chicken broth

⅓ cup coconut aminos

⅓ cup raw honey

2 tablespoons mirin

1 tablespoon sake

2 boneless, skinless chicken breasts

sea salt and black pepper, to taste

2 tablespoons extra-virgin olive oil, divided

2 red bell peppers, cored, seeded, and cut into ½-inch strips

1 recipe CAULIFLOWER RICE (page 171)

Steps

1. In a medium saucepan, combine the chicken broth, coconut aminos, honey, mirin, and sake. Bring the mixture to a boil, then decrease to a simmer for 20 minutes.

2. Pound the chicken (see the tip on page 99) and season with salt and pepper.

3. In a large skillet over medium-high heat, heat 1 tablespoon of the olive oil. Add the chicken and cook until browned, about 8 minutes, then turn and brown the other side, about another 8 minutes. Transfer the chicken to a cutting board or plate and slice crosswise into strips.

4. Wipe out the skillet and add the remaining 1 tablespoon olive oil. Add the bell peppers and cook over medium-high heat until crisp-tender and lightly charred, about 3 minutes.

5. Add the chicken strips and the sauce to the skillet and cook over low heat for 3–5 minutes, until the sauce has thickened. Serve warm over Cauliflower Rice.

(Per serving) Calories: 343 | Fat: 10g | Sodium: 496mg
Carbs: 35g | Fiber: 3g | Sugar: 28g | Protein: 27g

QUICK TIP

This teriyaki sauce is quite simple to mix together and simmer while the chicken and peppers cook. Instead of soy sauce, I've called for coconut aminos, and instead of the sugar (or corn syrup—yuck!) in many teriyaki sauces, I've used some raw honey. It's wholesome and delicious, and the kiddos can't get enough of it.

PIZZA-STUFFED CHICKEN

prep time: 20 minutes ● *cooking time:* 45 minutes ● *serves:* 6

What is it with kids and pizza? My kids could eat pizza any time, day or night, whether they were hungry or not. It's like kid catnip.

Too bad pizza isn't filled with the protein, fiber, vitamins, and minerals that kids need for a proper, nutritious meal, right? That was the thought that led me to the idea of turning chicken breast into "pizza."

By adding some pepperoni, dairy-free cheese spread, and pizza sauce, chicken breast is magically transformed into pizza—and is welcomed by the kids with opened mouths.

Ingredients

FOR THE DAIRY-FREE CHEESE SPREAD:

1 cup raw cashews, soaked in hot water for 10 minutes and drained

$^{1}/_{4}$ cup extra-virgin olive oil

1 tablespoon lemon juice

1 tablespoon water

1 teaspoon minced garlic

$^{1}/_{2}$ teaspoon sea salt

$^{1}/_{4}$ teaspoon onion powder

$^{1}/_{4}$ teaspoon sweet paprika

pinch of black pepper

FOR THE PIZZA ROLLS:

2 boneless, skinless chicken breasts

sea salt and black pepper, to taste

$^{1}/_{4}$ cup chopped fresh basil

20 nitrate- and sugar-free pepperoni slices

1 cup pizza sauce

Steps

FOR THE DAIRY-FREE CHEESE SPREAD:

Combine all of the ingredients in a food processor and pulse until smooth. Be patient, as it can take about 5 minutes—wait until it's really creamy.

FOR THE PIZZA ROLLS:

1. Preheat the oven to 350°F. Lightly grease a glass 10 × 15-inch casserole pan with olive oil and set aside.

2. Rinse the chicken breasts and pound them out to $^{1}/_{2}$ inch thick (see tip). Season both sides with salt and pepper, then spread 2 tablespoons of the Dairy-Free Cheese Spread on top of each chicken breast. Sprinkle with most of the basil, then arrange a few slices of the pepperoni on top of the chicken breasts in an even layer. Roll each breast and place, seam side down, in the prepared casserole pan.

3. Pour the pizza sauce over the rolled chicken breasts and sprinkle with the remaining basil. Bake for 35–45 minutes, or until cooked through.

4. Slice each chicken breast roll and serve warm.

(Per serving) Calories: 386 | Fat: 23g | Sodium: 736mg Carbs: 12g | Fiber: 2g | Sugar: 2g | Protein: 21g

QUICK TIP

It's important that you take the time to pound out the chicken breasts to $^{1}/_{2}$-inch thickness before covering with the yummy pizza toppings and rolling up. To easily do this, cover the chicken with plastic wrap or put it in a large zip-top bag, then place it on a cutting board. Use a sturdy skillet or saucepan and whack it gently until properly flattened. Yes, this part is fun.

ITALIAN SLOW COOKER CHICKEN

prep time: 15 minutes ● *cooking time:* 6 hours ● *serves:* 6

Back in the '90s, I was convinced that all types of fat were bad.

The media were constantly harping on us to rid our diets of any and all fats. Of course, in time we saw that despite our low-fat diets, obesity rates continued to rise. The fat-promoting culprit wasn't fat in general, but had (and still has) much more to do with sugars and processed foods.

We are still recovering from the fat-phobia, with many people still hesitant to include any fat at all in their diet. But it's dangerous to lump all fats together, as certain fats are essential to build lean muscle and promote optimal health.

Some fats, however, are harmful and should be avoided, such as trans fats and processed vegetable oils.

Here are three reasons you should NOT FEAR fat:

1. **Fat is essential.** Your body requires a certain amount of fat to function properly. Fat is needed to prevent deficiency of fat-soluble vitamins K, E, D, and A.

2. **Fat isn't fattening.** Forget everything you learned in the '90s about how fat will make you fat. In reality, healthy fat is no more fattening than carbs or protein. Emphasis on the word *healthy*, because harmful trans fats and refined vegetable oils do create inflammation, which can add pounds.

3. **Fat helps burn fat.** It's true—good fats help curb your appetite, improve overall health, and encourage fat burning and muscle building.

This recipe has more than 10 grams of fat per serving, but are you going to let that deter you from making it and enjoying all of the flavorful nutrition that it has to offer? No you aren't, my friend. You're going to embrace those wholesome fat grams with open arms.

Ingredients

1 (28-ounce) can whole tomatoes, undrained

1 yellow onion, diced

2 tablespoons minced garlic

½ cup kalamata olives, pitted and sliced

¼ cup dry white wine

1 tablespoon Italian seasoning blend

1 teaspoon black pepper

½ teaspoon sea salt

1 teaspoon dried basil

2 pounds boneless, skinless chicken thighs

¼ cup tomato paste

3 cups cubed butternut squash (about 2 medium squash)

chopped fresh parsley, for garnish

NAAN BREAD (page 156), for serving

Steps

1. Combine all of the ingredients except the parsley and naan in a slow cooker and stir to combine. Cover and cook on low for 6 hours, until the chicken is tender and cooked through.

2. Sprinkle with fresh parsley and serve with naan.

(Per serving) Calories: 315 | Fat: 11g | Sodium: 695mg
Carbs: 22g | Fiber: 5g | Sugar: 7g | Protein: 33g

QUICK
TIP

I love slow cooker recipes like this one for two reasons: First, it's a nearly effortless meal. Throw everything into the slow cooker in the morning, and then come home to a hot meal in the evening. Isn't that pretty much like having a personal chef? Ha! Second, there's a lot of flexibility in the ingredients you can use in a recipe like this. Don't have butternut squash? Use pretty much any other type of winter squash or even sweet potato. Don't have chicken thighs? Sub in beef or pork. No onions but have a bunch of bell peppers? Chop 'em up and throw 'em in!

GINGER-BRAISED CHICKEN MEATBALLS

prep time: 20 minutes
cooking time: 40 minutes
serves: 8

Confession time: I absolutely hate getting on a scale to check my weight. Even on days when I know I'm looking and feeling good, I'd rather do 100 burpees than check my weight.

The scale has been my nemesis ever since a memorable day back in the late '80s . . . I was in third grade in public school and the teacher shuffled us into the library, in a single-file line. A handful of moms had volunteered to measure our height and weight, and my neighbor Daniel was there with his beautiful mom, Coleen (who had dark hair and the brightest red lipstick), next to a scale with a vertical measuring stick looming overhead.

Hmmm, this could be fun, I thought to myself as I scrambled onto the scale. I stood perfectly still, with my side ponytail and purple Velcro sneakers, waiting for approval.

"Whoa!" I heard Daniel say, "Mom, she weighs over 70 pounds—that's more than me!" At eight years old, I knew that girls should weigh less than boys, especially a boy that was a head taller than me. "Shush, a girl's weight is a secret, honey," his mother laughed, ruffling his hair.

I looked at him, his thin waist and knobby knees, and then looked down at myself. For the first time I noticed the softness above my knees and the roundness of my waist. Hot shame started in my belly and crept up to my ears, and I knew without looking in the mirror that my face was bright red.

Ever since that day I've avoided scales the way some people avoid circus clowns. Stay. Away. For. Reals.

Lucky for me (and for you, if you're a fellow scale-a-phobic), real health is measured in our body's functionality, strength, and vitality, all of which flourish when fueled with nutrient-dense dishes like these Ginger-Braised Chicken Meatballs.

This dish is significantly lower in simple carbs than traditional rice bowls. The cauliflower rice offers the consistency of actual rice with a fraction of the calories. And I love the creamy coconut milk–based broth that's spiked with aromatic ginger and colored with vibrant yellow turmeric.

Ingredients

FOR THE MEATBALLS:

3 tablespoons blanched almond flour

3 tablespoons minced fresh ginger

3 cloves garlic, minced

2 teaspoons sea salt

2 pounds ground chicken

2 eggs

1 tablespoon fish sauce

FOR THE GINGER COCONUT BROTH:

1 (13.7-ounce) can full-fat coconut milk

2 cups chicken broth

2-inch knob fresh ginger, peeled and thinly sliced (about ¼ cup)

3 cloves garlic, thinly sliced

3 Anaheim chiles, seeded and thinly sliced

1 stalk lemongrass

1 tablespoon fish sauce

1 teaspoon ground turmeric

1 tablespoon coconut palm sugar

sea salt and black pepper, to taste

3 limes, divided

1 head cauliflower

1 teaspoon extra-virgin olive oil

2 tablespoons sliced fresh mint

¼ cup chopped fresh cilantro

Steps

FOR THE MEATBALLS:

1. Preheat the oven to 425°F. Lightly grease a large rimmed baking sheet with coconut oil and set aside.

2. Combine all of the meatball ingredients in a large bowl. Form the mixture into 40 meatballs, about 1½ inches across. Arrange them on the prepared baking sheet and bake for 15 minutes.

FOR THE GINGER COCONUT BROTH:

1. In a medium saucepan, combine the coconut milk, chicken broth, ginger, garlic, chiles, lemongrass, fish sauce, turmeric, coconut palm sugar, and a sprinkle of salt and pepper. Zest and juice 2 of the limes and add to the pot. Bring the mixture to a boil, decrease to a simmer, and remove the lemongrass. Add the meatballs to the broth and simmer for 15 minutes.

2. In the meantime, wash the cauliflower, trim the stem and leaves, and run it through the food processor with the grating attachment. Heat the olive oil in a large skillet and sauté the cauliflower over medium-high heat until tender, about 5 minutes. Season with salt and pepper.

3. Slice the remaining lime into 8 wedges. Spoon some cauliflower rice into each bowl, top with meatballs and broth, and garnish with the fresh mint, cilantro, and a lime wedge.

(Per 5 meatballs) Calories: 343 | Fat: 18g | Sodium: 1,093mg | Carbs: 16g | Fiber: 5g | Sugar: 5g | Protein: 27g

QUICK TIP

My best tip when it comes to this savory recipe is simply this: MAKE THIS DISH! It is hands-down one of my favorite dinner recipes and one that I crave and enjoy often. Go on then, get cooking!

ZEVIA COLA CHICKEN

prep time: 10 minutes ● *cooking time:* 50 minutes ● *serves:* 4

Have you ever wanted to reinvent yourself? To scrape away your less-than-admirable bits and pieces in order to expose the part of you that shines?

Changing your diet is a form of reinvention. The foods that you eat are quite literally a part of who you are. Going from a diet of processed foods to wholesome foods quickly transforms the shape of your body, and reinvention occurs with every pound shed.

Reinvention is exciting. It fills you with new hope and opens the way for new goals to be conceived and achieved.

However, in order for reinvention to occur, you must first say good-bye to your current self and bring down the curtain on all your nasty little habits that are keeping you from greatness.

Write those nasty habits an epitaph. Bid them adieu. Set them ablaze and push them out to sea.

It's time for the new you to shine.

Ingredients

- 1 (12-ounce) can Zevia cola
- 1 cup coconut aminos
- ¼ cup dry white wine
- 1 tablespoon apple cider vinegar
- 2 tablespoons raw honey
- ½-inch knob fresh ginger, peeled and minced (about 1 teaspoon)
- 1 tablespoon minced garlic (about 2 cloves)
- 4 boneless, skinless chicken breasts
- ½ teaspoon arrowroot starch
- ¼ cup cold water
- minced scallion, for garnish

Steps

1. Preheat the oven to 300°F.

2. In a large, oven-safe skillet, combine the Zevia, coconut aminos, wine, vinegar, honey, ginger, and garlic. Mix well. Place the chicken in the skillet in a single layer and bring the mixture to a simmer over medium heat. Cook for 5 minutes.

3. Transfer the skillet to the middle rack of the oven and bake, uncovered, for 30 minutes, until cooked through. Transfer the chicken to a plate.

4. Strain the cooking liquid into a large bowl through a fine-mesh strainer. Let the liquid stand for 5 minutes, then skim and discard the fat from the top.

5. Combine the arrowroot and cold water in a small bowl. Whisk to dissolve the arrowroot.

6. Transfer 1 cup of the cooking mixture and the arrowroot mixture to a clean skillet. Cook over medium heat, stirring often, until the sauce thickens, about 12 minutes. Serve the warm sauce over the chicken and garnish with scallions.

(Per serving) Calories: 328 | Fat: 2g | Sodium: 1,462mg
Carbs: 24g | Fiber: 1g | Sugar: 9g | Protein: 40g

QUICK TIP

Drinking soda pop that's filled with chemicals and corn syrup or other artificial sweeteners is a dangerous habit that many people struggle with. Those darn drinks are everywhere and have been tailored to please our taste buds. I have found a more wholesome and natural replacement for sugary and artificial sodas in the Zevia brand of soda pop. It's made with stevia, so it has zero calories without the harmful artificial sweeteners, and it's free of the calorie-dense, uber-sweet corn syrup that infamously causes weight gain. This recipe uses Zevia in place of mass-market cola in this classic chicken dish. It can be found at your local health food market or purchased on Amazon.

CREAMY TARRAGON CHICKEN AND GREEN BEANS

prep time: 15 minutes ● *cooking time:* 30 minutes
serves: 4

Here you go, another unique and flavorful way to serve wholesome chicken breast and veggies! What stands out about this dish is the savory flavor of fresh tarragon and the creaminess of the sauce. Serve it up on a big bed of CAULIFLOWER COUSCOUS (page 168) for a quick, healthy family dinner.

Ingredients

- ¼ **pound green beans, trimmed and halved**
- 2 **tablespoons extra-virgin olive oil, divided**
- 2 **boneless, skinless chicken breasts**
- **sea salt and black pepper, to taste**
- 3 **large shallots, minced**
- 3 **cloves garlic, minced**
- ½ **cup dry white wine**
- ¾ **cup chicken broth**
- ¼ **cup coconut cream**
- ¼ **cup minced fresh tarragon**
- 2 **tablespoons Dijon mustard**

Steps

1. In a large saucepan over high heat, bring 2 inches of water to a boil. Add the green beans and cook until tender, about 3 minutes. Drain and set aside.

2. In a grill pan, heat 1 tablespoon of the olive oil over medium-high heat. Rinse the chicken breasts and pat dry with paper towels. Season both sides with salt and pepper. Place the chicken breasts in the heated grill pan and cook, turning once, until golden and cooked through, about 8 minutes per side. Transfer to a cutting board or plate and, once cooled, cut into bite-size pieces.

3. In a large skillet, heat the remaining 1 tablespoon olive oil over medium-high heat. Add the shallots and garlic. After 3 minutes, add the wine; 3 minutes later, add the chicken broth, coconut cream, tarragon, and Dijon. Season with salt and pepper.

4. Add the green beans and chicken to the sauce. Mix well and serve.

(Per serving) Calories: 341 | Fat: 10g | Sodium: 297mg
Carbs: 10g | Fiber: 2g | Sugar: 3g | Protein: 41g

QUICK TIP

Cooking with fresh herbs, like tarragon, is a simple way to really turn up the flavor dial in a natural, wholesome way. Consider planting fresh herbs in your garden or if you don't have any outdoor space, you can grow your favorite herbs in little pots by your kitchen sink.

TERIYAKI-BRAISED SHORT RIBS

prep time: 10 minutes ● *cooking time:* 5–6 hours
serves: 10

On a recent Sunday, I took a break from cooking to enjoy a family dinner at a steakhouse in Costa Mesa. My son, Andrew, who is rapidly growing and has the appetite of a linebacker, ordered the short rib entrée, which arrived on a pile of buttered noodles with a side of sour cream.

I may have drooled a little, looking up from my grilled sea bass and salad.

The very next night at home I served up my own version of short ribs, buttered noodles, and sour cream—and this time I chowed down, too. Andrew was halfway through his heaping plate before he realized that it wasn't from the steakhouse!

 Ingredients

1 tablespoon sesame oil

8 beef short ribs (about 4 pounds)

½ cup coconut aminos

⅓ cup coconut palm sugar

¼ cup apple cider vinegar

1 tablespoon minced garlic

1 tablespoon grated fresh ginger

½ teaspoon ground cayenne pepper

1 head green cabbage, quartered

COCONUT SOUR CREAM **(page 201)**

BUTTERED NOODLES **(see tip)**

Steps

1. Heat the oil in a large skillet over medium-high heat. Add the short ribs and brown each side for 30 seconds. Transfer them to the slow cooker.

2. In a small bowl, combine the coconut aminos, coconut palm sugar, apple cider vinegar, garlic, ginger, and cayenne. Pour the mixture over the short ribs and add the quartered cabbage.

3. Cover the slow cooker and cook on high for 5–6 hours, until the meat is tender and falling off the bone. Enjoy with Coconut Sour Cream and Buttered Noodles.

(Per serving) Calories: 425 | Fat: 25g | Sodium: 381mg
Carbs: 14g | Fiber: 2g | Sugar: 9g | Protein: 43g

QUICK TIP

To make simple Buttered Noodles, you'll need 4 zucchini (peeled and turned into flat noodles with a veggie peeler), 2 tablespoons coconut butter (gently melted and browned in a skillet over low heat), 3 tablespoons minced fresh parsley, and a pinch of sea salt and black pepper. Combine all of the ingredients and heap the short ribs on top.

MOROCCAN TURKEY BURGERS WITH CARROT SLAW

prep time: 10 minutes ● *cooking time:* 10 minutes ● *serves:* 6

One of my favorite things to read in your emails and Facebook messages is how you've used my recipes to help you lose weight and transform your body. You should see the smile on my face when I hear that!

Your success stories motivate me to continue to create and share healthy, delicious recipes and provide so much inspiration to others who are also looking to transform their bodies and their lives.

I believe that you and your hard work should be praised and celebrated, because we all know that losing weight takes discipline and determination, and YOU DID THAT!

If you have experienced an amazing physical transformation with the help of my recipes, please email your most stunning before-and-after pictures to me at RealHealthyRecipes@gmail.com. I'd love to showcase your success stories on my website!

It's time for you to get the kudos that you deserve!

Ingredients

FOR THE CARROT SLAW:

3 cups shredded carrot (about 4 carrots)

3 celery stalks, thinly sliced

$1/2$ cup chopped fresh cilantro

2 teaspoons coconut palm sugar

$1/2$ teaspoon sea salt

$1/4$ teaspoon ground cumin

1 tablespoon lemon juice

1 tablespoon extra-virgin olive oil

1 tablespoon Muscat vinegar

FOR THE BURGERS:

1 pound ground turkey

$1/2$ cup diced yellow onion

$1/4$ cup diced red bell pepper

2 tablespoons minced fresh mint

2 tablespoons red curry paste

1 teaspoon ground cumin

1-inch knob fresh ginger, peeled and minced (about $1^1/2$ teaspoons)

$1/2$ teaspoon ground coriander

$1/2$ teaspoon sea salt

$1/4$ teaspoon black pepper

Steps

FOR THE CARROT SLAW:

Combine all of the slaw ingredients in a large bowl. Chill until ready to serve.

FOR THE BURGERS:

1. Line a baking sheet with parchment paper. Combine all the burger ingredients in a large bowl and mix well. Use your hands to shape the mixture into 6 even patties and lay them on the prepared baking sheet.

2. Preheat a grill pan over medium-high heat and generously grease with olive oil. Sear the patties for 5 minutes, flip, cover the pan, and cook for another 4 minutes, or until cooked through. Remove from the heat and serve with the Carrot Slaw.

(Per patty and serving of slaw) Calories: 234 | Fat: 8g | Sodium: 533mg Carbs: 21g | Fiber: 4g | Sugar: 7g | Protein: 16g

QUICK TIP

These Moroccan Turkey Burgers are fantastic served for dinner as lettuce-wrapped burgers or sandwiched between two pieces of **NAAN BREAD** (page 156). I highly recommend that you make this for dinner sometime. Or a bunch of other times. It's also one of my favorite recipes for snack time. Use the exact same ingredients, just form the meatballs into golf ball–size portions and bake at 350°F for 25 minutes, or until cooked through. It'll make about 20 meatballs.

STUFFED ZUCCHINI

prep time: 1 hour
cooking time: 1 hour
serves: 6

My mother-in-law, Suzy, is an *amazing* cook. This lady lives and breathes food.

Suzy was born in war-torn Armenia, grew up in Syria in the 1940s, and then moved back to Armenia to marry her husband, Joe, and raise a family before immigrating to the United States in the early 1980s, where she devoutly watches the Turkish cooking channel. Each of her geographical homes has influenced her cooking.

Her youth in Syria was spent living in an abbey, where she watched nuns cook mostly vegetarian food. If there was meat in a dish, it was boiled and discarded; the broth was used for soups. To this day, it's a rare occurrence to see Suzy eat meat.

In Armenia as a young bride, she focused on getting the best fresh fruits and vegetables available. They reminded her of the abbey grounds, which were covered with rows of fruit trees that she could see from her window. Vendors would go door-to-door selling their homegrown, seasonal produce, and Suzy got so excited that she would buy it all, even when that meant hiding some of the fruit under the bed! She now grows her own produce right in the backyard. Lucky for me, she's very generous with bags of fresh tomatoes, figs, grapefruits, cucumbers, lemons, oranges, passion fruits, guavas, and even pineapples. (And Joe is relieved that it's all free of charge!)

Suzy's kitchen is always the most active room of the house. Its tempting aromas offer a warm greeting, along with her friendly *shooneeks* (doggies), as soon as you step inside. No one leaves her house hungry. No. One.

You'll see Suzy's influence in my cooking, including this recipe for Stuffed Zucchini. My version is a few shades different than the one that she expertly cooks (hers involves white rice and a pat or two of butter, and she prefers to cook this on the stove, while I choose the "set it and forget it" oven method), but she's cool with my, as she puts it, "Skinny Lady" versions of her favorite foods.

Ingredients

FOR THE STUFFED ZUCCHINI:

8 medium zucchini

1 pound ground beef

¼ cup minced yellow onion

¼ cup uncooked quinoa

¼ cup minced fresh parsley

¼ cup minced fresh cilantro

2 tablespoons minced fresh dill

2 tablespoons minced fresh basil

2 tablespoons minced black raisins

1 teaspoon sea salt

⅛ teaspoon black pepper

2 tablespoons extra-virgin olive oil

2 tablespoons tomato paste

2 tablespoons lemon juice

1 onion, cut into 2-inch pieces (if needed)

FOR THE COOKING LIQUID:

½ cup boiling water

¼ cup lemon juice

2 tablespoons extra-virgin olive oil

½ teaspoon sea salt

Steps

FOR THE STUFFED ZUCCHINI:

1. Wash the zucchini and trim the ends. Cut the zucchini in half widthwise and use a zucchini corer to hollow out each piece, leaving a ¼-inch-thick wall. (Depending on the size of the zucchini, a melon baller could also work for doing this; however, the zucchini corer gets the job done in a fraction of the time.) Set aside.

2. In a large bowl, combine all the remaining ingredients except the onion. Mix well until fully combined.

3. Fill each hollowed zucchini with stuffing, leaving ¼ inch of room at the top. Place the zucchini upright in an 8 × 4-inch loaf pan and use pieces of onion as needed to keep the zucchini securely in place. Cover the pan with foil and place it in the fridge for at least an hour, so the flavors can mingle.

FOR THE COOKING LIQUID:

Preheat the oven to 400°F. Combine the cooking liquid ingredients in a large bowl and pour the mixture into the bottom of the loaf pan. Cover the pan tightly with foil and bake for 45–60 minutes, until the filling is cooked through and the zucchini are tender. Slice and serve.

(Per serving) Calories: 390 | Fat: 24g | Sodium: 664mg
Carbs: 19g | Fiber: 4g | Sugar: 7g | Protein: 26g

QUICK TIP

If you'd prefer to cook this on the stove top, you can do so by plugging the end of each zucchini with a smaller piece of onion, then lay all the zucchini on their sides in a large pot. Fill the pot with the cooking liquid, then add extra water, just until it covers all of the zucchini, and place a plate on top to weight down the zucchini. Bring the water to a boil over medium heat, then decrease the heat to low. Partially cover the pot with a lid and continue to cook over low heat for 40 minutes.

INSIDE-OUT STUFFED CABBAGE

prep time: 20 minutes ● *cooking time:* 3 hours ● *serves:* 12

If only I had some motivation . . . Have you ever uttered this phrase? Have you wished that motivation would drift down from the heavens and land right on you, preferably right when you're faced with a plate of chocolate chip cookies?

Guess what? There's a simple solution. In order to have *motivation*, you first need a *motive*. So what's your motive? Why do you want to eat healthier? Why do you want to lose the weight? Why do you want to become stronger? Why do you want to nourish your family with the best nutrition?

I can't answer those questions for you. Only you can tap into the core of what really matters to you. What I *can* do is share my motives with you: I eat healthy to keep my body in optimal health for as many years as possible, in order to spend quality time with the people I love. I eat healthy to be an example to my children and to those who enjoy my recipes, so that together we can make improvements in the toxic food culture in which we live. And I also love real food and truly believe that it's the most delicious way to eat!

Ingredients

FOR THE MEATBALLS:

$^1/_2$ **cup uncooked quinoa**

1 cup chicken broth

1 pound ground beef

2 eggs

$^1/_2$ **cup finely chopped yellow onion**

1 teaspoon sea salt

$^1/_4$ **teaspoon black pepper**

FOR THE CABBAGE:

1 tablespoon extra-virgin olive oil

2 yellow onions, sliced

1 (28-ounce) can whole tomatoes, undrained

$1^1/_4$ **teaspoons sea salt**

$^1/_4$ **teaspoon black pepper**

2 large green cabbage heads, cut into 1-inch pieces

2 tablespoons lemon juice

$^1/_3$ **cup golden raisins**

2 tablespoons coconut palm sugar

Steps

FOR THE MEATBALLS:

1. In a medium saucepan, combine the quinoa and chicken broth over medium-high heat. Bring to a boil, decrease to a simmer, cover, and cook for 20 minutes. Set aside.

2. In a large bowl, combine the cooked quinoa, ground beef, eggs, onion, salt, and pepper, and mix well. Form into golf ball–size meatballs and place them on a plate. Cover the plate with plastic wrap and chill the meatballs in the fridge for 20 minutes.

FOR THE CABBAGE:

1. Add the olive oil to a large pot over medium-high heat. Add the sliced onions and cook until translucent, about 8 minutes. Add the tomatoes, breaking up the big pieces with a wooden spoon. Add the salt and pepper, cover, and cook for 20 minutes.

2. Add the cabbage to the pot. Cover and simmer for 1 hour.

3. Place the meatballs on top of the cabbage mixture. Cover and simmer for 15 minutes, until the meatballs are cooked through. Then gently stir the meatballs into the cabbage mixture, cover, and simmer for 45 minutes.

4. Remove the lid and stir in the lemon juice, raisins, and coconut palm sugar. Cook for 15 more minutes, uncovered, and then serve hot.

(Per serving) Calories: 245 | Fat: 9g | Sodium: 282mg
Carbs: 17g | Fiber: 2g | Sugar: 9g | Protein: 13g

QUICK TIP

This recipe is for you if you love the idea of savory stuffed cabbage but simply don't have the time or desire to actually stuff cabbage. Inside-Out Stuffed Cabbage gives you flavorful, savory meat paired with tender cabbage and plump sweet raisins with far less work than regular Stuffed Cabbage (flip to the next page and give it a try, though; it's worth it if you have time!). Two notes on this recipe: 1) Feel free to make the meatball portion independently of the cabbage for a nice on-the-go snack or to serve over zucchini noodles (just bake the meatballs in the oven at 350°F for 25 minutes, or until cooked through), and 2) If you aren't a meat eater or you just want a tender, tasty veggie side dish, then just make the cabbage portion of this recipe. Yummy!

STUFFED CABBAGE

prep time: 1 hour
cooking time: 1 hour 45 minutes
serves: 10

If you're looking for a hearty and satisfying dinner that's free of grains and bursting with flavor, then your search is over.

This Stuffed Cabbage has it all—from the ground meat and cauliflower rice mixture wrapped inside tender cabbage, to the homemade savory sauce on top—you'll never want it to end! What I love most about this dish is how the flavors intensify overnight and how refreshing it is eaten cold as a quick lunch or dinner the next day.

Ingredients

2 heads savoy cabbage

2 tablespoons extra-virgin olive oil, divided

1 head cauliflower, shredded

$2\frac{1}{2}$ cups chicken broth, divided

3 tablespoons black raisins

sea salt and black pepper, to taste

1 pound ground beef

$\frac{1}{2}$ pound loose mild Italian sausage

1 yellow onion, chopped, divided

2 teaspoons minced garlic (about 2 cloves), divided

2 tablespoons chopped fresh sage

$\frac{1}{8}$ teaspoon ground nutmeg

4 ounces pancetta, minced (about 4 slices)

1 (14.5-ounce) can diced tomatoes, undrained

1 (8-ounce) can tomato sauce

$\frac{1}{4}$ cup toasted and chopped pecans

$\frac{1}{4}$ cup chopped fresh parsley

$\frac{1}{4}$ cup nutritional yeast

1 egg, beaten

Steps

1. Bring a large pot of salted water to a boil. Separate 15 large cabbage leaves (reserve the leftover smaller leaves) and wash. Boil the leaves for 3 minutes, drain, and let them cool on dish towels. Chop 1 cup of the reserved smaller cabbage leaves. Set aside.

2. Heat 1 tablespoon of the olive oil in a large skillet over medium heat. Add the shredded cauliflower and cook for 3 minutes, stirring often. Add 1 cup of the chicken broth and the raisins. Season with salt and pepper to taste. Cook for another 3 minutes, or until the broth has been absorbed, then remove the pan from the heat. Transfer the cauliflower rice mixture to a very large bowl and set aside. Wipe out the skillet.

3. Heat the remaining 1 tablespoon olive oil in the skillet over medium heat. Add the beef and sausage, breaking it up with a large spoon or spatula as it browns. Drain off any liquid and add half of the onion and half of the garlic. Stir in the sage, nutmeg, and reserved chopped cabbage. Season with salt and pepper to taste and cook for another 5 minutes. Remove the pan from the heat and add the meat mixture to the bowl of cauliflower rice. Wipe out the skillet.

4. Cook the pancetta in the skillet over medium heat, stirring, until cooked through, about 5 minutes. Add the remaining onion and garlic. Cook for 5 minutes longer, or until tender. Add the remaining $1\frac{1}{2}$ cups chicken broth, the diced tomatoes, and the tomato sauce. Season with salt and pepper and simmer for 15–20 minutes, until the sauce has thickened. Remove the pan from the heat.

5. Preheat the oven to 350°F. Lightly grease a 9 × 13-inch casserole pan with olive oil and spread $\frac{1}{2}$ cup of the tomato sauce over the bottom of the pan.

6. Add the pecans, parsley, nutritional yeast, egg, and $\frac{1}{2}$ cup of the tomato sauce to the bowl of rice and meat. Mix well and season with salt and pepper. Place a generous spoonful of the mixture at the center of each cabbage leaf and roll it up like a burrito, tucking in the sides as you roll. Place each stuffed cabbage leaf seam side down in the casserole pan. Pour the remaining tomato sauce over the top, cover with foil, and bake for 45 minutes, until the meat is cooked through.

(Per serving) Calories: 313 | Fat: 21g | Sodium: 795mg | Carbs: 14g | Fiber: 3g | Sugar: 6g | Protein: 21g

QUICK TIP

Stuffed Cabbage freezes very well, so it's a great idea to make a double batch and, once it cools, place it in a freezer bag with some extra red sauce. To reheat, simply remove from the bag and heat in the oven or in a saucepan over medium-low heat.

EASY SPAGHETTI

prep time: 10 minutes ● *cooking time:* 30 minutes ● *serves:* 6

For many, pasta is the perfect answer to the age-old question: "What's for dinner?" But consider this: pasta consumption and obesity—where one goes, the other follows. Traditional pasta is composed primarily of carbohydrates. One cup of noodles contains roughly 390 calories, with 78 grams of simple carbs. Realistically, you'd eat two cups of noodles when pasta is your main dish, so this would put your carb count close to 200 grams, not counting sauce and the remainder of your meal. All those simple carbohydrates are quickly stored in your body as fat. So to reduce body fat, eliminating meals that are high in carbohydrates is a simple and effective strategy.

But don't give up on pasta just yet! Allow me to introduce you to the new age of pasta . . . noodles made from vegetables slash the calories in half!

Why make high-calorie, high-carbohydrate noodles from flour when we can simply and easily make low-calorie, low-carbohydrate noodles from vegetables?

Brilliant, right?!

A fresh zucchini, when peeled and run through a spiral slicer, turns into white noodles that are just like the ones you grew up on . . . give it a try!

Ingredients

Steps

FOR THE SPAGHETTI SAUCE:

1 tablespoon extra-virgin olive oil

1 tablespoon minced garlic (about 3 cloves)

1 yellow onion, chopped

2 tablespoons minced fresh thyme, plus more for serving

2 tablespoons minced fresh rosemary, plus more for serving

2 bell peppers (I used orange and red), cored, seeded, and chopped

1 pound ground beef

1 (24-ounce) jar spaghetti sauce (no added sugar)

1 cup halved cherry tomatoes

FOR THE NOODLES:

5 zucchini

FOR THE SPAGHETTI SAUCE:

1. In an extra-large nonstick skillet or medium saucepan over medium heat, warm the olive oil for 3 minutes. Add the garlic, onion, thyme, and rosemary. Sauté, mixing often, for 5 minutes, until the onion is tender. Add the bell peppers and continue to cook for 5 minutes.

2. Add the ground beef and cook, stirring and breaking the beef apart with your spoon or spatula, until all the pink is gone. Drain the fat, then return the pan to medium heat.

3. Add the spaghetti sauce and cherry tomatoes and mix until well combined. Decrease the heat to low and simmer for 15 minutes.

FOR THE NOODLES:

Wash the zucchini and use a veggie peeler to remove all of the green skin. Use the veggie peeler to create long, flat "noodle" strips of zucchini. Collect in a large bowl. There's no need to cook these noodles. Simply serve with a large helping of the warmed spaghetti sauce and a sprinkle of fresh herbs on top.

(Per serving) Calories: 371 | Fat: 18g | Sodium: 570mg
Carbs: 23g | Fiber: 6g | Sugar: 14g | Protein: 24g

HEALTHY EATING TIP

Don't stop at zucchini; butternut squash, spaghetti squash, asparagus, jicama, and cucumbers are all exciting options for healthy noodles.

BUTTERNUT SQUASH SPAGHETTI

prep time: 25 minutes ● *cooking time:* 8 hours ● *serves:* 12

It's a happy day for low-carb noodle lovers! We've got a whole new noodle to love: butternut squash noodles. *Gee, this recipe is going to take me longer to make than regular spaghetti,* you may be thinking. Yes, this is true. It will take more effort. And yes, the noodles do look a little different and taste a little different than the noodles your kids are used to. So why do it?

I don't think that healthy eating should mean salads for dinner every night. As a mom, I know firsthand what a fight that would be! So by making simple, real-food swaps—like using butternut squash for noodles, rather than processed, boxed noodles—we can serve our families the foods they love while making a real improvement in our health. Let's make a difference in the lives of those we love—one meal at a time!

Now, there's a little bit of technique involved with cutting your squash so that you can run it through a spiral slicer, but the rest is super-duper easy. I've found that the narrow part of the squash—the "neck"—is the piece that works best. Slice or peel off the skin first, and then simply run the squash flesh through the slicer. Then either reserve the remaining squash for another use or scoop out the seeds and thinly slice the flesh to serve alongside the long noodle strands.

Ingredients

FOR THE SPAGHETTI SAUCE:

1 tablespoon extra-virgin olive oil

1 pound ground beef

1 pound loose pork sausage

2 large yellow onions, chopped

3 cloves garlic, minced

1 (28-ounce) can diced tomatoes, undrained

2 (15-ounce) cans tomato sauce

1 (6-ounce) can tomato paste

1 tablespoon herbes de Provence or dried basil

1 teaspoon dried oregano

$^1/_2$ teaspoon sea salt

$^1/_2$ teaspoon black pepper

$^1/_2$ teaspoon sweet paprika

FOR THE BUTTERNUT SQUASH NOODLES:

6 medium butternut squash

1 teaspoon extra-virgin olive oil

sea salt and black pepper, to taste

Steps

FOR THE SPAGHETTI SAUCE:

1. Heat the olive oil in a large skillet over medium-high heat. Add the beef, sausage, onions, and garlic, and cook for about 10 minutes, stirring often, until the sausage is no longer pink.

2. Transfer the contents of the skillet to a slow cooker and add the remaining sauce ingredients. Stir, cover, and cook on low for 8 hours.

FOR THE BUTTERNUT SQUASH NOODLES:

1. Preheat the oven to 350°F. Cut off the narrow part of both squash and peel the skin using a knife or vegetable peeler. You should have 6 nice, solid pieces of squash (with no hollow, seed-filled section). Run these through a spiral slicer to create long, thin noodles. Toss the noodles with the olive oil and season with salt and pepper. Spread over an 18 × 26-inch rimmed baking sheet and bake for 5–8 minutes, until tender.

2. Serve a pile of tender butternut squash noodles with the warm spaghetti sauce.

(Per serving) Calories: 278 | Fat: 18g | Sodium: 732mg
Carbs: 19g | Fiber: 6g | Sugar: 7g | Protein: 20g

QUICK TIP

The spaghetti sauce recipe here is awesome because it simmers all day in the slow cooker while you are hard at work doin' what you do, so the house smells amazing when you get home. The noodles only take about 20 minutes, so you can cook 'em right before you eat.

HAMBURGER CASSEROLE

prep time: 10 minutes ● *cooking time:* 30 minutes ● *serves:* 6

Changing your diet is never easy—especially when it means giving up some of your favorite foods. Sure, it helps to know that your efforts will be rewarded as you begin to look and feel better, but temptations and old habits may still threaten to land you right back where you started.

A great strategy to assist with changing your diet is to make wholesome versions of your unhealthy favorites. It's like training wheels for healthy eating! Love Hamburger Helper night? Well, this Hamburger Casserole is a real-food version of that concept. While traditional Hamburger Helper contains grain-based noodles, artificial ingredient–laden sauce, and dairy-based mix-ins, this wholesome version combines simply shredded sweet potatoes with fresh spices, natural ketchup and mustard, and onions, pickles, and tomatoes. It tastes pretty awesome, too!

Ingredients

FOR THE SPICE BLEND:

2 tablespoons minced fresh parsley

2 teaspoons smoked paprika

1 teaspoon coconut sugar

1/2 teaspoon garlic powder

1/2 teaspoon black pepper

FOR THE HAMBURGER:

3 sweet potatoes

1 pound ground beef

1/2 cup minced yellow onion

1/4 teaspoon sea salt

1/4 teaspoon black pepper

1/2 cup natural ketchup

1/4 cup yellow mustard

1/4 cup diced sweet pickles

1/4 cup diced tomatoes

Steps

FOR THE SPICE BLEND:

Combine the spice blend ingredients in a small bowl.

FOR THE HAMBURGER:

1. Preheat the oven to 450°F. Grease a 10 × 15-inch glass casserole pan with olive oil.

2. Peel the sweet potatoes and cut them into pieces small enough to fit through the food processor feed tube. Using the grating attachment, shred the sweet potatoes, then set aside.

3. Combine the ground beef with the onion, salt, pepper, ketchup, and yellow mustard in the casserole pan. Use a spoon or spatula to break up the mixture until it's well combined.

4. Add the spice blend to the shredded sweet potatoes and spread the mixture over the ground beef. Cover the casserole tightly with foil and bake for 25 minutes. Turn on the broiler to high. Remove the foil and place the pan under the broiler for a few minutes, until the tops of the sweet potatoes are golden. Sprinkle with the pickles and tomatoes and serve warm.

(Per serving) Calories: 285 | Fat: 12g | Sodium: 593mg
Carbs: 19g | Fiber: 3g | Sugar: 10g | Protein: 22g

HEALTHY EATING TIP

As a rule of thumb, avoid purchasing foods that begin in a box, such as Hamburger Helper or boxed cake and brownie mixes. Sure, it's convenient to simply follow the directions on the back of the box, but as you're learning in the pages of this book, real-food cooking can become as convenient as you want it to be.

PIZZA CASSEROLE

prep time: 20 minutes ● *cooking time:* 50 minutes ●*serves:* 10

There's a popular recipe for pizza casserole (maybe you've tried it) that combines spaghetti noodles, pizza toppings, and cheese to create a very tasty, very kid-friendly dinner.

The problem with this traditional recipe for pizza casserole is that it's lacking in nutrition while bursting with fat-inducing calories. And though the kids may take a few bites, Mommy and Daddy end up eating all the leftovers . . . and hating themselves for it the next day. Not cool. So I created this Pizza Casserole that you can polish off and still feel great.

In place of the spaghetti noodles, I call for making noodles out of sweet potato using a spiral slicer. The reason for using sweet potato, rather than zucchini, is that the sweet potato is firmer and will become tender with the baking time, whereas zucchini noodles would get soggy and most likely break apart. You could also use butternut squash noodles.

Ingredients

5 small sweet potatoes

sea salt and black pepper, to taste

2 teaspoons extra-virgin olive oil

1 teaspoon minced garlic (about 1 clove)

1 yellow onion, chopped

1 bell pepper, cored, seeded, and chopped

1 pound loose sweet pork sausage

1 (2.25-ounce) can sliced olives, drained

2–4 vine-ripened tomatoes, diced (optional)

1 (16-ounce) jar tomato basil pasta sauce (no added sugar)

30 nitrate- and sugar-free pepperoni slices, halved

¼ cup chopped fresh basil

Steps

1. Preheat the oven to 425°F. Lightly grease a 10 × 15-inch glass casserole pan with olive oil.

2. Peel the sweet potatoes and trim them to a size appropriate for your spiral slicer. Run all of the pieces through the slicer to create long, spaghetti-like noodles. Put the noodles in the prepared pan and toss with salt and pepper.

3. In a large skillet over medium-high heat, sauté the olive oil and garlic for 3 minutes. Add the onion and sauté until translucent, about 8 minutes. Add the bell pepper and pork sausage and cook, breaking up the sausage into small pieces with your spoon or spatula, until all of the pink is gone. Drain the fat from the skillet.

4. Stir in the olives, tomatoes if using, pasta sauce, pepperoni, and basil. Cook for another 3 minutes, then pour the tomato mixture over the pan of noodles. Cover the pan tightly with foil and bake for 25 minutes, or until the noodles are tender.

(Per serving) Calories: 297 | Fat: 17g | Sodium: 966mg
Carbs: 13g | Fiber: 4g | Sugar: 6g | Protein: 15g

QUICK TIP

Choose nitrate- and sugar-free pepperoni slices for this dish. Or, if you're not a fan of pepperoni, then feel free to leave it out completely. You could also get creative with the ground meat—use whatever kind you prefer, and vary it from time to time.

MAPLE APPLE BRISKET WITH GARLIC MASHED ROOT VEGGIES

prep time: 20 minutes
cooking time: 5 hours 15 minutes
serves: 12

I grew up in a restored farmhouse with a white picket fence on a hill overlooking Padilla Bay in northern Washington State. Green fields, patches of forest, and an estuary filled with little catchable critters were my playground. When it wasn't raining, you could bet that I was outdoors playing with my younger brother, Pete.

We built forts with scraps of plywood, created mazes through the tall grass in Mr. Zimmerman's field, collected tadpoles from the ditch across the street, rode our bikes down to the water, and played baseball in the front yard.

I'll never forget the day when our neighbor, a little boy named Rhett, joined us as my dad was pitching. After about half an hour of play, he looked up at my dad (who was in his early forties at the time) and said with breathless awe, "Wow, you are really good! Are you going to be a baseball player when you grow up?"

We nearly died laughing.

The idea that an adult could do anything other than what they'd always done was just too much to handle. But now I think Rhett was on to something . . .

Who says you can't reinvent yourself at forty? Or fifty? Or ninety?

Ask yourself: *What am I going to do when I grow up?* And go do it.

Ingredients

FOR THE BRISKET:

4 strips bacon

1 (3-pound) brisket

1 yellow onion, chopped

8 cloves garlic, smashed

1 tablespoon tomato paste

2 cups fresh-pressed apple juice, divided

¼ cup pure maple syrup

FOR THE GARLIC MASHED ROOT VEGGIES:

2 medium parsnips

6 medium carrots

2 green apples

1 medium sweet potato

2 tablespoons coconut oil

1 tablespoon fresh rosemary

1 teaspoon dried thyme

FOR THE MAPLE APPLE GLAZE:

2 tablespoons arrowroot starch

1 tablespoon apple cider vinegar

1 tablespoon water

sea salt and black pepper, to taste

FOR THE BRISKET:

1. In a large skillet, cook the bacon over medium-high heat until crispy. Transfer to a paper towel to drain and set aside.

2. Return the skillet to the stove over medium-high heat and brown the brisket in the bacon drippings on all sides, about 4 minutes per side. Remove the pan from the heat and transfer to a slow cooker.

3. Return the skillet to the stove over medium heat and add the onion, garlic, and tomato paste. Cook for 5 minutes, until tender. Add $\frac{1}{2}$ cup of the apple juice to deglaze the skillet, then transfer all of the skillet contents to the slow cooker. Add the remaining $1\frac{1}{2}$ cups apple juice and the maple syrup to the slow cooker, cover, and cook on high for $3\frac{1}{2}$ hours.

FOR THE GARLIC MASHED ROOT VEGGIES:

1. After the brisket has been cooking for $3\frac{1}{2}$ hours, peel and chop the parsnips, carrots, apples, and sweet potato, and add them to the slow cooker. Continue cooking on high for an additional hour.

2. Remove the brisket from the slow cooker and allow it to rest under a foil tent for 15 minutes. Transfer the veggies from the slow cooker to a food processor or high-speed blender along with the coconut oil, rosemary, and thyme. Blend until smooth and creamy.

FOR THE MAPLE APPLE GLAZE:

1. Strain the liquid from the slow cooker using a cheesecloth or fine-mesh strainer. Add the strained liquid to a medium skillet and cook over medium-low heat, covered, for 12 minutes, until the mixture reduces to approximately 2 cups. Whisk in the arrowroot starch, vinegar, and water. Bring to a boil for a full minute and season with salt and pepper to taste. Remove from the heat.

2. Slice the brisket and serve with a side of the mashed root veggies and a drizzle of the glaze.

(Per serving) Calories: 196 | Fat: 6g | Sodium: 160mg | Carbs: 34g | Fiber: 7g | Sugar: 12g | Protein: 27g

QUICK TIP

Here's a meat-'n'-potatoes dinner that truly satisfies. The Maple Apple Brisket simmers away in the slow cooker along with the root veggies in a delightfully low-maintenance way until it's falling-apart tender. And I'm not kidding when I say that the Garlic Mashed Root Veggies are one of my all-time favorite side dishes. On holidays you won't find white mashed potatoes at my dinner table; instead, you'll see a big bowl of fluffy Garlic Mashed Root Veggies!

APPLE AND GINGER–GLAZED PORK LOIN

prep time: 15 minutes ● *cooking time:* 2 hours 10 minutes ● *serves:* 6

It's hard to describe just how delicious this Apple and Ginger–Glazed Pork Loin is . . . hold on, let me sample another slice . . .

OK, I'm back. This recipe is a healthy spin on the classic combination of savory and sweet, topped with little pieces of candied ginger—surprisingly delightful! It took more than a little willpower for me to keep my hands off this dish long enough to snap a couple of glamour shots.

In order to lighten up the glaze in this recipe, I used fresh-pressed apple juice (made with my juice press) and reduced it down with ginger and spices to create the perfect sweet topping.

Ingredients

Steps

FOR THE APPLE-GINGER GLAZE:

1 tablespoon coconut oil

3 tablespoons minced fresh ginger

3 cups fresh-pressed apple juice

1 tablespoon raw honey

4 whole black peppercorns

4 whole cloves

FOR THE PORK LOIN:

1 (1½-pound) boneless pork loin

9 cloves garlic, peeled and halved lengthwise

sea salt and black pepper, to taste

2 tablespoons coconut oil

3 tablespoons chicken broth

FOR THE APPLE-GINGER GLAZE

In a small pot, warm the coconut oil over low heat. Add the minced ginger and sauté for 3 minutes, stirring often. Stir in the remaining glaze ingredients and simmer until it reduces to a syrupy glaze, about 45 minutes. It should end up being about 1 cup of glaze.

FOR THE PORK LOIN:

1. Preheat the oven to 350°F. Rinse the pork loin and pat dry with paper towels. Make 18 small, 1-inch-deep slits evenly over the top of the pork loin and insert the garlic halves. Season generously with salt and pepper.

2. Warm the coconut oil in a large skillet over medium-high heat. Add the pork and sear well on all sides, about 5 minutes per side. Transfer the pork to a roasting pan. Pour the remaining oil from the skillet and the chicken broth into the roasting pan. Roast, basting frequently, for 45 minutes.

3. Baste the pork with the glaze (remove the peppercorns and cloves) every 5 minutes, continuing to roast the pork for an additional 20–25 minutes, until the center is mostly white with a slight hint of pale pink. Reserve the remaining glaze and tent the roast with foil for 15 minutes before serving. Slice thinly and use a clean spoon to serve with the glaze. Enjoy!

(Per serving) Calories: 426 | Fat: 17g | Sodium: 112mg
Carbs: 20g | Fiber: 1g | Sugar: 17g | Protein: 34g

QUICK TIP

Complete the meal by serving your Apple and Ginger–Glazed Pork Loin with this simple and delightful recipe for Spiced Pear Collard Greens: Heat 2 tablespoons coconut oil in a large skillet over medium heat. Add ¼ teaspoon ground cinnamon and a pinch of ground cayenne and ground cloves. Stir the spices, then add 2 sliced Bosc pears and 4 minced shallots. Sprinkle with sea salt and cook undisturbed for 5 minutes. Flip the pears and cook for 5 minutes on the other side, until golden, then remove from the skillet. Add to the skillet 2 tablespoons olive oil and 2 bunches chopped, stemmed collard greens. Sauté until wilted, about 8 minutes. Add ¼ cup chicken broth, cover, and braise for 30 minutes, or until tender. Serve the tender greens topped with the spiced pears and a sprinkle of chopped toasted pecans.

BEAN-LESS PORK SAUSAGE CHILI ON PURPLE SWEET POTATO

prep time: 20 minutes
cooking time: 2 hours 15 minutes
serves: 12

As the group of firefighters approached, in crisp pressed navy blue uniforms, my stomach did a funny tumble. The fire chief pulled off his sunglasses and peered down at me. "So, what do we have here?" he asked in a booming voice. I grabbed a cup of steaming chili, dropped a plastic spoon into it, and held it out, hands trembling.

"This is a bean-less pork sausage chili served over purple sweet potato and topped with avocado," I said, my voice coming out as a squeak. He took a bite and his eyes widened. "Wow, this is really good! Gomez, Brown, try this one!" I breathed a sigh of relief and served up chili samples to the rest of his fire crew—and a couple of hours later received the news that my chili had won the chili cook-off by a landslide!

Oh man, it was nerve-wracking to have my cooking judged, and sweetly satisfying to win first place. Sure, it was just a friendly little chili cook-off at Andrew and Chloe's school . . . but I approached it like it was the cooking Olympics. And my determination paid off.

You'll notice that my chili doesn't contain any beans. Beans contain phytates, which inhibit nutrient absorption and cause inflammation. Ever heard the term "musical fruit"? That's the phytates at work, wreaking havoc on the digestive system. Beans also contain lectins, which can mess with healthy hormonal functions. And to top it off, beans are high in carbohydrates.

Beans (also known as legumes) are promoted as a healthy food because of their fiber, vitamins and minerals, and "high" protein content. In fact, beans aren't a dense protein source, because most contain two or three times as many carbs as protein. When compared to vegetables and fruits, beans are lacking in both fiber and micronutrient density. The protein found in meat, seafood, and eggs is much more dense and complete, which is why I'd rather stick with these as main protein sources and only use beans occasionally.

It's important to commit to your own concept of healthy eating, regardless of the input or judgment of others. Look, you know your body better than anyone else does and so you instinctively know which foods give you the most energy to thrive on. You also know which foods don't settle well and give you discomfort. Don't let anyone else on this planet impose his or her own ideas or rules for eating on you. We are all uniquely made with our own set of inborn preferences. I choose to make bean-less chili because I know that a big bowl of beans is going to make me feel bloated, lethargic, and gassy. If beans fill you with boundless energy, then by all means add some to your own pot of award-winning chili.

Ingredients

- **4 purple sweet potatoes**
- **2 tablespoons extra-virgin olive oil**
- **3 cloves garlic, minced**
- **3 bell peppers (I like 1 red, 1 orange, and 1 yellow), cored, seeded, and chopped**
- **1 yellow onion, chopped**
- **1$^1/_2$ pounds loose pork sausage (or your preferred ground meat)**
- **1 tablespoon chili powder**
- **1 tablespoon sweet paprika, plus more for serving**
- **$^1/_2$ teaspoon ground allspice**
- **pinch of ground cloves**
- **1$^1/_2$ tablespoons unsweetened cocoa**
- **2 teaspoons ground cumin, plus more for serving**
- **2 teaspoons ground cinnamon**
- **$^1/_2$ teaspoon sea salt, plus more for serving**
- **2 (15-ounce) cans tomato sauce**
- **1 tablespoon apple cider vinegar**
- **$^1/_2$ cup water**
- **1 avocado, pitted, peeled, and chopped**

Steps

1. Preheat the oven to 400°F. Rinse and pat dry the sweet potatoes and pierce the skin in several places with a fork. Place on an 18 × 26-inch rimmed baking sheet and bake for 45 minutes. Once cooled, cut each sweet potato into 3 even pieces and set aside.

2. In a large pot, heat the olive oil over medium heat. Add the garlic, bell peppers, and onion, and cook until tender, about 5 minutes. Add the pork and chili powder and cook until the meat is no longer pink. Add the rest of the ingredients except for the avocado. Bring the mixture to a simmer, then decrease the heat to low and simmer, uncovered, for 1$^1/_2$ hours.

3. Serve the chili over each of the pieces of baked sweet potatoes and top with the chopped avocado and a sprinkle of cumin, paprika, and salt.

(Per serving) Calories: 339 | Fat: 23g | Sodium: 866mg
Carbs: 19g | Fiber: 5g | Sugar: 7g | Protein: 14g

QUICK TIP

This recipe calls for purple sweet potatoes, which my local market often carries. I enjoy serving this vibrantly colored potato because it catches the eye and engages the senses. The nutritional properties are very similar to orange- or white-fleshed sweet potatoes, so there's no need to get hung up over the unusual color. It's all good!

CHINESE NOODLE BOWL

prep time: 30 minutes ● *cooking time:* 50 minutes ● *serves:* 6

There's a strategy in selling called *reduce it down to the ridiculous.*

This is when a buyer shows resistance so you draw her attention away from the total cost by reframing it as a daily cost. *"Mrs. Jones, your monthly membership to this gym would come out to only $1.45 per day. That's less than what you spend at Starbucks every morning!"*

Gee, $1.45 per day is a much easier pill to swallow than $45 per month . . . even though it's really the exact same amount.

It's possible to use this reframing technique with yourself, as you learn to eat and love healthy foods. When you find yourself becoming overwhelmed with the idea of eating zucchini noodles for the rest of your life rather than your favorites, stop and reduce it down to the ridiculous.

Could you get through the next hour without a big plate of traditional noodles? Of course you can. Could you get through the next day? Certainly.

And for the times you're really missing those grain-based noodles? Give this Chinese Noodle Bowl recipe a try. It delivers all the satisfaction of a big bowl of your favorite noodles with the bonus of ginger-spiked meatballs!

Ingredients

FOR THE MEATBALLS:

1 pound ground pork

1 teaspoon Chinese
   five-spice powder

**sea salt and black
   pepper, to taste**

1 tablespoon minced
   fresh ginger (about
   1-inch knob)

½ teaspoon minced
   garlic

¼ cup almond flour

2 scallions, whites and
   greens, minced

2 teaspoons sesame oil

FOR THE NOODLE BOWLS:

1 tablespoon sesame oil,
   plus more for drizzling

1-inch knob fresh
   ginger, peeled and
   thinly sliced

1 teaspoon minced
   garlic

4 scallions, whites and
   greens, thinly sliced,
   plus more for garnish

1 red bell pepper, cored,
   seeded, and thinly
   sliced

4 baby bok choy, thinly
   sliced

6 cups chicken broth

2 tablespoons coconut
   aminos

5 zucchini, peeled and
   run through a spiral
   slicer

Steps

FOR THE MEATBALLS:

1. Preheat the oven to 400°F. Place a wire rack on a large rimmed baking sheet and set aside.

2. In a medium bowl, combine all of the meatball ingredients. Mix well with your hands, form into 16 golf ball–size meatballs, and place on the wire rack. Bake for 25–30 minutes, until fully cooked.

FOR THE NOODLE BOWLS:

1. In a large soup pot, heat the sesame oil over medium-high heat. Add the ginger, garlic, scallions, and bell pepper. Cook for 4 minutes. Add the bok choy and cook for another 4 minutes. Add the broth and coconut aminos and decrease the heat to medium-low.

2. Add the zucchini noodles and the cooked meatballs to the soup pot. Simmer over medium-low heat for 10 minutes. Serve in shallow bowls, drizzled with sesame oil and sprinkled with scallions.

*(Per serving) Calories: 403 | Fat: 23g | Sodium: 644mg
Carbs: 10g | Fiber: 3g | Sugar: 5g | Protein: 28g*

QUICK TIP

I make a large batch of meatballs on most weekends, to stock the fridge with on-the-go, protein-based snacks. These meatballs have fantastic stand-alone flavor, so give 'em a try without the noodle bowl sometime.

CHORIZO-STUFFED PEPPERS

prep time: 40 minutes ● *cooking time:* 1 hour 15 minutes ● *serves:* 6

Jerry Seinfeld is my favorite comedian of all time.

Back when B and I were first married, our budget was so limited that we couldn't afford a TV subscription, so every night we would watch one Seinfeld episode on DVD. I could probably recite each one . . . *No soup for you!*

Last month, we saw Jerry perform at Caesar's Palace in Las Vegas. It was surreal to see him live onstage, cracking jokes and making the audience roll with laughter. He did a hilarious bit on being harped on to hydrate that is constantly being repeated in our house now:

"You've got to HY-D-ER-ATE, Jerry!" (Said with your best Seinfeld voice.)

And while his joshing on the subject is hilarious, hydration really is a serious topic.

Drinking plenty of water throughout the day is one of the quickest, easiest, and most practical ways to improve your health. Carry a water bottle with you while exercising, make a point to set a glass of water at your work station, and have water with your meals. Once water consumption becomes a habit, you'll be able to fully appreciate the synergistic powers of hydration.

When in doubt . . . *HY-D-ER-ATE, Jerry!*

There's nothing funny about this recipe. It's a seriously delicious combination of chorizo, quinoa, and tender bell peppers. I dare you not to smile while eating it.

Ingredients

½ cup uncooked quinoa

1 cup chicken broth

6 bell peppers, stem ends sliced off, seeded

1 pound chorizo

1 celery stalk, diced

1 large carrot, diced

½ cup diced yellow onion

4 cloves garlic, minced

½ cup chopped fresh cilantro

1 cup spaghetti sauce

sea salt and black pepper, to taste

1 small, sweet red chile, thinly sliced, for garnish

Steps

1. Preheat the oven to 350°F. Lightly grease a 10 × 15-inch glass casserole pan with olive oil.

2. In a medium saucepan, combine the quinoa and broth over medium-high heat. Bring to a boil, decrease to a simmer, cover, and cook for 20 minutes. Set aside.

3. Bring a large pot of water to a boil. Add the bell peppers, cover, and cook for 5 minutes. Remove the peppers with tongs and set aside.

4. In a large skillet over medium-high heat, cook the chorizo until almost brown. Drain the fat and add the celery, carrot, onion, garlic, cilantro, and spaghetti sauce. Season with salt and pepper and cook for 5 minutes. Stir in the cooked quinoa and cook for another 3 minutes.

5. Place the peppers on the prepared pan and fill them with the chorizo mixture. Cover the pan with foil and bake for 30 minutes, until cooked through and tender. Garnish with chile slices.

(Per stuffed pepper) Calories: 466 | Fat: 31g | Sodium: 1,170mg
Carbs: 18g | Fiber: 3g | Sugar: 7g | Protein: 29g

QUICK TIP

When I make this recipe, I double the chorizo-quinoa mixture and use the leftovers to make a taco salad the next day. Here's what else goes into my taco salad:

- Chopped romaine lettuce
- Chopped scallions
- Chopped avocados
- Chopped cucumbers
- Peeled and sliced jicama
- Pico de gallo
- COCONUT SOUR CREAM (page 201)

SLOW COOKER LAMB DINNER

prep time: 15 minutes ● *cooking time:* 6 hours ● *serves:* 16

B and I were born on opposite sides of the world: He arrived in a little village in Armenia, and I arrived in Bellingham, Washington. At the time of his birth, Armenia was under the control of the Soviet Union.

He has memories of surprise raids on their home, of standing in long lines for food with his mom, and of the fear and uncertainty that went along with a life lived under communist rule.

Arriving in the United States at the age of six, he was instantly taken by the abundance and opportunity here, and a few short decades later, he brought his very own American dream into reality.

B has an earnest love for his adopted homeland, with true patriotism running through his veins. Even so, the taste of simple, rustic braised lamb—an Armenian classic—still tops his list of favorite foods.

This dish is the perfect comforting weekday meal. Just throw the ingredients in the slow cooker before you rush off to start your day. There's depth in the spices and a touch of sweet as rich figs mingle with bites of tender lamb.

Ingredients

- 2 tablespoons coconut oil
- 1 yellow onion, chopped
- 2 tablespoons minced fresh ginger
- 1 tablespoon minced garlic (about 2 cloves)
- 1/4 cup apple cider vinegar
- 1 tablespoon coconut palm sugar
- 1 tablespoon ground coriander
- 1 tablespoon ground cumin
- 1 teaspoon ground cinnamon
- 1 teaspoon black pepper
- 1 teaspoon ground cardamom
- 1/8 teaspoon saffron strands, crushed
- 1/4 teaspoon ground cloves
- 1 teaspoon sea salt
- 1/2 cup dried apricots
- 1/4 cup sliced almonds
- 1 (15-ounce) can tomato sauce
- 1 cup peeled and cubed sweet potato
- 1 cup peeled, seeded, and cubed butternut squash
- 1/2 cup dried Mission figs
- 4 pounds bone-in lamb shoulder
- NAAN BREAD (page 156), for serving

Steps

1. In a large skillet, heat the coconut oil over medium-high heat. Add the onion, ginger, and garlic, and cook until the onion is translucent, about 12 minutes. Transfer to a slow cooker.

2. Add the vinegar, coconut palm sugar, spices, apricots, almonds, tomato sauce, sweet potato, squash, and figs to the slow cooker. Mix until fully combined.

3. Rinse the lamb and pat dry with a paper towel. Season generously with salt and pepper. Press the lamb into the slow cooker, covering the meat completely with the other ingredients. Cover and cook on low for 6 hours.

4. Remove the lamb from the slow cooker, debone, and mix the meat back into the slow cooker. Serve with naan.

(Per serving) Calories: 318 | Fat: 10g | Sodium: 406mg
Carbs: 11g | Fiber: 5g | Sugar: 7g | Protein: 36g

HEALTHY EATING TIP

You've probably heard this expression: "Success is a journey, not a destination." This sentiment perfectly applies to how you eat. Healthy eating is a journey that is made one home-cooked meal at a time.

BUTTERNUT SQUASH WITH KALE AND SAUSAGE

prep time: 15 minutes ● *cooking time:* 25 minutes
serves: 4

You'll be hard-pressed to find a simpler way to prepare fresh butternut squash as a hearty, satisfying dinner than this. The sweetness of the butternut squash blends perfectly with the savory sausage and earthy kale. It really beckons fall to emerge—bring on the brisk air, swirling leaves, cozy sweaters, and cute boots!

This dish is delicious hot and even more so chilled the next day because the flavors intensify as they sit.

Ingredients

- 1 pound loose sweet Italian sausage
- 1 tablespoon extra-virgin olive oil
- 1 yellow onion, chopped
- 3 cups cubed butternut squash (about 2 medium squash)
- 1/4 cup dry white wine
- 2 teaspoons minced garlic
- 1 teaspoon dried marjoram
- 1 1/2 cups chicken broth, divided
- 1 bunch lacinato kale, stemmed and chopped

Steps

1. In a large skillet over medium-high heat, cook the sausage for 5 minutes, breaking it up into small pieces with a spoon or spatula. Once all the pink is gone, push the sausage to the sides of the pan, leaving a clear cooking area in the center.

2. Add the olive oil and the onion and cook for 5 minutes. Add the butternut squash, wine, garlic, marjoram, and 3/4 cup of the chicken broth. Cook for 5 minutes, until the squash is tender.

3. Stir in the kale and the remaining 3/4 cup chicken broth. Cover the pan and decrease the heat to low. Cook for 10 minutes, until the kale is tender.

(Per serving) Calories: 310 | Fat: 14g | Sodium: 836mg Carbs: 25g | Fiber: 5g | Sugar: 6g | Protein: 23g

HEALTHY EATING TIP

Never give up. If you don't ever quit, then you'll NEVER fail. Get up, dust yourself off, and keep moving forward.

CRISPY FISH

prep time: 25 minutes ● ***cooking time:*** 8 minutes
serves: 4

Do you only eat when you're hungry?

This is an interesting thing to consider each time you reach for food. It's amazing how many extra calories we can accumulate for reasons other than hunger.

You could be eating out of habit. You could be eating out of boredom. You could be eating out of social obligation. You could be eating for comfort. You could be eating for fun.

Part of your real-food journey is to get to a place where your primary motivation for consumption is hunger.

Enjoy this recipe . . . but only if you're actually hungry!

This is the grown-up version of the fried fish sticks that you enjoyed as a kid. It still has the crave-worthy crunchy breaded outside, but with the addition of sophisticated herbs and spices.

Ingredients

2 tablespoons coconut flour

¼ teaspoon garlic powder

2 eggs

¼ cup full-fat coconut milk

½ cup blanched almond flour

½ cup flax meal

⅓ cup nutritional yeast

1 tablespoon dried oregano

2 tablespoons extra-virgin olive oil

4 (6-ounce) white fish fillets

TARTAR SAUCE (**page 201**), for serving

Steps

1. In a shallow bowl, combine the coconut flour and garlic powder. In a second shallow bowl, whisk together the eggs and coconut milk. In a third shallow bowl, combine the blanched almond flour, flax meal, nutritional yeast, and dried oregano.

2. Arrange the 3 bowls within arm's reach of your stove. Heat the olive oil in a skillet over medium-high heat.

3. Dip each fish fillet in the coconut flour mixture, then in the egg mixture, and finally in the almond flour mixture so it's well coated. Add the fish to the pan, working in batches if necessary, and sauté for 8 minutes, until golden and cooked through, turning once. Serve immediately.

(Per fillet) Calories: 404 | Fat: 23g | Sodium: 227mg
Carbs: 11g | Fiber: 8g | Sugar: 1g | Protein: 43g

QUICK TIP

The success of your Crispy Fish hinges entirely on the quality of the fillets that you use. Buy only the freshest, highest-quality fish.

PECAN-CRUSTED SEA BASS

prep time: 15 minutes ● *cooking time:* 20 minutes ● *serves:* 4

As a college student, I worked as a personal trainer to make ends meet. The large gym where I spent most afternoons and evenings was a very interesting place with its own socio-ecological system. The front of the gym was inhabited by the membership sales team, with their slicked-back hair, collared shirts, and practiced smiles (avoid interaction at all costs, even if it means walking five minutes out of your way). The aerobics room was filled with the caffeinated group instructors, with their neon spandex, microphone-enhanced voices, and boundless energy (don't get too close or they'll yell at you to join in). The weight room belonged to the tough, muscle-bound guys, with their weight belts, wrist wraps, and loud, painful grunts (kinda smells in there). And then there was the trainer desk, populated by my fellow blue polo shirt–clad trainers, with our training notebooks, stopwatches, and plastic containers filled with chicken breast and broccoli (we thought we were *so* cool!).

Back then it seemed like chicken breast and broccoli was the only thing that we told our clients to eat . . . and the only thing we ate ourselves. Boring! Boring! Boring!

Today I like to find lots of different (read: delicious) ways to serve up protein and fiber. And it rarely involves broccoli.

This recipe for Pecan-Crusted Sea Bass is the perfect example of a tasty dish that delivers in flavor without adding refined carbs or bad fats. Enjoy it guilt-free and share it with your favorite personal trainer!

Ingredients

FOR THE PECAN-CRUSTED SEA BASS:

⅓ **cup coconut flour**

½ **teaspoon sea salt**

¼ **teaspoon black pepper**

2 eggs

2 teaspoons Dijon mustard

1 teaspoon pure maple syrup

½ **cup pecans, toasted and finely chopped**

4 (6-ounce) sea bass fillets

1 tablespoon coconut oil, or more as needed

FOR THE CREAMY DIJON SAUCE:

½ **cup coconut cream**

¼ **cup stone-ground Dijon mustard**

Steps

FOR THE PECAN-CRUSTED SEA BASS:

1. Preheat the oven to 350°F. Line a baking sheet with foil and set aside.

2. Combine the flour, salt, and pepper in a shallow bowl. In a second shallow bowl, whisk together the eggs, mustard, and syrup. Fill a third shallow bowl with the pecans.

3. Dredge each sea bass fillet in the flour mixture, dip it into the egg mixture until it's fully coated, and then press it into the pecans to evenly coat. Place on a clean plate.

4. Melt the coconut oil in a large skillet over medium heat. Add the fillets, in batches if necessary, and cook for 2 minutes on each side, or until lightly browned, adding more coconut oil as needed. Arrange the fillets on the prepared baking sheet and bake for 10 minutes, or until flaky.

FOR THE CREAMY DIJON SAUCE:

In a bowl, whisk together the coconut cream and mustard with a fork. Chill in the fridge for at least 15 minutes and serve with the hot fish.

(Per fillet) Calories: 387 | Fat: 18g | Sodium: 750mg
Carbs: 9g | Fiber: 5g | Sugar: 3g | Protein: 37g

QUICK TIP

This recipe comes together quickly, so be sure to get all your sides ready beforehand, and wait on cooking the fish until right before you're ready to serve. It's also important to chop the pecans quite fine in order to get a nice, even crust.

EASY SALMON WITH GINGER AND LEMON

prep time: 10 minutes ● *cooking time:* 15 minutes ● *serves:* 4

Salmon is a rich source of vitamin B_{12} and omega-3 fatty acids—both vital nutrients that we could use more of in our diets. It's also a phenomenal source of protein and beneficial fats.

In my home state of Washington, the beginning of spring marks the start of salmon season. As the majestic, silvery beasts begin their migration from the frigid depths of the Pacific Ocean to the scenic rivers from which they were hatched, we humans stock up on cedar planks and pull out our favorite salmon recipes.

While salmon roasted on cedar over a roaring outdoor fire is the tastiest way that I know to prepare salmon, this oven-baked recipe gives you all of the tender, flaky salmon flavor that you love with a fraction of the effort. By wrapping each fillet in a little parchment paper parcel, the salmon stays perfectly juicy while being infused with ginger and garlic.

Ingredients

- 4 (6-ounce) salmon fillets
- 3-inch knob ginger, peeled and minced (about 1 tablespoon)
- 4 cloves garlic, thinly sliced
- 4 scallions, greens only, thinly sliced
- 1 red bell pepper, cored, seeded, and sliced
- 4 lemons, sliced

Steps

1. Preheat the oven to 400°F.
2. Cut out four 8 × 10-inch rectangles of parchment paper. Place each of the salmon fillets in the center of a rectangle. Divide the ginger, garlic, scallions, bell pepper, and lemon slices evenly among the fillets. Fold both long sides of parchment paper over each fillet, and tuck the shorter edges underneath to form a parcel. Place on a baking sheet and bake for 15 minutes, until flaky.

(Per fillet) Calories: 291 | Fat: 14g | Sodium: 127mg
Carbs: 12g | Fiber: 4g | Sugar: 1g | Protein: 31g

HEALTHY EATING TIP

Healthy eating is simple: Avoid processed and packaged foods. Cook and eat meals at home. Drink water. Eat fresh veggies, fruits, meat, eggs, nuts, and seeds. Stop eating sugar. It's not *easy*, but it's simple.

MAPLE BACON–WRAPPED SALMON

prep time: 15 minutes ● *cooking time:* 20 minutes ● *serves:* 4

Want the secret to achieving any goal?

Model success.

Find someone else who has done the same thing you're aiming to do and ask him or her for the blueprint. Observe what worked for others and implement those things in your own life.

There's no need to reinvent the wheel. Simply model success. (And do it with your own flavor.)

When it comes to creating over-the-top-awesome recipes, I decided to take my own advice and model the success of other over-the-top-awesome recipes. It all came down to one ingredient . . . BACON!

Ingredients

- **1 teaspoon minced garlic**
- **¹/₂ teaspoon sea salt**
- **¹/₄ teaspoon black pepper**
- **¹/₂ cup plus 2 tablespoons pure maple syrup, divided**
- **¹/₄ cup coconut aminos**
- **4 (6-ounce) salmon fillets, skin removed**
- **8 strips bacon**
- **1 tablespoon Dijon mustard**
- **¹/₂ teaspoon lemon zest**

Steps

1. In a small bowl, combine the garlic, salt, pepper, ¹/₂ cup of the maple syrup, and coconut aminos. Place the salmon in a shallow casserole pan and coat with the marinade. Cover the dish with plastic wrap and let the salmon marinate in the fridge for 30 minutes, turning once.

2. Preheat the broiler to high. Lightly grease a 10 × 15-inch baking dish with olive oil.

3. Wrap each fillet with 2 strips of bacon, securing the bacon with 2 skewers. In a small bowl, combine the remaining 2 tablespoons maple syrup, mustard, and lemon zest. Brush the mustard mixture over the bacon-wrapped fillets.

4. Place the bacon-wrapped fillets in the prepared baking dish and broil, watching closely. Once the bacon has crisped, about 10 minutes, adjust the oven temperature to 400°F, place the salmon on the center rack, and bake for 5–10 minutes, until cooked through and flaky.

(Per fillet) Calories: 553 | Fat: 26g | Sodium: 697mg
Carbs: 27g | Fiber: 0g | Sugar: 18g | Protein: 38g

QUICK TIP

An alternative to wrapping your salmon fillets in bacon is to cook the bacon separately, chop it up, and sprinkle it over the fillets. To do so, line a rimmed baking sheet with foil and place a wire rack on top. Lay the bacon strips over the wire rack and brush them with the maple-mustard sauce. Bake at 400°F for 20 minutes, or until crispy. This sweet glazed bacon makes an awesome treat all by itself, too!

SIDES, SNACKS, AND PANTRY STAPLES

We are more than halfway through this book, so now's a good time to check in and see how you're feeling about the new recipes. How are you doing, friend? Are you pumped up to start cooking some of this stuff? Have you flagged a few pages to try and jotted down some of the new ingredients to purchase during your next run to the market?

I hope so!

I really want you to succeed and hope that this little book of mine is helping you make positive, measurable changes to how you cook and eat. The best time for you to take action with this new information is now, while you're excited about it. Really, the ONLY time to take action is now. All you have is now.

Procrastination is the number one reason for failure in life.

So bust out your pots and pans, preheat that oven, and let's get cooking! No waiting for tomorrow—this is going down tonight!

EVERYTHING CRACKERS

prep time: 15 minutes ● *cooking time:* 14 minutes ● *makes:* 80 crackers

When you make the decision to start eating healthy, your entire diet goes under review. Upon reflection, it's often surprising how many unhealthy snack items have taken up residence in your daily routine.

By their nature, snacks have to be quick and easy, a short pause to refuel so that hunger leaves you alone for a few more hours. This is why unhealthy items are so often selected—a package from a vending machine or a bag grabbed from a drive-thru window.

But all of those unhealthy snacks are robbing you of your ideal body, of your best health, and of that real, pure energy boost that only wholesome food delivers. The good news is that wholesome snacking can be just as quick, simple, and convenient as junk food snacking. Really!

All it takes is a little bit of forethought.

Taking a couple of hours on the weekend to bake a batch or two of these Everything Crackers, a pan of GINGERSNAPS (page 216), some GLAZED MEATBALLS (page 76), and a batch of QUINOA ENERGY BARS (page 46) and to slice organic fruit and hard-boil a dozen eggs will set you up for a week filled with smart, healthy snacking. And just like that, you take another giant step toward that leaner, healthier, more energetic you—the best version of you.

Ingredients

FOR THE CRACKERS:

4 cups blanched almond flour

2 eggs

1 teaspoon sea salt

1 tablespoon coconut palm sugar

FOR THE EVERYTHING TOPPING:

1 tablespoon sesame seeds

1 tablespoon fennel seeds

1 tablespoon poppy seeds

1 teaspoon coarse sea salt

1 tablespoon dried garlic

1 tablespoon dried onion

Steps

FOR THE CRACKERS:

1. Preheat the oven to 350°F. Cut out 2 large rectangles of parchment paper that fit on an 18 × 26-inch rimmed baking sheet.

2. Combine the almond flour, eggs, salt, and coconut palm sugar in the bowl of a food processor. Pulse until a dough forms.

FOR THE EVERYTHING TOPPING:

1. In a small bowl, combine the topping ingredients.

2. Place the dough ball between the 2 sheets of parchment paper. Roll out the dough to ⅛ inch thick. Transfer the parchment and dough to the baking sheet and remove the top layer of parchment paper. Lightly brush the dough with water and sprinkle with the topping mixture.

3. Using a fluted pastry wheel, cut the dough into 1-inch squares and pierce the center of each square with a fork. Bake for 12–14 minutes, until golden.

(Per 8 crackers) Calories: 146 | Fat: 12g | Sodium: 218mg
Carbs: 6g | Fiber: 3g | Sugar: 2g | Protein: 6g

QUICK TIP

Using parchment paper to roll the dough out may seem like a hassle, but trust me on this one. The dough is pretty sticky, so the parchment paper really helps you roll it out nice and thin.

CHEEZY CRACKERS

prep time: 15 minutes ● *cooking time:* 15 minutes ● *makes:* 80 crackers

I'm going to let you in on a little secret, so lean in really close . . .

It's not about reaching a number on the scale.

You've been duped! The number on the scale is an empty, meaningless goal. Which is probably why so many dieters fail to ever reach that idealized number.

So what is it about? What is the prize that awaits the dedicated? What is this intangible carrot that we chase?

It's about how you feel when you're eating right and exercising.

When you're on track, eating right, exercising regularly, making wholesome food choices, and being proactive for your health, this *feeling* comes over you.

It's hard to describe, but once you experience it you'll know . . .

It's a buzzing in your cells. It's a tickle of excitement. It's a steady flow of energy. It's a confidence. It's a satisfaction in your bones. It's a peace of mind and heart.

It's about living in that feeling.

Ingredients

- **1 cup blanched almond flour**
- **1 teaspoon sea salt**
- **1 cup FANCY CHEESE BALL mixture (page 64)**
- **3 tablespoons coconut oil, melted**
- **2 tablespoons ice water**
- **1 tablespoon full-fat coconut milk**

Steps

1. Preheat the oven to 350°F. Cut out 2 large rectangles of parchment paper that fit on an 18 × 26-inch rimmed baking sheet.

2. Combine all the ingredients in the bowl of a food processor and pulse until a dough forms.

3. Place the dough ball between the 2 sheets of parchment paper and roll out to ⅛ inch thick. Transfer the parchment and dough to the baking sheet and remove the top layer of paper. Using a fluted pastry wheel, cut the dough into 1-inch squares and pierce the center of each square with a fork. Bake for 12–15 minutes, until golden.

(Per 8 crackers) Calories: 147 | Fat: 14g | Sodium: 209mg
Carbs: 3g | Fiber: 1g | Sugar: 1g | Protein: 4g

QUICK TIP

Yes, these crackers are for real! And yes, these really do taste like Cheez-It crackers! These Cheezy Crackers are tasty and so much fun. It's important to let the crackers cool all the way before removing from the pan, in order to prevent crumbling. Also, keep the leftovers in the fridge to keep 'em fresh and intact (remember, coconut oil gets firm when chilled). These crackers taste best when freshly baked. Enjoy!

PIZZA KALE CHIPS

prep time: 10 minutes ● *cooking time:* 5 hours ● *serves:* 6

B and I are friends with a really cool couple who recently moved to California from the East Coast. They've taught us the fascinating social modality of tailgating, which involves gathering in a parking lot before a concert and sharing food and drinks.

Last week, during one such tailgating session, someone pulled out a bag of "Pizza Kale Chips" from a natural foods supermarket. We all skeptically tried some, but sure enough, they really tasted like pizza. (There was also a bag of "Chocolate Kale Chips" passed around; see page 152.) I took a picture of the ingredients list with my phone and got to work on creating this homemade recipe.

If you're a fan of pizza and a fan of chips, then you will enjoy this recipe—even if you're not a fan of regular kale chips. They smell uncannily like pizza as they dehydrate in the oven, and the taste really hits that spot when you need a salty, savory snack. And they're perfect for enjoying while loitering in a parking lot.

Ingredients

1 bunch curly kale

1 cup raw unsalted cashews, soaked in hot water for 15 minutes and drained

$1/3$ cup water

$1/4$ cup tomato paste

3 tablespoons nutritional yeast

1 tablespoon coconut palm sugar

1 tablespoon Italian seasoning blend

1 teaspoon garlic powder

$1/2$ teaspoon sea salt

pinch of red pepper flakes

2 tablespoons lemon juice

1 teaspoon apple cider vinegar

1 tablespoon extra-virgin olive oil

Steps

1. Preheat the oven to 170°F. Line an 18 × 26-inch rimmed baking sheet with parchment paper and set aside.

2. Wash the kale and pat dry. Cut out the long, thick stems and tear the leaves into 2- to 3-inch-wide pieces. Put them in a large bowl and set aside.

3. Add all of the remaining ingredients to the bowl of a food processor and blend until smooth.

4. Add the creamy cashew mixture to the bowl of kale. Use your hands to mix well, coating each piece of kale. Spread the kale evenly on the prepared baking sheet.

5. Put the baking sheet in the oven and use a wooden spoon to prop the oven door open a couple of inches (this allows moisture to escape). Check on the kale every hour, flipping the kale pieces after 2 hours. It should take about 5 hours for the kale to become really crispy. Store in an airtight container at room temperature for up to 5 days.

(Per serving) Calories: 90 | Fat: 5g | Sodium: 211mg
Carbs: 9g | Fiber: 3g | Sugar: 3g | Protein: 6g

QUICK TIP

After a day or two, your kale chips will lose much of their crispiness. To bring back the crunch, simply spread the chips on a rimmed baking sheet and place in the oven at 300°F for 5 minutes.

CHOCOLATE KALE CHIPS

prep time: 10 minutes ● *cooking time:* 5 hours ● *serves:* 6

Chocolate Kale Chips?! Have I completely lost my mind? Have I taken the concept of healthy snacks too far? Only you can decide how you feel about these crispy, sweet, chocolaty, green chips . . . and if you're anything like the eight taste testers who tried this recipe for me, then you're going to eat this one up . . . literally!

Let's face it, chocolate is awesome, and life is not fully lived without a bite or two of choco-late every now and then . . . as in *right now*! But you don't want to throw your diet into disarray to get your chocolate fix. No way! You deserve wholesome, beneficial chocolate treats that will enhance your health while pleasing your taste buds—and I support you. #LoftyChocolateGoals

Ingredients

1 bunch curly kale

1 cup raw unsalted pecans

5 dates, pitted, soaked in hot water for 15 minutes, and drained

2 tablespoons coconut palm sugar

$^1/_3$ cup unsweetened cocoa powder

1 teaspoon vanilla extract

$^1/_2$ teaspoon sea salt

$^1/_2$ cup water

Steps

1. Preheat the oven to 170°F. Line an 18 × 26-inch rimmed baking sheet with parchment paper and set aside.

2. Wash the kale and pat dry. Cut out the long, thick stems and tear the leaves into 2-to 3-inch-wide pieces. Put them in a large bowl and set aside.

3. Add the remaining ingredients to a food processor and pulse to create a soft chocolate mixture with the consistency of frosting.

4. Add the chocolate mixture to the bowl of kale leaves and then get your hands nice and gooey by mixing the frosting-like chocolate into the leaves. Take your time and mix gently, so that the kale leaves aren't crushed. Spread the kale evenly on the prepared baking sheet.

5. Put the baking sheet in the oven and use a wooden spoon to prop the oven door open a couple of inches (this allows moisture to escape). Check on the kale every hour, flipping the kale pieces after 2 hours. It should take about 5 hours for the kale to become really crispy. Store in an airtight container at room temperature for up to 5 days.

(Per serving) Calories: 147 | Fat: 3g | Sodium: 221mg
Carbs: 29g | Fiber: 3g | Sugar: 5g | Protein: 4g

CAJUN-ROASTED PUMPKIN SEEDS

prep time: 10 minutes ● *cooking time:* 20 minutes ● *serves:* 4

This morning at 7 A.M. I walked into Chloe's room to find her sitting on the floor, bent over a notebook, writing in silence with a serious expression on her face. If you've ever met Chloe, then you'd know that silence and serious are rarities for her! The girl is a whirlwind of sound effects and dance moves, her laughter lighting up every room she walks into. Seeing her in such a stoic pose instantly grabbed my attention, and I bent over her shoulder to catch a glimpse of what she was writing . . .

WHAT I KNOW

I know that whatever you do, your mind says No first. Like if you had no mind, your body would be able to do anything it wants. So what you want to do, make it happen. Have fun with your mind and help it grow.

I'm not sure how she came up with this—if it was something she heard at school or picked up from the Napoleon Hill audiobooks I play in the kitchen—but the wisdom in her words stopped me in my tracks. Out of the mouths of babes! This is a message that we adults too often forget.

Let's pause and absorb this wisdom of an eight-year-old . . . **Limitations only exist in our minds.**

How have you imposed limitations on your ability to skip processed foods in favor of healthy, real foods? What expectations would you have if you had successfully avoided processed food for twelve months? You would expect more! And you would know with conviction that it was possible.

These wholesome Cajun-Roasted Pumpkin Seeds are a great place to start your real-food journey—or another tasty chapter of a journey that you're already on. Eating snacks like this, instead of processed and packaged junk food, is the key to transforming your diet into one that promotes good health, natural weight loss, and boundless energy. And they're pretty darn tasty, too.

Ingredients

- **1 tablespoon coconut oil**
- **1 cup fresh pumpkin seeds, washed and dried**
- **1 tablespoon Cajun seasoning**
- **1/4 teaspoon sea salt**

Steps

1. Preheat the oven to 325°F. Line a baking sheet with parchment paper and set aside.

2. Place a skillet over medium heat. Heat the coconut oil, and then add the pumpkin seeds and sauté for 5 minutes, until golden brown. Sprinkle with the Cajun seasoning and salt, mix until fully incorporated, and then spread the seeds on the prepared baking sheet.

3. Roast for 15–20 minutes, until golden and crisp. Store in an airtight container at room temperature for up to 1 week.

(Per serving) Calories: 213 | Fat: 19g | Sodium: 533mg
Carbs: 4g | Fiber: 7g | Sugar: 0g | Protein: 9g

QUICK TIP

Pumpkin seeds aren't the only seeds worth roasting. You could also roast the seeds from butternut squash or acorn squash.

NAAN BREAD

prep time: 80 minutes ● *cooking time:* 7 minutes per batch ● *makes:* 20 naan

When going grain-free, one of the biggest cravings people get is typically for bread products. While there are plenty of grain-free bread recipes out there, most of them take quite a while to bake. This recipe is great because it cooks quickly on a grill pan, and it has the authentic, yeasty flavor that scratches the bread itch.

Naan is a light, yeasty flat bread that's great served with dinner or used to make a little sandwich. It's best while still hot off the grill.

Ingredients

1 cup warm water

1 tablespoon raw honey

1 (1/4-ounce) packet active dry yeast

3 tablespoons coconut cream

1 egg, beaten

2 teaspoons sea salt

3 1/2 cups blanched almond flour

4 cups arrowroot starch, plus more for dusting

1/4 cup coconut oil

extra-virgin olive oil, for cooking

Steps

1. In a small bowl, combine the warm water with the honey. Sprinkle the yeast on top, then gently mix it into the warm honey water. Set aside for 10 minutes to allow it to foam up.

2. In a large bowl, combine the coconut cream, egg, and salt. Add the yeast mixture, almond flour, arrowroot starch, and coconut oil. Mix until fully combined.

3. Sprinkle arrowroot starch over a cutting board and carefully knead the dough, using plenty of arrowroot starch to prevent sticking.

4. Oil the inside of a large bowl and put the dough ball inside. Cover the bowl with a damp cloth and set aside in a warm place for 1 hour. The mixture won't rise as much as traditional bread, but we still leave the yeast alone to work a little magic.

5. Heat a grill pan over medium-high and lightly grease it with olive oil. Pinch off a golf ball–size piece of the dough, flatten it in your hands into a roughly 6-inch-wide pancake, and place it on the grill pan. Cook for 2–3 minutes, until the dough is puffy and lightly browned. Brush the uncooked side of the dough with olive oil, flip, and cook for another 2–4 minutes. Continue the process until all of the dough has been cooked. Store in an airtight container in the fridge for up to 1 week.

(Per naan) Calories: 239 | Fat: 10g | Sodium: 229mg
Carbs: 28g | Fiber: 4g | Sugar: 2g | Protein: 5g

QUICK TIP

I use active dry yeast in this recipe, which adds authentic breadlike flavor while also making the dough fluffy. A couple of things usually come up when I post bread recipes with yeast online, so let's tackle 'em now: First, active dry yeast does NOT contain gluten or grains, so you can rest easy. Second, the dough is not going to rise to the level that grain-based dough would, but it still will rise some, giving you a nice and light finished product.

WALNUT RAISIN ROLLS

prep time: 15 minutes ● *cooking time:* 18 minutes ● *makes:* 18 rolls

These Walnut Raisin Rolls were inspired by two different bread rolls, one from Prime 112 in Miami and one from Starbucks. Both are soft, moist, and dotted with chopped walnuts and black raisins. However, both also included grains, gluten, and cane sugar.

This is the perfect recipe to try if you're new to grain-free baking, because it's really, really simple. Just mix up the ingredients, shape the dough into flattened golf balls, and bake. Done and done. The flavor and consistency are fantastic—I always know I have a winner on my hands when B and the kids keep reaching for more! They're also really versatile—you could grab one for breakfast or a snack or serve them fresh from the oven at your next fancy dinner party.

Ingredients

2 eggs

1/2 cup coconut oil, melted

1/4 cup filtered water

2 tablespoons raw honey, gently melted

1 teaspoon apple cider vinegar

2 cups almond meal

1/3 cup coconut flour

1/4 cup arrowroot starch

1/2 teaspoon baking soda

1/2 teaspoon sea salt

1/2 cup chopped raw walnuts

1/3 cup black raisins

Steps

1. Preheat the oven to 350°F. Line a baking sheet with parchment paper and lightly grease the paper with coconut oil. Set aside.

2. In a medium mixing bowl, combine the eggs, coconut oil, water, honey, and vinegar. Mix until fully combined.

3. In another medium mixing bowl, combine the almond meal, coconut flour, arrowroot starch, baking soda, and salt. Mix until fully combined.

4. Add the egg mixture to the almond meal mixture and mix until fully incorporated. Stir in the walnuts and raisins.

5. Use your hands to form golf ball–size rounds of dough and flatten them slightly as you place them on the prepared baking sheet. Bake for 15–18 minutes, until cooked through and lightly golden on the bottom.

(Per roll) Calories: 201 | Fat: 16g | Sodium: 110mg
Carbs: 10g | Fiber: 3g | Sugar: 4g | Protein: 6g

QUICK TIP

Make a double batch of these rolls to keep in the freezer for a rainy day. Once cooled, put the baked rolls in an airtight container and freeze for up to 3 months.

PLANTAIN CHIPS

prep time: 15 minutes   *cooking time:* 30 minutes
serves: 6

Most popular snack foods are of the crunchy and salty variety, which are super-tasty . . . and super-unhealthy. This simple recipe for Plantain Chips really saves the day when your inner crunchy, salty, snacking monster wakes up. The seasoning is pretty simple, so feel free to enhance it with flavors of your choice—you could add some paprika and red pepper for spice or cinnamon and coconut palm sugar for sweetness.

Ingredients

3 large green plantains

1 tablespoon extra-virgin olive oil

juice of 1 lemon

sea salt and black pepper, to taste

Steps

1. Preheat the oven to 350°F. Line two 18 × 26-inch rimmed baking sheets with parchment paper and set aside.

2. Using a sharp knife, carefully cut the plantains in half widthwise, then slice off the green skin by cutting straight down onto a cutting board. Use a mandoline to thinly slice the plantains widthwise.

3. Put the sliced plantains in a bowl and add the olive oil and lemon juice, then season with salt and pepper. Mix well.

4. Arrange the plantains in a single layer on the prepared baking sheets. Bake for 30 minutes, or until golden and crisp.

*(Per serving) Calories: 112 | Fat: 3g | Sodium: 97mg
Carbs: 24g | Fiber: 2g | Sugar: 11g | Protein: 1g*

QUICK TIP

You'll definitely need to use a mandoline in order to slice the plantains quickly, safely, and evenly. (Be very careful when using this slicer for the first time—protect those fingertips!) Practice making your plantain slices as thin as possible for the crispiest chips.

SPICY COCONUT CURRY SOUP

prep time: 15 minutes ● *cooking time:* 25 minutes
serves: 6

Oh man, this recipe is the bomb!

It's perfectly creamy, spicy, and dotted with tender veggies. My inner vegetarian is doing cartwheels right now.

Give this soup a try on a cold and dreary day—it's sure to cheer you up.

Ingredients

2 cups pearl onions

2 tablespoons extra-virgin olive oil

2 red bell peppers, cored, seeded, and diced

1 medium rutabaga, peeled and diced

1 medium sweet potato, peeled and diced

3 cloves garlic, minced

2 tablespoons minced fresh ginger

2 tablespoons red chile paste

3 cups vegetable or chicken broth

¾ cup unsweetened coconut milk

2 tablespoons lime juice

2 tablespoons minced fresh cilantro

sea salt and white pepper, to taste

Steps

1. Bring a medium pot of water to a boil. Add the pearl onions and blanch (boil) for 4 minutes. Drain the pot. Once the onions have cooled, halve them and remove their outer skin.

2. Place a large soup pot over medium-high heat. Add the olive oil, pearl onion halves, and bell peppers. Sauté for 5 minutes. Add the rutabaga, sweet potato, garlic, ginger, and chile paste. Continue to cook, stirring often, for 5 minutes, or until the vegetables are tender.

3. Stir in the chicken broth, cover, and cook for 12 minutes. Remove the lid, mix in the coconut milk, and bring the liquid to a simmer. Stir in the lime juice and fresh cilantro, season with salt and white pepper, and serve.

(Per serving) Calories: 195 | Fat: 6g | Sodium: 467mg
Carbs: 22g | Fiber: 5g | Sugar: 8g | Protein: 9g

QUICK TIP

Let's talk about ingredient substitutions in this soup: The rutabaga and sweet potato can be successfully swapped out for your favorite winter squash or root veggie. Butternut squash, acorn squash, parsnips, carrots, zucchini—it'd all be delicious. You'll notice that this recipe calls for white pepper instead of black. White pepper has more spice, which takes the flavor up a notch in a way that black pepper simply can't.

CHICKEN SOUP WITH QUINOA
AND ROASTED RED PEPPERS

prep time: 20 minutes *cooking time:* 5 minutes *serves:* 5

"So what made you go to the doctor? How did you know?" he asks, then takes a sip of his drink. The din of conversation, laughter, and clinking glasses fills the air around us. It's Friday night social hour and once again the conversation has turned to my recent experience with cancer.

I don't mind talking about it—it's usually cathartic—but I never know quite how to answer that question.

How did I know to go in for that skin exam?

There were no symptoms, no discomfort, no flashing neon signs pointing to the small, non-descript mole on my back that was harboring malignant melanoma.

It was simply a feeling. A soft internal nudging. A knowing.

As I try to describe this to my friend, I can see his eyebrows raise. He's too nice to roll his eyes, but I can sense that what I'm saying is quickly getting lost on him. And I can understand how the idea of heeding messages from the depths of our essence might sound a little hokey . . . and yet at the same time, it makes the most sense of all.

Don't you know, deep in your gut, when something is wrong with a loved one?

Can't you feel it, as a buzzing in your cells, when there's an action you need to take?

Your body has a lot to tell you—when you slow down enough to listen.

I find this especially true when it comes to the food and drink that we consume. By pausing for just a moment before eating or drinking, you will find clarity and wisdom about what your body really needs—and there's often a chasm between what your appetite says it *wants* and what your body knows it *needs*.

A warm bowl of homemade soup comes close to perfection when you combine the comfort of what we want with the nutrition that our bodies need. This soup provides equal amounts nourishment and excitement.

Wouldn't it be great if all dinner recipes were ready in 15 minutes flat? By using flavorful ingredients, like roasted red bell peppers and white bean hummus, this soup tastes like you slaved over it all afternoon, but it really takes less than 20 minutes to throw together.

Ingredients

1 cup roasted red bell peppers (about 2 peppers, see Quick Tip)

3/4 cup ROASTED GARLIC WHITE BEAN HUMMUS **(page 62), or store-bought**

2 cups chicken broth

1/2 cup cooked quinoa (see step 2 on page 75 for cooking instructions)

1 cup shredded rotisserie chicken

sea salt and black pepper, to taste

2 tablespoons chopped fresh parsley

Steps

1. Slice enough of the roasted peppers to fill 1/4 cup. Set aside.

2. Put the remaining red peppers in a blender along with the hummus and broth. Blend until smooth.

3. Transfer the mixture to a medium saucepan. Add the quinoa and chicken and season with a pinch of salt and pepper. Bring to a boil over medium-high heat.

4. Ladle the soup into bowls and garnish with the reserved red pepper slices and the chopped parsley.

(Per serving) Calories: 236 | Fat: 7g | Sodium: 626mg
Carbs: 20g | Fiber: 3g | Sugar: 2g | Protein: 23g

QUICK TIP

To roast bell peppers: Wash and dry the peppers and place them whole on a preheated grill pan over medium-high heat. They will sizzle and pop and your kitchen will fill with a delightful aroma. After a few minutes, use tongs to turn the peppers. After a few more minutes, repeat. Continue until all of the skin is blackened. Transfer the peppers to a paper bag, crimp the top shut, and leave for 5 minutes. Remove the skin from the peppers, along with the stem and seeds.

ASPARAGUS SOUP

prep time: 5 minutes ● *cooking time:* 20 minutes ● *serves:* 4

Full disclosure: I first made this recipe with low expectations. My goal was to eat asparagus as a light, cleansing meal, so instead of chewing on a big pile of green stalks, I made soup.

I expected to feel good about reaping all the nutritional benefits of asparagus, such as detoxing and antioxidants, but I did NOT expect to slurp down my bowl of soup, lick the bottom of the bowl, and then go for seconds . . .

This soup has a comforting, satisfying quality that's hard to explain. It's a combination of tasty sautéed leeks, shallots, and garlic served up warm, creamy, and soothing. This is one cleansing, light meal that is completely worth your time to make and enjoy.

Just don't be surprised when you go back for seconds!

Ingredients

8 cups vegetable or chicken broth

2 tablespoons extra-virgin olive oil

4 shallots, chopped (about 1 cup)

2 leeks, white parts only, chopped

1 tablespoon minced garlic

3 pounds fresh asparagus (3 bunches)

$1/2$ teaspoon sea salt

$1/4$ teaspoon white pepper

coconut cream, for garnish

fresh dill, for garnish

Steps

1. In a medium soup pot, warm the broth over low heat.

2. Heat the olive oil in a large skillet over medium-high heat. Add the shallots and leeks. Cook, stirring often, for about 5 minutes, until tender. Add the garlic and continue to cook while you prepare the asparagus.

3. Wash the asparagus, dry it, then trim off the woody end of the stalks. Chop the remainder of the asparagus into 2-inch pieces. Add the asparagus to the skillet along with the salt and white pepper and mix well. Cook for 8 minutes, until quite tender.

4. Add the cooked asparagus mixture to the pot of broth. Bring to a boil, then remove the pot from the heat and use an immersion blender to blend the mixture until smooth. Return the pot to the heat and simmer until you are ready to serve.

5. For garnish, add a spoonful of coconut cream and a sprinkle of fresh dill.

*(Per roll) Calories: 128 | Fat: 7g | Sodium: 1,807mg
Carbs: 10g | Fiber: 9g | Sugar: 3g | Protein: 9g*

HEALTHY EATING TIP

A bowl of homemade soup makes a wonderfully light meal and is the perfect follow-up to a weekend or vacation of not-so-wholesome eating. It's a good idea to have a few soup recipes on hand for just such a purpose, with this recipe for Asparagus Soup at the top of the list.

BALSAMIC MUSHROOMS

prep time: 5 minutes ● *cooking time:* 30 minutes ● *serves:* 4

Don't tell anyone, but some mornings, instead of typing on our respective sides of the living room, B and I will strap a couple of longboards on top of the car and head toward the ocean. We sip coffee and enjoy the scenery as the hills give way to the coast and the horizon becomes the sparkly blue Pacific.

I apply merciful amounts of sunscreen to my face, don a long-sleeved wet suit, then paddle out to join the cluster of other surfers bobbing in the water. The invigorating, cleansing feel of the ocean is highlighted by thrilling moments of gliding on air and then underwater tumbles. After a couple of hours, we are satisfied, spent . . . and famished.

We put on dry clothes, shake off the sand, and make our way to a little French bistro with patio seating. One of the first times we went, we ordered up a feast. Fancy omelets, fresh fruit, and mixed greens come out with a side of . . . mushrooms? I was immediately skeptical—mushrooms having been on my list of least-favorite foods for most of my life—but I gave them a try anyway. They were tender, savory, and a little tangy. I couldn't believe my taste buds. The mushrooms were so enjoyable that I snuck back to the tiny kitchen and talked the charmingly French-accented chef into giving me the recipe.

Ingredients

3 tablespoons extra-virgin olive oil

3 cloves garlic, minced

1 pound mushrooms, halved (about 5 cups)

¹/₄ cup balsamic vinegar

¹/₄ cup dry white wine

sea salt and black pepper, to taste

1 tablespoon BALSAMIC GLAZE (page 200)

2 tablespoons minced fresh parsley

Steps

1. Heat the olive oil in a medium skillet over medium heat. Add the garlic and sauté until soft, but not browned, about 5 minutes.

2. Add the mushrooms, balsamic vinegar, wine, and a sprinkle of salt and pepper. Decrease the heat to medium-low and simmer for 20–30 minutes, until the mushrooms are very tender.

3. Drizzle Balsamic Glaze over the mushrooms, mix well, and remove the pan from the heat. Garnish with the parsley and serve.

(Per serving) Calories: 145 | Fat: 11g | Sodium: 81mg
Carbs: 7g | Fiber: 3g | Sugar: 7g | Protein: 4g

HEALTHY EATING TIP

As healthy eating becomes second nature, you'll find that vegetables naturally begin to take center stage in your diet. Most of your meals will be a compilation of different veggie side dishes with one main protein. These addicting Balsamic Mushrooms are a wonderful way to cook up fresh mushrooms and are delicious served over an omelet, steak, or burger, or simply as a stand-alone side to your next meal.

CAULIFLOWER COUSCOUS

prep time: 15 minutes ● *cooking time:* 15 minutes ● *serves:* 6

Cauliflower rice is a concept that has been in the healthy eating world for quite a while. I have made a whole bunch of different cauliflower rice recipes, with everything from Asian flavors to Mexican flavors to Hawaiian flavors.

But nothing compares to this recipe that I accidentally created. Instead of shredding the cauliflower raw and then throwing it into a skillet for a few minutes, I started with a boiled head of cauliflower that resulted in plumper, softer rice—more like couscous. Wowsa! Both the flavor and the consistency blew me away—and the kids gobbled it down when I served grilled salmon fillets over it.

So, my friend, you see that it is so very possible to eat a diet that is lighter, filled with wholesome fiber, and void of the naughty stuff that gets us in trouble with our weight and health. I hope that you give this recipe a try really soon and that your family loves it.

Ingredients

- 2 heads cauliflower
- 2 tablespoons extra-virgin olive oil, divided
- 1 teaspoon minced garlic
- 1 zucchini, cut into matchsticks
- 4 carrots, cut into matchsticks
- 1 red onion, diced into 1-inch pieces
- 2 teaspoons lemon juice
- 1/4 cup minced fresh parsley
- 1/2 teaspoon sea salt
- 1/4 teaspoon black pepper

Steps

1. Bring a large pot of water to a boil. Meanwhile, trim the leaves and stems from the cauliflower heads and place both heads in the boiling water, covered, for 5 minutes. Carefully remove the cauliflower with tongs and set aside until cooled.

2. In a skillet, heat 1 tablespoon of the olive oil over medium-high heat. Add the garlic, zucchini, carrots, and red onion. Sauté for 10 minutes, until the vegetables are golden and tender. Set aside.

3. Cut the cooled cauliflower heads into florets, then run them through the food processor fitted with the grating attachment. Transfer the shredded cauliflower to a large bowl and mix in the remaining 1 tablespoon olive oil, plus the lemon juice, fresh parsley, salt, and pepper. Mix in the sautéed veggies and serve. Enjoy!

(Per serving) Calories: 139 | Fat: 8g | Sodium: 313mg
Carbs: 16g | Fiber: 12g | Sugar: 6g | Protein: 8g

HEALTHY EATING TIP

You are the sixth. If your closest five friends watch more than two hours of TV each day, frequent fast-food restaurants for lunch, and avoid exercise like the plague, then chances are you do, too. On the other hand, if your five closest friends seek out wholesome food, cook meals at home, and live a fit and active lifestyle at their ideal weight, then chances are you do, too. Choose your five closest friends wisely because whether you like it or not, you will be the sixth.

BROCCOLI AND ALMOND
CAULIFLOWER RICE

prep time: 25 minutes ● *cooking time:* 30 minutes ● *serves:* 8

Cauliflower rice is a staple side dish in my kitchen that takes the place of grain-based rice dishes. It is just as it sounds—cauliflower shredded into little "rice" pieces and served just as you would serve traditional rice. It's fantastic for losing weight and increasing the fiber content of your diet, and it's easy to get used to once you've stuck with it for a month or so.

I like to think of cauliflower rice as a blank canvas on which to bestow whatever flavors marry well with my main dish. In this recipe, we use an orange dressing to lend sweet and spicy flavor. Feel free to add any veggies, herbs, spices, or even a couple of eggs to your cauliflower rice.

Ingredients

FOR THE SWEET AND SPICY ORANGE DRESSING:

2 tablespoons fruit-only orange marmalade

1 tablespoon minced pickled sweet cherry peppers

1 tablespoon pickled sweet cherry pepper juice

1 tablespoon apple cider vinegar

2 teaspoons coconut aminos

1 teaspoon bottled cane sugar–free chili garlic sauce

FOR THE CAULIFLOWER RICE:

1 head cauliflower, stem and leaves trimmed, cut into small pieces

1 teaspoon toasted sesame oil

1 teaspoon minced garlic

1 yellow onion, diced

1 cup diced carrot

1 head broccoli, chopped into small florets

¹/₂ cup chicken broth

¹/₂ cup sliced almonds, toasted

Steps

FOR THE SWEET AND SPICY ORANGE DRESSING:

Combine the dressing ingredients in a small bowl and set aside.

FOR THE CAULIFLOWER RICE:

1. Using a food processor with the grating blade, grate all of the cauliflower.

2. In a large skillet, heat the sesame oil over medium heat. Add the garlic and cook until golden, about 3 minutes, being careful not to let it burn. Add the onion and carrot and cook until tender, about 12 minutes. Mix in the cauliflower, broccoli, and chicken broth. Cover the pan and decrease the heat to low. Cook for 10 minutes, stirring occasionally.

3. Remove the lid and mix in the Sweet and Spicy Orange Dressing. Cook, uncovered, for another 3 minutes. Stir in the sliced almonds and serve hot.

(Per serving) Calories: 87 | Fat: 4g | Sodium: 138mg
Carbs: 11g | Fiber: 6g | Sugar: 6g | Protein: 6g

QUICK TIP

The Sweet and Spicy Orange Dressing is also fantastic when used as a marinade for chicken! Triple the recipe, cook your chicken in a skillet, and once the pink is all gone, add the dressing and simmer for a few minutes. Delish!

VEGGIE STIR-FRIED RICE

prep time: 15 minutes ● *cooking time:* 15 minutes
serves: 8

Can you picture yourself in your new-and-improved body?

You know, the one you'll attain after healthy eating becomes second nature, when you've been living and breathing the real-food lifestyle so long that it's changed you from the inside out?

What will you wear? How will you feel? What will be different about your daily life?

Hold this image in your mind. Fixate on it with each and every bite of cauliflower rice that you cook and enjoy.

You've got this!

Ingredients

1¹/₂ cups chopped carrot

1 cup frozen peas

2 heads cauliflower, stems and leaves trimmed, cut into small pieces

2 tablespoons extra-virgin olive oil

3 eggs, beaten

3 tablespoons coconut aminos

sea salt and black pepper, to taste

Steps

1. Bring a medium pot of water to a boil. Add the carrot and boil for 3 minutes. Add the frozen peas and boil for another 2 minutes. Drain the water and set the veggies aside.

2. Using a food processor with the grating blade, grate all of the cauliflower.

3. Heat the olive oil in a large skillet or wok over medium heat. Add the carrots and peas and sauté for 3 minutes. Stir in the eggs. When they've set, add the grated cauliflower and stir to combine.

4. Season the rice mixture with the coconut aminos, salt, and pepper. Decrease the heat to low, cover, and cook for another 5 minutes.

5. Add more coconut aminos, salt, and pepper, if desired, and serve.

(Per serving) Calories: 103 | Fat: 6g | Sodium: 212mg
Carbs: 8g | Fiber: 7g | Sugar: 3g | Protein: 8g

QUICK TIP

Feel free to play around with the amount of coconut aminos, salt, and pepper in this recipe to find the level of seasoning that suits your palate.

LOADED BAKED SWEET POTATO

prep time: 15 minutes *cooking time:* 1 hour
serves: 4

With some CHEESY SAUCE (page 200) and COCONUT SOUR CREAM (page 201), this is a legit loaded potato! Add some chopped scallions and crumbled bacon, and you'll forget there ever was a greasy, fatty alternative.

The method of thinly slicing the potato almost all the way through is my trick for getting a tender-yet-crispy finished product. Yum and yum.

Ingredients

- **4 medium sweet potatoes**
- **4 tablespoons coconut oil**
- **4 cloves garlic, thinly sliced**
- **sea salt and black pepper, to taste**
- **1 cup** CHEESY SAUCE **(page 200)**
- **¹/₄ cup** COCONUT SOUR CREAM **(page 201)**
- **4 strips bacon, cooked and crumbled**
- **¹/₄ cup sliced scallions, greens only**

Steps

1. Preheat the oven to 400°F. Line an 18 × 26-inch rimmed baking sheet with foil and set aside.

2. Scrub the sweet potatoes and pat dry. Make horizontal slices the entire length of the potato, about ¹/₈ inch apart, making sure not to cut all the way through the base of the potato.

3. Place the potatoes on the prepared baking sheet. Rub them all over with the coconut oil and tuck the slices of garlic in between the potato slices. Season with salt and pepper and bake for 1 hour, until tender.

4. Slather the Cheesy Sauce all over each baked potato and top with Coconut Sour Cream, bacon, and scallions.

(Per potato) Calories: 363 | Fat: 21g | Sodium: 393mg
Carbs: 31g | Fiber: 6g | Sugar: 10g | Protein: 10g

QUICK TIP

Give this recipe a try with both white sweet potatoes and orange sweet potatoes.

SUMMER QUINOA SALAD

prep time: 15 minutes ● *cooking time:* 20 minutes ● *serves:* 16

Quinoa is quite the superfood. Often mistaken for a grain, quinoa is actually a protein-packed seed. It's gluten-free (yay!) and is a complete protein, containing all nine essential amino acids. It is also filled with magnesium and fiber, as if the other benefits weren't enough to convince us.

The one drawback to this amazing food is the carbohydrate volume. While it is lower than rice and other traditional grains, it is high enough that you'll want to limit the amount you eat. Of course, the kids need plenty of carbohydrates to support their active, growing bodies, so it's totally fine if they want to load up.

This Summer Quinoa Salad is the ultimate potluck salad. It's colorful and flavorful, dotted with crisp, colorful veggies. Enjoy it all summer long.

Ingredients

FOR THE QUINOA SALAD:

2 cups uncooked quinoa

4 cups vegetable or chicken broth

1 red bell pepper, cored, seeded, and chopped

1 yellow bell pepper, cored, seeded, and chopped

$^1/_2$ red onion, diced

3 large carrots, diced

2 zucchini, diced

$^1/_2$ cup peeled and chopped jicama

2 avocados, pitted, peeled, and chopped

$^1/_2$ cup sun-dried tomatoes, minced

$^1/_2$ cup chopped fresh cilantro

8 heads endive, for serving (optional)

FOR THE DRESSING:

$^1/_2$ teaspoon minced garlic

1 packet or $^1/_2$ teaspoon stevia

$^1/_4$ teaspoon sea salt

2 tablespoons apple cider vinegar

3 tablespoons extra-virgin olive oil

zest and juice of 2 limes

1 tablespoon raw honey, melted

Steps

FOR THE QUINOA SALAD:

1. In a medium saucepan, combine the quinoa and broth over medium-high heat. Bring to a boil, then decrease to a simmer. Cover and cook for 20 minutes. Set aside.

2. In a large bowl, combine the bell peppers, onion, carrots, zucchini, jicama, avocado, sun-dried tomatoes, and cilantro. Stir in the quinoa.

FOR THE DRESSING:

1. In a small bowl, combine the dressing ingredients and mix well. Pour the dressing over the quinoa mixture and stir to combine. Chill in the fridge for 15 minutes.

2. If desired, separate the endive into individual cups and fill with the salad. Alternatively, serve in a big bowl.

(Per serving) Calories: 174 | Fat: 7g | Sodium: 139mg
Carbs: 14g | Fiber: 6g | Sugar: 5g | Protein: 6g

QUICK TIP

Without the avocado, this salad will keep for up to 5 days in the fridge. If you'd like to enjoy it all week long, make a nice big batch without avocado and then simply add fresh avocado to each serving.

WINTER QUINOA SALAD
WITH POMEGRANATE DRESSING

prep time: 30 minutes ● *cooking time:* 1 hour ● *serves:* 16

I couldn't leave you hanging with just a summer quinoa salad recipe! This wintertime version is filled with warm, roasted veggies and is fancied up with festive pomegranate seeds.

My in-laws, having spent most of their lives living in Armenia, where pomegranates abound, have planted two very productive pomegranate trees in my yard. We all but have pomegranates coming out of our ears during the fall and winter months, so I love finding new ways to highlight their bright, acidic-but-sweet flavor. By adding them to this salad, they lend lightness to the deep, rich, roasty wintery goodness of the cold-weather veggies.

Ingredients

FOR THE SALAD:

1 medium butternut squash, peeled, seeded, and cut into bite-size pieces

extra-virgin olive oil

sea salt and black pepper, to taste

ground nutmeg, to taste

1 fennel bulb, bulb and fronds chopped

1 green zucchini, chopped

1 yellow zucchini, chopped

1 orange bell pepper, cored, seeded, and chopped

1 red onion, chopped

2 cups uncooked rainbow quinoa (see note on page 35 about quinoa variations)

4 cups chicken broth

FOR THE POMEGRANATE DRESSING:

1 pomegranate

3 tablespoons lemon juice

2 cloves garlic, minced

3 tablespoons extra-virgin olive oil

1 scallion, whites and greens, minced

1 cup minced fresh parsley

$1/3$ cup minced fresh mint

Steps

FOR THE SALAD:

1. Preheat the oven to 425°F. Lightly grease a 10 × 15-inch rimmed baking pan and an 18 × 26-inch rimmed baking sheet with olive oil.

2. Toss the squash with a drizzle of olive oil and season generously with salt, pepper, and nutmeg. Arrange in a single layer on the smaller baking pan and roast in the oven for 20–35 minutes.

3. In a large bowl, combine the fennel, zucchini, bell pepper, and onion. Toss with olive oil and season with salt and pepper. Spread the vegetables in a single layer on the large baking sheet and roast for 15–20 minutes.

4. Combine the quinoa and chicken broth in a small pot and bring to a low boil over medium-high heat. Decrease the heat to low, cover, and cook for 15 minutes. Remove the pot from the heat and fluff the quinoa with a fork. Set aside.

FOR THE POMEGRANATE DRESSING:

1. Fill a medium bowl with water. Cut the pomegranate in half, place both halves in the water, and use your fingers to separate all of the seeds from the skins. Drain the water and transfer the seeds to a small bowl.

2. Add the remaining dressing ingredients to the small bowl and mix to combine.

3. In a large salad bowl, combine the cooked quinoa with the dressing. Add the roasted butternut squash and veggies. Mix well and, if needed, season with additional salt and pepper.

(Per serving) Calories: 157 | Fat: 6g | Sodium: 64mg
Carbs: 22g | Fiber: 4g | Sugar: 4g | Protein: 5g

HEALTHY EATING TIP

Stop buying bottled salad dressing. Stop. It. Right. Now. Processed dressing is filled with toxic ingredients (such as MSG and potassium sorbate) and doesn't even taste as good as a simple homemade dressing. Here's the formula for making your own: 3 parts high-quality oil (olive or sesame), 1 part lemon juice or vinegar (try champagne, white wine, or brown rice), a pinch of sea salt and black pepper, and a few tablespoons minced fresh herbs (such as oregano or thyme) or a few teaspoons dried herbs.

MASSAGED KALE AND APPLE SALAD

prep time: 15 minutes ● *serves:* 4

Kale is one of my favorite superfoods. I drink it in my daily green juice and often sauté it in savory dishes. It's low in calories, high in fiber, and crammed with nutrients in a way that simply gets my cells buzzing with green energy. Enjoying kale in a salad, however, can be a challenge. Oftentimes the leaves are too tough to comfortably chew and the raw flavor can overwhelm the other ingredients.

That's why I came up with this salad, which showcases everything that I love about kale. The leaves are chopped into very fine ribbons and then "massaged," which makes them easy to chew while bringing out their delicate, refreshing flavor.

Ingredients

1 bunch curly kale

2 scallions, whites and greens, minced

1 Fuji apple, cored and chopped

1 tablespoon dried mint

2 tablespoons lemon juice

$1/4$ teaspoon sea salt

pinch of black pepper

2 tablespoons extra-virgin olive oil

Steps

1. Wash the kale and pat dry. Remove the stems and finely chop the leaves. Put them in a large salad bowl. Massage the kale with the back of a large spoon (see tip) until visibly softened.

2. Add the scallions, apple, mint, lemon juice, salt, and pepper to the bowl. Drizzle in the olive oil, mix well, and serve.

(Per serving) Calories: 116 | Fat: 7g | Sodium: 169mg
Carbs: 10g | Fiber: 3g | Sugar: 2g | Protein: 3g

QUICK TIP

Massage kale? Sounds a little silly, doesn't it? The technique of massaging the kale helps break down the fibers in the leaves, making it easier to digest. This also improves the mouthfeel of the kale and makes it easier to chew a nice big mouthful of these super greens. While you massage the kale, you'll actually see it start to change—it will become softer and more vibrantly green. To massage, simply use the back of a large spoon to press down on the kale. Then mix the leaves and press down again. Keep repeating until the kale is noticeably softened.

KALE SALAD WITH POPPY SEED DRESSING

prep time: 15 minutes ● *serves:* 10

Relapse: To suffer deterioration after a temporary improvement.

Has it happened to you yet? You're coasting along, making good choices and enjoying the results, and then—WHAM!—you fall off the wagon and spiral back into your old eating habits.

Oy vey. What do you do now?

You stand up, dust yourself off, and jump right back on the wagon. Shake off the shame, embarrassment, and disappointment. Forget about your mistakes and regain your forward momentum.

Relapses happen to the best of us. It's what you do after the relapse that really matters.

What will you do? Further the damage with more poor eating choices? Or sit down to a hearty serving of this Kale Salad with Poppy Seed Dressing?

Ingredients

FOR THE POPPY SEED DRESSING:

2 tablespoons finely grated yellow onion

2 teaspoons poppy seeds

1/2 teaspoon stevia powder

1/2 teaspoon sea salt

1/4 teaspoon mustard powder

1/2 cup extra-virgin olive oil

1/4 cup Muscat sherry vinegar

2 tablespoons lemon juice

FOR THE SALAD:

1 bunch curly kale, sliced into thin ribbons

1/2 head red cabbage, sliced into thin ribbons

10 Brussels sprouts, sliced into thin ribbons

1 head broccoli, finely chopped

Steps

FOR THE POPPY SEED DRESSING:

Combine all of the dressing ingredients in a small jar, then make like Taylor Swift and shake, shake, shake!

FOR THE SALAD:

Combine all of the roughage in a large bowl. Add the dressing and toss to coat. Eat a big bowl and instantly feel sexier.

(Per serving) Calories: 108 | Fat: 8g | Sodium: 165mg
Carbs: 15g | Fiber: 5g | Sugar: 6g | Protein: 4g

QUICK TIP

This salad is a great way to cleanse your system after a healthy eating relapse. It's packed with nutritious fiber to flush out the toxins and to get you back on track with your healthy lifestyle.

BEET SALAD WITH PICKLED EGGS

prep time: 15 minutes ● *cooking time:* 30 minutes ● *serves:* 6

Please only attempt this recipe if you are in a really fancy mood. Put on your gourmet, award-winning-chef hat and fancy things up.

Remember, this salad is only for the fanciest of moods. Mkay?

Ingredients

4 medium red beets

4 medium golden beets

²/₃ cup apple cider vinegar

2 tablespoons raw honey

2 teaspoons extra-virgin olive oil

2 teaspoons balsamic vinegar

¹/₃ cup shelled pistachios

6 PICKLED EGGS (page 80), quartered

1 cup micro greens

¹/₄ cup BALSAMIC GLAZE (page 200)

Steps

1. Wash and peel the beets. Cut smaller beets into quarters and larger beets into eighths.

2. In 2 separate pots, bring 2 cups water to a boil. Add the red beets to one pot and the yellow beets to the other. Cover the pots and boil for 15 minutes, until the beets are fork-tender. Drain the water and return the beets to their respective pots.

3. In a medium bowl, whisk together the apple cider vinegar, honey, olive oil, and balsamic vinegar. Divide the mixture evenly between the 2 pots of beets. Return the pots to medium heat, and simmer for 5 minutes. Let the beets cool slightly, and then transfer them to separate covered containers in the fridge to chill until immediately before plating the salad.

4. Toast the pistachios in a dry skillet over medium heat for 8 minutes, stirring often. Remove once golden. Let them cool slightly and then chop.

5. To plate the salad, arrange each plate with both types of beet, wedges of Pickled Egg, a sprinkling of micro greens and chopped pistachios, and a drizzle of Balsamic Glaze.

(Per serving) Calories: 177 | Fat: 6g | Sodium: 218mg
Carbs: 25g | Fiber: 5g | Sugar: 18g | Protein: 9g

QUICK TIP

To keep the vibrant yellow of the golden beets untainted by the red beets, all of the steps with the two different kinds of beets need to be done separately. This does take a little extra time and dirties up some extra dishes, but if you're going for a stunning presentation, then it's worth it. If you're just cooking for taste, then mix it all together.

FIELD GREENS AND PEAR SALAD WITH BALSAMIC DRESSING

prep time: 15 minutes
serves: 4

Sixteen years ago, during a two-day drive down the 5 Freeway—from Skagit Valley, Washington, to La Mirada, California—I took an aptitude test in the hopes of figuring out what I should do with my life. I had just turned eighteen, graduated high school, and was on my way to the big city to start college. My life had just begun! But I still hadn't the faintest clue of what I wanted to do with it.

I filled out page after page of questions about my abilities, tendencies, and preferences as farmlands whizzed by, followed by forested mountains, cow fields, and then—the big concrete city.

My heart raced as I moved my belongings into a small, shared dorm room and started to learn my way around the campus that was crawling with thousands of students. Having come from a tiny school with just twenty-six students in my graduating high school class, the large lecture halls were overwhelming. All of my childhood friends were thousands of miles away, attending schools in either Washington or the Midwest or already starting out in the workplace. I was scared and alone and eager to get the results to that test. Somehow I knew it would provide the direction that I needed to move on to the next phase of my life.

When I look back on what happened next, it makes me chuckle. But at the time, it wasn't the answer I was looking for. When the results to my aptitude test came back, I opened the letter with enthusiasm. I think I was expecting my appointed profession to be printed out across the top, giving me the answer to the annoying question that everyone seemed to be asking: "What's your major?" But instead there was a list of my skills and interests (*writing, photography, cooking, nutrition, fitness, business, children, animals*), followed by an even longer list of professions related to each skill. I was more lost than ever.

As I journeyed through my college years, earning a degree in pre-sports physical therapy, I realized two things: 1) I wanted to work for myself, and 2) I didn't want to choose a single skill or interest to build my work around. I wanted to do them all!

Today when someone asks me "What do you do?" it's never easy to answer. I'm a writer. I'm a photographer. I'm a recipe blogger. I'm a cookbook author. I'm a business owner. I'm a stay-at-home mom. I'm a dog and kitty mommy. So maybe none of it has anything to do with my pre-sports physical therapy major, but every single day I get to wake up and spend time doing all of the things that I love most. Like creating this refreshing, wholesome version of my favorite salad from California Pizza Kitchen. This recipe has a simple, delicious balsamic dressing, nuts candied with coconut sugar, organic greens, and crisp pears. Honestly, it's tastier than the original.

Ingredients

FOR THE SALAD:

1 tablespoon coconut oil

¹/₃ cup roughly chopped pecans

3 tablespoons coconut palm sugar

4 cups mixed greens

1 Bosc pear, cored and sliced

FOR THE DRESSING:

¹/₃ cup extra-virgin olive oil

¹/₄ cup BALSAMIC GLAZE (page 200)

1 packet or ¹/₂ teaspoon stevia

1 tablespoon fresh thyme

1 teaspoon Dijon mustard

1 clove garlic, minced

pinch of black pepper

Steps

FOR THE SALAD:

1. Melt the coconut oil in a small skillet over low heat. Add the pecans and cook, stirring constantly, for 3 minutes. Add the coconut palm sugar and continue to cook, stirring constantly, for about 4 minutes, until the sugar has melted and the pecans are golden. Remove from the heat and set aside.

2. Divide the greens and sliced pear among 4 plates. Top with the candied pecans.

FOR THE DRESSING:

Combine the dressing ingredients in a small jar or bowl. Shake or mix well, then drizzle over the salad.

(Per serving) Calories: 326 | Fat: 18g | Sodium: 195mg
Carbs: 27g | Fiber: 5g | Sugar: 14g | Protein: 2g

QUICK TIP

By making a big batch of glazed pecans and dressing at the beginning of the week you'll be able to quickly throw this salad together in the evenings before dinner.

BLT PASTA SALAD

prep time: 20 minutes ● *cooking time:* 10 minutes ● *serves:* 6

According to Wikipedia, the BLT is the second most popular sandwich in the United States and is *the* most popular sandwich in the UK. Of course, you didn't need me to spout off statistics to convince you of the enchanting delight that comes when we combine the smoky flavor of bacon with sweet, juicy tomato and crisp lettuce.

So of course I had to add this deli classic to my hack list. While it's very possible to create a BLT sandwich on ALMOND BREAD (page 43) or NAAN BREAD (page 156), I thought it would be twice as fun to make it into an exciting pasta salad, complete with zucchini noodles and home-made pesto. The true flavors of a BLT shine through this salad with the additional notes of fresh basil and the fun of noodles. (Try it and you'll see just *how much* fun!)

And I've added an extra "L"—there's Lettuce AND Leeks. Layer in some tender, cooked cherry tomatoes and bacon crumbles, and you've got a BLT made in heaven. You won't even miss the bread.

Ingredients

6 zucchini

1 head butter lettuce

2 cups basil leaves

pinch of sea salt

$1/4$ cup pine nuts

$1/4$ cup nutritional yeast

1 teaspoon lemon juice

$1/4$ cup plus 1 teaspoon extra-virgin olive oil

2 leeks, whites and greens, thinly sliced

4 cloves garlic, minced

1 cup halved cherry tomatoes

pinch of black pepper

$1/2$ cup dry white wine

4 strips bacon, cooked and chopped

Steps

1. Wash the zucchini and use a veggie peeler to remove the green skin. Run the zucchini through a spiral slicer to create long, thin noodles. Put them in a large bowl. Thinly chop the lettuce and add it to the bowl.

2. In a food processor, combine the basil, salt, pine nuts, nutritional yeast, lemon juice, and $1/4$ cup of the olive oil. Pulse until a paste forms. Add the pesto to the bowl of noodles and lettuce.

3. In a small skillet, heat the remaining 1 teaspoon olive oil over medium heat. Add the leeks and garlic and sauté for 3 minutes, or until the leeks are soft. Add the cherry tomatoes, stir, cover, and cook for 8 minutes, until the tomatoes burst. Season with salt and pepper, then add the wine and simmer to cook it off. Add the mixture to the bowl.

4. Mix the contents of the bowl well and stir in the bacon pieces.

(Per serving) Calories: 216 | Fat: 9g | Sodium: 107mg
Carbs: 16g | Fiber: 8g | Sugar: 6g | Protein: 11g

QUICK TIP

You have a trustworthy spiral slicer by now, don't you? I hope you're nodding, but if you aren't, then go to Amazon.com and get ordering! Spiral slicers take ordinary vegetables and turn them into perfect spaghetti-like noodles—which is fantastic for recipes like this one. Sure, you could always use a simple veggie peeler to create long, flat noodles, but there's something awesome about having veggie noodles that look just like the real thing!

COCONUT CURRY NOODLE BOWL

prep time: 15 minutes ● *cooking time:* 10 minutes ● *serves:* 4

I know that traditional pasta dishes aren't solely responsible for the obesity in our society. The toxicity in our food culture extends way beyond simple bowls of starchy noodles. There are the sugar-packed drinks served up at coffee shops. The fried fast-food meals being handed through car windows. The packaged snacks falling out of vending machines. The supersized portions that our stomachs have slowly become accustomed to. And the list goes on.

No, pasta isn't the only problem.

But by making the switch from traditional noodles to noodles made with vegetables, you will be taking a step in the right direction. One small step toward shedding those accumulated pounds. One small step toward reclaiming your energy. One small step in your quest for good health. One small step toward showing your kids a better way to eat.

This dish tastes like a bowl of flavorful, naughty take-out noodles that should be only eaten for a cheat meal. And yet it's really made with wholesome, fiber-filled veggies.

Ingredients

1 tablespoon coconut oil

1 red onion, halved lengthwise and thinly sliced

2 red bell peppers, cored, seeded, and thinly sliced lengthwise

$1/4$ cup filtered water

sea salt and black pepper, to taste

2 tablespoons Thai red curry paste

1 (13.7-ounce) can unsweetened coconut milk

1 cup fresh basil leaves

1 tablespoon lime juice

6 zucchini, peeled and made into noodles with a spiral slicer

Steps

1. In a large skillet, warm the coconut oil over medium-high heat. Add the onion, bell peppers, and water. Season with salt and pepper. Cook, stirring occasionally, until the vegetables are tender, about 4 minutes. Add the curry paste and cook for another minute, stirring constantly.

2. Add the coconut milk and simmer as the sauce thickens, 4–5 minutes. Remove the pan from the heat and stir in the basil, lime juice, and zucchini noodles. Season with salt and pepper and serve warm.

(Per serving) Calories: 164 | Fat: 9g | Sodium: 211mg
Carbs: 23g | Fiber: 9g | Sugar: 13g | Protein: 9g

QUICK TIP

This dish was made vegan, but you could easily add strips of sautéed beef that have been seasoned generously with salt and pepper. Brown the beef in the skillet first, remove it from the pan, and then toss it in with the noodles right before serving. And feel free to play around with the amount of red curry paste, which plays a starring role in the dish but can be adjusted depending on your desired spice level. Two tablespoons' worth will give you tons of flavor without being too spicy for the kids.

ROASTED CARROTS

prep time: 15 minutes ● *cooking time:* 20 minutes ● *serves:* 6

This recipe is for my fellow carrot lovers out there. It's tender; it's colorful; it's savory; it's sweet. It's the perfect side dish for just about any meal where meat is the main dish. And as a bonus, the kiddos simply love it.

Ingredients

20 rainbow carrots

1 tablespoon extra-virgin olive oil

1 tablespoon lemon juice

1 teaspoon raw honey, melted

$^1/_4$ teaspoon sea salt

$^1/_2$ cup golden raisins

$^1/_2$ cup dry white wine

1 teaspoon coconut palm sugar

$^1/_4$ cup raw pepitas

$^1/_4$ cup shelled pistachios

$^1/_4$ cup chopped fresh parsley

Steps

1. Preheat the oven to 400°F. Line a large rimmed baking sheet with parchment paper.

2. Wash and peel the carrots. Cut them into 2- to 3-inch pieces, then cut each piece in half lengthwise on the diagonal. Put the carrots in a large bowl and set aside.

3. In a small bowl, whisk together the olive oil, lemon juice, honey, and salt. Pour the mixture over the carrots and toss to coat. Arrange the coated carrots cut side down on the prepared baking sheet. Roast for 20 minutes, or until the carrots are tender.

4. Meanwhile, combine the raisins, wine, and coconut palm sugar in a small pot over medium-low heat. Bring to a simmer and cook for 10 minutes. Remove the pot from the heat and drain, discarding the liquid. Transfer the raisins to a paper towel–lined plate.

5. In a small, dry skillet, toast the pepitas and pistachios over low heat. Stir often for 5 minutes, until golden.

6. Combine the roasted carrots, plumped raisins, toasted nuts, and chopped fresh parsley in a serving bowl.

(Per serving) Calories: 188 | Fat: 6g | Sodium: 104mg
Carbs: 27g | Fiber: 6g | Sugar: 15g | Protein: 5g

QUICK TIP

It's really stunning to make this recipe with rainbow carrots, which include an assortment of colors, from palest yellow to deepest purple; however, it's wholly unnecessary. Got a big bag of classic orange carrots? Coolio, that works, too.

SHAVED AND ROASTED ASPARAGUS

prep time: 10 minutes   *cooking time:* 15 minutes
serves: 6

Why shave your asparagus before roasting it? Here's why:

> It looks fancy.
> It's easier to chew.
> It's fun.
> It cooks more quickly.
> It's served like this in swanky steakhouses, so it must be cool.

Ingredients

2 bunches asparagus, tough ends trimmed

1 tablespoon extra-virgin olive oil

¼ teaspoon sea salt

pinch of black pepper

1 tablespoon lemon juice

1 teaspoon minced garlic

Steps

1. Preheat the oven to 425°F. Lightly grease a large rimmed baking sheet with olive oil.

2. Lay each asparagus spear flat on a cutting board and use a vegetable peeler to shave off the skin 2 inches from the tip all the way to the ends.

3. Toss the shaved asparagus stalks in a large bowl with the remaining ingredients until fully coated. Spread them on the prepared pan and bake until just tender, 12–15 minutes.

(Per serving) Calories: 33 | Fat: 2g | Sodium: 127mg
Carbs: 2g | Fiber: 3g | Sugar: 1g | Protein: 2g

 QUICK TIP

Be careful of your fingertips while shaving the asparagus. I've found that placing the stalks flat against a cutting board and using a veggie peeler to swipe away from your body is the best method.

OVEN-STEAMED BEETS

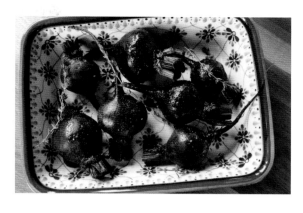

prep time: 10 minutes *cooking time:* 1 hour
serves: 8

This might be the easiest recipe for beets that you'll ever come across. And also the most delish. The simple steaming method intensifies the natural flavor and sweetness of the beets.

I highly recommend making these Oven-Steamed Beets the next time you have friends and family over for dinner. It pairs well with steak and tastes like you slaved over it all day!

Ingredients

8 medium red beets

1 tablespoon extra-virgin olive oil

sea salt and black pepper, to taste

6 sprigs fresh thyme

¼ cup water

Steps

1. Preheat the oven to 425°F. Remove the beet greens (if still attached) and scrub the beets.

2. In a 9 × 13-inch glass casserole dish, toss the beets with the olive oil. Season with salt and pepper and add the sprigs of thyme and water. Cover the dish tightly with foil and roast in the oven for an hour, or until the beets are fork-tender.

3. Let the beets cool in the covered pan, then rub off the beet skins with paper towels. Season to taste with salt and pepper. Serve warm.

(Per serving) Calories: 59 | Fat: 2g | Sodium: 101mg
Carbs: 10g | Fiber: 3g | Sugar: 6g | Protein: 2g

QUICK TIP

Save those beet greens to steam and season with sea salt and black pepper. They're highly nutritious, with loads of immune-boosting vitamin C, and make for a downright delicious side.

BACON BRUSSELS SPROUTS

prep time: 20 minutes ● *cooking time:* 35 minutes ● *serves:* 6

Whenever I get out of the bubble of my RHR Kitchen, it strikes me just how unhealthy most of us eat. Packaged snacks, soda pops, fried foods, and sugary desserts are almost all that you can purchase at the zoo and other attractions, and that's what most people are filling up on.

Lately I've seen some improvements, with healthy options being added to places here and there, like the roasted chicken skewers and fresh fruit available at Disneyland now, and I love seeing that.

But we have miles and miles to go . . .

The sad truth is that we are living in a toxic food culture. Much of our food supply has been processed, packaged, and pumped full of artificial and harmful ingredients. Youngsters with developing palates are learning to prefer flavors manufactured in a laboratory to flavors grown in nature.

Obesity and diet-related illnesses and ailments are degrading our quality of life . . . and, in many cases, robbing us *of* our lives. I don't want that for myself, for my loved ones, or for you.

These are the thoughts that keep me up at night.

All the work that I do with Real Healthy Recipes has a purpose . . . to make wholesome, nutritious food more accessible and practical for us to build our diets around, and I've dedicated myself to this mission.

Our bodies thrive on wholesome, real foods; when prepared right, the healthy stuff tastes even better than convenience meals. If you want to see just how powerful real foods are, then eliminate packaged foods for seven days and see how you feel . . . it's remarkable!

My intention today is to remind you that we are in this together, and that all of our efforts to eat healthy will culminate into something bigger than ourselves. Lives will be touched; bodies will be transformed. We are changing the world, one real-food meal at a time. Starting with a bowl of these Bacon Brussels Sprouts.

Ingredients

4 strips bacon

1 yellow onion, chopped

2 tablespoons pure maple syrup

$\frac{1}{4}$ cup dry white wine

1 tablespoon Dijon mustard

sea salt and black pepper, to taste

1 pound Brussels sprouts, thinly sliced (about 4 cups)

Steps

1. Preheat the oven to 425°F. Line a large rimmed baking sheet with parchment paper and set aside.

2. In a large skillet, cook the bacon over medium-high heat until crisp. Remove the bacon from the skillet and blot with paper towels. Set aside, leaving the bacon grease in the skillet.

3. Add the onion to the skillet and cook over medium-high heat until soft, about 3 minutes. Mix in the maple syrup, wine, Dijon, a pinch of salt and pepper, and the Brussels sprouts. Cook for 5 more minutes, then crumble the bacon and mix it in. Remove the pan from the heat.

4. Spread the mixture on the prepared pan and roast for 20 minutes, stirring after 10 minutes. Once the Brussels sprouts are very tender, remove them from the oven and serve warm.

(Per serving) Calories: 87 | Fat: 1g | Sodium: 116mg
Carbs: 16g | Fiber: 5g | Sugar: 7g | Protein: 4g

HEALTHY EATING TIP

Today eat in a way that your future self with thank you for.

GREEN BEANS AND EGGS

prep time: 25 minutes ● *cooking time:* 45 minutes ● *serves:* 8

Here's a recipe to help you use your garden's summer bounty or to use up all those farmers' market treasures, for those of us who never got around to planting a garden this year. Tender green beans, plump tomatoes, fresh dill, and organic eggs come together in a savory, mouthwatering fashion in this simple dish.

Credit must go to my mother-in-law, Suzy, for this one, since this is another recipe that originated in her kitchen and has been lightened up in mine. The first time I made it I had to call her twice for her input and guidance. Our phone calls are pretty comical, neither of us being fluent in the other's native tongue. We converse in part-English, part-Armenian, and are pretty much reliant on using gestures and context to fill in the blanks. Over the phone, though, that's just not possible . . . I should probably set her up with a Skype account! In the meantime, I am learning how to say many ingredients in Armenian.

This dish is filled with fiber, vitamins, minerals, and protein. It's wonderful alongside dinner, but the leftovers taste even better as the flavors mingle and marinate. You can bet that if I'm serving this for dinner, I'll be enjoying a scoop or two of this tasty dish the next day.

Ingredients

1 tablespoon extra-virgin olive oil

1 yellow onion, thinly sliced into half-moons

3 cups chopped fresh tomatoes

2 pounds green beans, trimmed and cut into 1-inch pieces (about 8 cups)

$^1/_2$ cup chopped fresh dill

$^1/_2$ teaspoon sea salt

$^1/_8$ teaspoon black pepper

3 eggs, beaten

Steps

1. Heat the olive oil in a medium pot over low heat. Add the onion and cook for 3 minutes. Add the tomatoes and cook, stirring often, for 5 minutes. Add the green beans and enough water so that it's not quite covering the beans. Cover the pot and cook over low heat for 25–30 minutes, stirring every 5 minutes or so.

2. Once the beans are tender, drain off the water. Return the pot to low heat and add the dill, salt, and pepper. Mix well, cover, and cook for 3 minutes.

3. Mix the eggs into the green beans and cook for 5 minutes while stirring. Remove from the heat and serve.

(Per serving) Calories: 85 | Fat: 4g | Sodium: 175mg
Carbs: 10g | Fiber: 5g | Sugar: 3g | Protein: 6g

HEALTHY EATING TIP

Nothing in life is accomplished without definitiveness of purpose, and this applies to fat loss and diet reform as much as it does to running a successful business or writing a novel. Define exactly what your ideal diet is and then live by that definition.

MOROCCAN-SPICED BUTTERNUT SQUASH

prep time: 15 minutes ● *cooking time:* 30 minutes ● *serves:* 6

Butternut squash is one of my favorite fresh ingredients to use in the fall and winter months. There are endless ways to enjoy this buttery vegetable: eat it in a breakfast hash (page 22), bake it into a vegetable tart (page 86), turn it into noodles (page 118), sauté it with kale and sausage (page 136), or if you'd like to keep things a little more simple (and a little more spiced!), then cube and roast it with these rich and bright Moroccan spices. Serve it with a side of KALE SALAD WITH POPPY SEED DRESSING (page 180) and MOROCCAN TURKEY BURGERS (page 108) to make it a meal.

Ingredients

- 2 butternut squash, peeled, seeded, and cubed
- $1/4$ cup extra-virgin olive oil
- 1 teaspoon ground cumin
- 1 teaspoon ground coriander
- $1/2$ teaspoon ground ginger
- $1/2$ teaspoon sea salt
- $1/4$ teaspoon white pepper
- $1/2$ teaspoon ground cinnamon
- $1/4$ teaspoon ground allspice
- $1/8$ teaspoon ground cayenne pepper
- 1 tablespoon minced fresh rosemary

Steps

1. Preheat the oven to 425°F. Line a large rimmed baking sheet with parchment paper and set aside.

2. In a large bowl, toss the cubed squash with all of the remaining ingredients. Spread the squash in a single layer on the prepared baking sheet.

3. Roast for 25–30 minutes, without stirring, until the squash is golden on the outside and tender all the way through.

(Per serving) Calories: 118 | Fat: 7g | Sodium: 193mg
Carbs: 12g | Fiber: 6g | Sugar: 1g | Protein: 1g

QUICK TIP

Spread the cubed squash far enough apart on the baking sheet so that the pieces aren't touching, and you'll ensure that your squash comes out crispy on the outside and creamy on the inside. If the squash is roasted all piled together, with pieces touching, it ends up steaming instead.

BALSAMIC GLAZE

prep time: 5 minutes
cooking time: 20 minutes
makes: ½ cup

Ingredients

1½ cups balsamic vinegar
pinch of sea salt

Steps

1. Combine the balsamic vinegar and salt in a small skillet over medium heat. Bring the mixture to a boil, then decrease to a simmer.

2. Allow the mixture to simmer over low heat for 20 minutes, until the volume has reduced by more than half. Store in an airtight container in the fridge for up to 2 weeks.

(Per 1 tablespoon) Calories: 40 | Fat: 0g | Sodium: 5mg Carbs: 7g | Fiber: 0g | Sugar: 3g | Protein: 0g

CHEESY SAUCE

prep time: 10 minutes
cooking time: 30 minutes
makes: 3 cups

Ingredients

2 cups filtered water
2 cups cauliflower florets
1 teaspoon onion powder
1 teaspoon minced garlic
¼ teaspoon sweet paprika
2 teaspoons yellow mustard
¼ teaspoon ground turmeric
½ cup nutritional yeast
1 heaping tablespoon tahini
2 tablespoons arrowroot starch
2 teaspoons lemon juice
½ teaspoon sea salt, plus more to taste
¼ cup sun-dried tomatoes
2 tablespoons dry white wine

Steps

1. In a small saucepan, combine the water, cauliflower, onion powder, garlic, paprika, mustard, and turmeric over medium heat. Cover and boil for 20 minutes.

2. Add the nutritional yeast, tahini, arrowroot, lemon juice, salt, sun-dried tomatoes, and wine, and simmer for 10 minutes.

3. Using an immersion blender, blend the ingredients until smooth. Allow to bubble for a couple more minutes over low heat and season to taste with salt.

(Per ⅓ cup) Calories: 65 | Fat: 1g | Sodium: 119mg Carbs: 12g | Fiber: 4g | Sugar: 1g | Protein: 9g

TARTAR SAUCE

prep time: 5 minutes
makes: $^3/_4$ cup

Ingredients

$^1/_2$ cup coconut cream
2 tablespoons diced dill pickles
1 tablespoon apple cider vinegar
1 tablespoon capers
2 teaspoons Dijon mustard
pinch of sea salt and black pepper

Steps

Combine all of the ingredients in a food processor and pulse several times until the ingredients are well mixed but not pureed. Chill before using. Store in the refrigerator for up to 1 week.

(Per 2 tablespoons) Calories: 36 | Fat: 3g | Sodium: 120mg Carbs: 2g | Fiber: 0g | Sugar: 1g | Protein: 0g

COCONUT SOUR CREAM

prep time: 10 minutes
makes: $^1/_2$ cup

Ingredients

1 (13.7-ounce) can full-fat coconut milk, chilled overnight
2 tablespoons lemon juice
$^1/_4$ teaspoon apple cider vinegar
$^1/_8$ teaspoon sea salt

Steps

1. Turn the can upside down and use a can opener to carefully remove the bottom. Drain off the liquid (be sure to catch it in a bowl to use for something else), and scrape the thick coconut cream into a food processor or blender.

2. Add the lemon juice, vinegar, and salt. Blend until smooth, taste, and add more salt as desired. Store in the refrigerator for up to 1 week.

(Per 1 tablespoon) Calories: 46 | Fat: 4g | Sodium: 102mg Carbs: 1g | Fiber: 0g | Sugar: 0g | Protein: 0g

DESSERTS

Know what's insane?

It's insane to eat the same way you've always eaten and think that you're going to change the shape of your body.

When you eat the same way you've always eaten, the ONLY outcome is to have the same body that you've always had.

Want a slimmer, healthier, sexier body? Then you're gonna have to eat differently, dear.

Start by cutting out grains, gluten, dairy, soy and cane sugar for the next 30 days. Sure, it'll be tough at first. Yes, you'll crave your old favorites. Of course, there will be days when you want to quit.

But stick with it.

After 30 days you'll see the difference.

(You'd have to be insane not to . . .)

Eating desserts that are filled with refined sugar, like traditional candy bars and other baked goods, creates an ongoing cycle of awful food choices, spikes your blood sugar, and primes your body to store fat all day long.

You'll feel SO MUCH BETTER when you cut refined sugar out of your diet, especially when you cut it out of your desserts. Your energy will be steady and soar. Your headaches will go away. Your weight will drop. Even your outlook on life will brighten.

And the best part? Soon you won't even think about your old go-to treats. When I decided to give up refined sugar, one of my goals was to create a cane sugar–free recipe for each and every sweet treat that I missed. And once you start reaping the benefits of a low-sugar diet—while eating these delicious and indulgent yet wholesome desserts—you won't miss refined sugar or its effects on your mind and body.

APRICOT PRESERVES

prep time: 20 minutes ● *cooking time:* 17 minutes ● *makes:* 2 cups

Apricots are said to have originated in Armenia, and the scientific name for apricot is *Prunus armeniaca,* which translates to "Armenian prune." So it's no wonder that my Armenian husband loves anything and everything related to apricots.

Most store-bought apricot jams, jellies, and preserves contain loads of refined sugar that actually detract from the naturally sweet-and-tart flavor of apricots, not to mention their nutrition. Lucky for us, making fresh apricot preserves that are free of refined sugar is a really simple and quick process.

It's also a wonderful way to preserve fresh stone fruit that may be at that overly ripe stage, on the brink of getting moldy. If you take a handful of fruit at that mushy stage and make a batch of these preserves, you'll get at least another few weeks out of it (if you don't eat it all sooner).

How shall we enjoy our Apricot Preserves? Let me count the ways . . .

> › Roll it up in a **COCONUT FLOUR TORTILLA** (page 89) or **COCONUT FLOUR CREPE** (page 58) with some homemade **ALMOND BUTTER** (see tip).

> Slather some on a piece of **NAAN BREAD** (page 156), **ALMOND BREAD** (page 43), or a **WALNUT RAISIN ROLL** (page 158).

Feel free to adjust the sweetness to your taste. I call for 2 tablespoons honey, but if you think the preserves still taste a little tart, add either more honey or a little liquid stevia.

Ingredients

8 ripe apricots, pitted and quartered

1 tablespoon lemon juice

$\frac{1}{2}$ teaspoon lemon zest

2 tablespoons raw honey, plus more to taste

1 teaspoon powdered gelatin

Steps

1. Put the apricots in a small saucepan over medium-low heat. Cook for 10 minutes, stirring often. Once the apricots have broken up and their released juices start boiling, add the lemon juice and zest and honey. Mix well and continue to boil for 4 minutes.

2. Sprinkle the gelatin over the top of the boiling apricots, mixing well to break up any clumps. Continue to cook for another 3 minutes after the gelatin has been worked into the preserves, then remove from the heat. Taste the preserves, adjusting the sweetness as desired. Store the preserves in a sealed container in the fridge for up to 10 days.

(Per $\frac{1}{4}$ cup) Calories: 45 | Fat: 0g | Sodium: 2mg
Carbs: 11g | Fiber: 1g | Sugar: 10g | Protein: 1g

QUICK TIP

Blending your own Almond Butter at home is super easy if you have a food processor. Combine 3 cups roasted, unsalted almonds in your food processor with $\frac{1}{4}$ teaspoon sea salt and 1 tablespoon coconut oil. Blend until creamy, and have some patience—this could take up to 10 minutes. Now to make an Almond Butter and Apricot Sandwich . . .

PEAR COBBLER WITH BALSAMIC SYRUP

prep time: 15 minutes ● *cooking time:* 30 minutes ● *serves:* 6

If I were to give a single food item the **Makes Us Fattest Award**, hands down the winner would be refined sugar . . . under all its aliases: evaporated cane sugar, corn syrup, dextrose, and fructose.

The sad fact is that we are not aware of how deadly sugar is—both in causing rapid weight gain and in degrading our health by damaging all our major organs. As if that isn't bad enough, sugar also feeds the bacteria in your body—a process that increases your risk for disease. It's even been shown to feed cancer cells. We put so much effort into getting fit, and yet the sugar that's in nearly everything we eat is a Trojan horse, cutting our health-promoting efforts off at the knees.

Desserts like this Pear Cobbler with Balsamic Syrup are a tasty way to enjoy a little something sweet after dinner without bombarding our bodies with a wave of refined sugar. It's just sweet enough to satisfy that tooth . . .

Ingredients

8 Bosc pears, peeled, cored, and sliced into $\frac{1}{4}$-inch-thick wedges

3 tablespoons plus $\frac{1}{4}$ cup coconut palm sugar, divided

$\frac{1}{2}$ cup blanched almond flour

$\frac{1}{4}$ teaspoon baking soda

$\frac{1}{4}$ teaspoon sea salt

3 tablespoons coconut oil, chilled

1 tablespoon coconut cream

1 large egg yolk

$\frac{1}{4}$ teaspoon vanilla extract

1 tablespoon lemon juice

COCONUT MILK ICE CREAM **(see Quick Tip)**

$\frac{1}{4}$ cup BALSAMIC GLAZE **(page 200)**

Steps

1. Preheat the broiler to high. In a medium bowl, toss the pear wedges with 3 tablespoons of the coconut palm sugar. Spread the pears over a large rimmed baking sheet and broil for 10 minutes in the middle of the oven, flipping them halfway through. Remove the pan from the oven and adjust the heat to 375°F.

2. In a large bowl, combine the almond flour, remaining $\frac{1}{4}$ cup coconut sugar, baking soda, and salt. Add the coconut oil and, with your fingers, rubbing it into the mixture evenly until it reaches a crumbly texture. Stir in the coconut cream, yolk, and vanilla until fully combined. Chill the topping in the fridge.

3. In a bowl, toss the cooled pears with the lemon juice and divide among six 8-ounce ramekins. Sprinkle them with the crumb topping and bake until the topping is golden and the pears are bubbling, about 20 minutes. Cool for 5 minutes, then serve with Coconut Milk Ice Cream and a drizzle of Balsamic Glaze.

(Per serving) Calories: 322 | Fat: 14g | Sodium: 125mg
Carbs: 43g | Fiber: 6g | Sugar: 23g | Protein: 6g

QUICK TIP

It's really easy to make your own Coconut Milk Ice Cream at home. Simply combine the following ingredients in a food processor: the cream from 2 (13.7-ounce) cans coconut milk that have been chilled overnight in the fridge and then drained, 2 frozen bananas (peeled), 3 tablespoons coconut palm sugar, and 1 tablespoon vanilla extract. Blend until smooth and then pour the mixture into an ice cream maker and run it until the mixture is creamy.

THANKSGIVING FRUIT SALAD

prep time: 15 minutes ● *serves:* 12

When I was a child, giving thanks on Thanksgiving meant picking out the one thing I was most thankful for and then squirming in my chair as I waited for it to be my turn to announce it to the family—secretly hoping that my brothers or cousins wouldn't say it first. Giving thanks was about giving the *right* answer, the one that would please Mom, Dad, and my grandparents. *I'm thankful for my family. I'm thankful for our house. I'm thankful for our pets. I'm thankful for my friends at school.*

In early adulthood, I'd wait my turn in the same chair, but the focus had shifted from pleasing the elders to a deeper reflection of what was truly significant in my life. Giving thanks was about putting my finger on what was most important to *me*, what I cared about most in the moment. *I'm thankful the university accepted me. I'm thankful I got the job. I'm thankful he proposed. I'm thankful we saved enough for the down payment.*

After the births of my children, I hosted the feast in my own home. My perspective further evolved: Giving thanks was no longer a checklist of items organized in my mind; it was a bouquet of emotion deeply felt in my chest. *I am thankful for the intense wonder, joy, awe, and love emanating from my heart as I gaze around the table at the faces of those I love.*

The waves of time persist, continuing to smooth out my rough edges and pulling me toward maturity. Experiencing shattering loss, heartbreak, and a brush with mortality became resilience that spurred growth and a newfound strength. Eventually, giving thanks was no longer an activity reserved for the fourth Thursday of November. It was no longer about giving the right answer, creating a list, or even reflecting on how I was feeling one day out of the year. Instead, giving thanks has become the lens through which I experience every new day.

May you always view the world around you through the lens of gratitude—from the smallest tickle of warm sun on your face and food in your belly to the deepest delight of family, love, and legacy.

This medley of harvest-time fruits—pineapple, pears, persimmons, oranges, pomegranate, and kiwis—is always served with pumpkin pie at my house on Thanksgiving. However, it's also wonderful served with your holiday feast or simply as a wholesome sweet treat any day during the fall and winter months when these vibrant fruits are in season.

Happy Thanksgiving to you and yours. xoxo

Ingredients

1 pineapple, peeled, cored, and chopped

2 Asian pears, seeded and sliced

4 persimmons, seeded and sliced

4 kiwis, peeled and sliced

4 mandarin oranges, peeled and seeded

12 dates, seeded and chopped

2 cups black grapes

Seeds from 1 pomegranate

Steps

Combine all of the fruit in a large bowl.

(Per serving) Calories: 134 | Fat: 1g | Sodium: 6mg
Carbs: 34g | Fiber: 6g | Sugar: 23g | Protein: 2g

QUICK TIP

Feel free to modify the fruit used in this recipe. It's always best to use fruit that is in season and grown locally. Picked from the back yard is even better!

FIG COOKIES

prep time: 20 minutes ● *cooking time:* 15 minutes ● *makes:* 24 cookies

There's nothing quite as comforting as biting into a cakey, moist Fig Newton. For me, it brings back all kinds of nostalgic childhood memories. The trouble with traditional Fig Newtons, though—even the ones baked at your local health food market—is that the dough is made with grains and the filling is tainted with refined sugar. Nothing comforting about that!

These babies, however, use blanched almond and coconut flours, and the sweetness in the filling comes from figs, apples, and apple juice. The dough is sturdy and easy to roll out, and the cookies end up golden and crispy on the outside while tender and plump on the inside. Delicious *and* nutritious!

Ingredients

FOR THE FIG FILLING:

1 cup chopped dried figs

$\frac{1}{2}$ cup shredded Fuji apple

$\frac{1}{4}$ cup lemon juice

$\frac{1}{4}$ cup apple juice

FOR THE COOKIE DOUGH:

$2\frac{1}{2}$ cups blanched almond flour

$\frac{1}{3}$ cup coconut palm sugar

$\frac{1}{4}$ cup coconut flour

$\frac{1}{4}$ teaspoon baking soda

$\frac{1}{2}$ teaspoon sea salt

$\frac{1}{4}$ cup coconut oil

2 eggs, at room temperature, beaten

1 tablespoon vanilla extract

Steps

FOR THE FIG FILLING:

1. Combine all of the filling ingredients in a small saucepan over medium-low heat. Simmer for 10 minutes, stirring occasionally. Remove the pot from the heat and let the filling cool for 5 minutes.

2. Transfer the fig mixture to a food processor and pulse until smooth. Set aside.

FOR THE COOKIE DOUGH:

1. Preheat the oven to 350°F.

2. Combine the almond flour, coconut palm sugar, coconut flour, baking soda, and salt in a medium bowl and mix to remove any lumps. In another medium bowl, combine the oil, eggs, and vanilla. Mix well. Stir the wet ingredients into the dry and mix well until a dough forms. Divide the dough into 4 even balls. Transfer them to the fridge to chill for 15 minutes.

3. Cut out eight 6 × 15-inch pieces of parchment paper and place one ball of dough in between two of them. Use a rolling pin to flatten the dough evenly into a 12 × 5-inch rectangle. Do the same with the remaining balls of dough, so that you have 4 rectangles almost identical in size.

4. Cover two of the rectangles with the filling, keeping a $\frac{1}{4}$-inch border free of filling. Carefully place the remaining rectangles of dough over the filling-coated rectangles. Pinch the edges of the 2 dough pieces all the way around to form a seal.

5. Transfer the logs of dough, along with the parchment paper that they are on, to a rimmed baking sheet. Slice each log into twelve 1-inch cookies. Separate them slightly so that none of the cookies are touching each other.

6. Bake for 15–20 minutes, until the dough turns golden.

(Per cookie) Calories: 129 | Fat: 8g | Sodium: 69mg
Carbs: 10g | Fiber: 3g | Sugar: 6g | Protein: 3g

QUICK TIP

I love packing these cookies in our lunches because one cookie provides hours of energy. Also, feel free to freeze your leftover cookies in an air-tight container to keep them for up to 2 months.

ROSE APPLE PASTRIES

prep time: 30 minutes
cooking time: 15 minutes
makes: 10 pastries

Do you want to know something really cool? It's something that I've stumbled upon after years of experimenting in the kitchen and poring over nutrition books and cookbooks. Here it is: Any food can be turned into something wholesome, nutritious, and delicious. ANY FOOD!

It was this way of thinking that earned me the name of "The Recipe Hacker," and it's the philosophy that I live and eat by.

Take this recipe for Rose Apple Pastries as an example: They're normally filled with simple sugars, unhealthy fats, grains, and dairy. Sure, the unhealthy version tastes delicious, but there's no substantial benefit to eating it. I had to challenge this antiquated concept of dessert by asking the question, "Why can't pastries be delicious, fun, flavorful, *and* packed with wholesome, nutritious, usable calories?"

The answer: THEY CAN! (And in my humble opinion, they SHOULD.)

This recipe for elegant Rose Apple Pastries is made with grain-free, refined sugar–free, and dairy-free ingredients. It's everything you could ask for in a pastry . . . and more.

It's important to ask for more from your food. Demand more! More flavor, more nutrition, more fun, more excitement.

Ingredients

2 Fuji apples

1 cup plus 1 tablespoon cold water, divided

juice of 1 lemon

³/₄ cup blanched almond flour

3 tablespoons coconut flour, plus more for dusting

¹/₂ cup arrowroot starch

¹/₂ teaspoon sea salt

¹/₄ cup hot water

2 tablespoons raw honey

1 egg

1 tablespoon extra-virgin olive oil

1 teaspoon apple cider vinegar

¹/₂ cup fruit-only apricot preserves

Steps

1. Preheat the oven to 400°F. Generously grease 10 muffin cups with coconut oil and set aside.

2. Slice the apples into quarters lengthwise. Carve out the core, and thinly slice the quarters into half-moons. Put the slices in a medium skillet with 1 cup of the cold water and lemon juice. Bring to a low simmer, then remove from the heat and drain, reserving only the apple slices. Set aside.

3. In a large bowl, combine the almond flour, coconut flour, arrowroot starch, and salt. Mix well. In a small bowl, combine the hot water with the honey and whisk with a fork until the honey has dissolved. Beat in the egg, olive oil, and apple cider vinegar.

4. Add the honey mixture to the flour mixture and mix with a large spoon or your hands to form a dough ball. Lightly knead the dough in the bowl until smooth, divide into two balls, then wrap them in plastic, and chill in the fridge for 10 minutes.

5. Individually roll the dough balls between two pieces of coconut flour–dusted parchment paper into two 10 × 6-inch rectangles with ¼-inch thickness. Slice each rectangle into five 6 × 2-inch strips.

6. Line 3–4 slices of apple along each strip of dough, with the peel side facing out. Roll each strip, pressing the dough together as you go. Place each rolled pastry in a muffin cup and bake for 15 minutes, until golden. Transfer to a wire rack to cool.

7. In small saucepan, warm the apricot preserves over low heat, adding the remaining 1 tablespoon cold water to thin it to a glaze. Dip each cooked Rose Apple Pastry into the glaze before serving.

(Per cookie) Calories: 173 | Fat: 6g | Sodium: 131mg | Carbs: 28g | Fiber: 2g | Sugar: 11g | Protein: 4g

QUICK TIP

The commercial version of this recipe calls for frozen puff pastry dough that's been shaped into squares. Due to the gluten in that frozen dough, it sticks together perfectly, and once thawed, it's quickly and easily shaped. Our grain- and gluten-free dough, on the other hand, isn't commercially made or perfect. So when it comes to the shaping of your pastries, it helps to have a nice dose of patience and to realize that these don't have to come out looking perfect. Just squish the dough together as you roll each rose up, and it will work!

Rolling and shaping your dough is a wonderful time to practice some relaxing breathing techniques . . . taking deep breaths in, exhaling every last drop of air, then holding for as long as is comfortable before taking another deep breath in. Now put on some tea and enjoy those pastries in your state of deep relaxation.

CHOCOLATE PEANUT BUTTER COOKIES

prep time: 15 minutes ● *cooking time:* 18 minutes ● *makes:* 24 cookies

It's hard to beat the chocolate–peanut butter flavor combination. And because I live with three peanut-butter-holics, you'll notice that I've included peanuts in a few of my recipes. If you love peanuts too, then have some fun with it!

However, if you are one of the many people with peanut allergies or sensitivities, then please know that peanuts can be subbed out for pretty much any other nut or seed.

Ingredients

1 cup blanched almond flour

1 tablespoon coconut flour

$^2/_3$ cup unsweetened cocoa powder

1 teaspoon baking soda

$^1/_2$ teaspoon sea salt

$^1/_4$ cup plus 2 tablespoons coconut oil

2 tablespoons full-fat coconut milk

$^3/_4$ cup creamy peanut butter or almond butter (look for a version with nuts and salt as the only listed ingredients, no sugar or corn syrup)

1 cup coconut palm sugar

2 eggs

1 teaspoon vanilla extract

1 cup dry-roasted peanuts (or your preferred nut or seed), chopped

Steps

1. Preheat the oven to 350°F. Line a large rimmed baking sheet with parchment paper and set aside.

2. In a large bowl, whisk together the almond flour, coconut flour, cocoa powder, baking soda, and salt. Set aside.

3. In the bowl of an electric mixer fitted with the paddle attachment, beat together the coconut oil, coconut milk, peanut butter, and coconut palm sugar. Add the flour mixture to the batter and mix until fully combined.

4. Add the eggs and vanilla to the batter and cream until fully combined.

5. Form the batter into small balls, about $1^1/_2$ tablespoons each. Roll the balls in the chopped nuts and arrange them on the prepared baking sheet, leaving about an inch between each cookie. Press the balls slightly. Bake for 15–18 minutes, until golden. Cool for 5 minutes before removing from the baking sheet.

(Per cookie) Calories: 171 | Fat: 13g | Sodium: 170mg
Carbs: 11g | Fiber: 3g | Sugar: 7g | Protein: 6g

· · · · · · · · · WHY COCONUT PALM SUGAR? · · · · · · · · ·

Coconut palm sugar rather than refined cane sugar?

For starters, coconut palm sugar is a nutritionally whole product—meaning that nothing has been stripped away from it, so our bodies are able to process it easily.

Since refined cane sugar has been totally altered from its natural state, it robs our body of valuable nutrients during the digestion process. I don't know about you, but I only want to eat foods that add nutritional value to my body, not rob me of it!

The other big benefit to coconut palm sugar is that it doesn't spike your blood sugar the way that refined cane sugar does. This means that your body is not going to go into "fat storage mode" the way it would when snacking on the refined sugar version of this sweet snack. Pretty great, right? I think so. ☺

QUICK TIP

You know what else would be tasty? Rolling these cookies in chopped **CANDIED PECANS** (page 242) rather than peanuts. Mmmmm . . .

GINGERSNAPS

prep time: 30 minutes ● *cooking time:* 15 minutes ● *makes:* 50 cookies

I'm going to come clean with you: It took me a couple of times to get this recipe right. I've gotten pretty good at coming up with grain-free recipes that are great on the first try, but these tricky little Gingersnaps made me work for it!

It was completely worth the persistence, though, because these cookies pack some serious ginger flavor.

Ingredients

2 cups raw pecans

$^1/_4$ cup coconut flour

$^1/_2$ cup blanched almond flour

$^1/_2$ cup arrowroot starch

2 teaspoons baking soda

$^1/_2$ teaspoon sea salt

1 tablespoon ground ginger

$^1/_2$ teaspoon ground cardamom

$^1/_2$ teaspoon black pepper

$^1/_3$ cup coconut oil

$^1/_4$ cup coconut cream

1 cup coconut palm sugar, divided

$^1/_4$ cup plus 2 tablespoons molasses

1 egg

Steps

1. Preheat the oven to 350°F. Line a large rimmed baking sheet with parchment paper and set aside.

2. Toast the pecans in a dry skillet over medium heat, stirring often, for 5 minutes, until fragrant and golden. Set aside to cool.

3. Pulse the pecans in a food processor until finely ground. Add the coconut flour, almond flour, arrowroot, baking soda, salt, ginger, cardamom, pepper, coconut oil, coconut cream, $^3/_4$ cup of the coconut palm sugar, molasses, and egg. Pulse until fully combined.

4. Gather the dough into a ball, wrap it with plastic wrap, and place it in the freezer for 20 minutes.

5. Place the remaining $^1/_4$ cup coconut palm sugar in a bowl. Form the dough into 1-tablespoon-size balls and roll them in the sugar. Arrange the dough balls on the prepared baking sheet about 3 inches apart and do not press the dough down. Bake for 8–12 minutes, until golden.

(Per cookie) Calories: 84 | Fat: 5g | Sodium: 88mg
Carbs: 9g | Fiber: 1g | Sugar: 6g | Protein: 1g

QUICK TIP

Keep in mind that the dough really expands while baking, which is why you'll need to space the cookies at least 3 inches apart on the baking sheet. Don't flatten out the balls when you put them on the pan, either. Let them expand naturally in the baking process and enjoy the pretty cracks that come as a result.

MONSTER COOKIES

prep time: 10 minutes ● *cooking time:* 12 minutes ● *makes:* 50 cookies

"Traditional" Monster Cookie recipes call for M&M's, oats, wheat flour, and refined sugar—so I took this as a worthy challenge to hack into something healthier.

In place of the M&M's, we are using colorful, dried fruit.

In place of the oats, we are using unsweetened, shredded coconut.

And in place of the flour and sugar, we are using almond flour and coconut palm sugar.

Don't want to use peanut butter? No worries; creamy almond butter works great, too.

You know what? This wholesome version came out pretty awesome! Give it a try.

Ingredients

3 eggs

1 cup coconut palm sugar

1/2 teaspoon sea salt

1/2 teaspoon vanilla extract

1 (12-ounce) jar creamy peanut or almond butter (look for a version with nuts and salt as the only listed ingredients, no sugar or corn syrup)

1/2 cup coconut oil

1/4 cup coconut cream

2 teaspoons baking soda

2 cups unsweetened shredded coconut

2 cups blanched almond flour

1/4 cup dried blueberries

1/4 cup dried cranberries

4 dried apricots, diced

1/2 cup stevia-sweetened chocolate chips

Steps

1. Preheat the oven to 350°F. Line a large rimmed baking sheet with parchment paper and set aside.

2. In a food processor, combine the eggs, coconut palm sugar, salt, vanilla, peanut butter, coconut oil, coconut cream, baking soda, shredded coconut, and almond flour. Pulse until fully combined. Fold in the dried fruit and chocolate chips.

3. Scoop the dough in 1-tablespoon mounds on the prepared baking sheet. Bake for 8–12 minutes, until golden.

(Per cookie) Calories: 151 | Fat: 10g | Sodium: 90mg
Carbs: 12g | Fiber: 3g | Sugar: 8g | Protein: 5g

QUICK TIP

Often, packaged dried fruit contains added sugars, so make sure to check the label and only purchase naturally sweetened, zero-sugar-added dried fruit. Because dried fruit is plenty sweet enough all on its own!

COOKIE DOUGH BONBONS

prep time: 30 minutes
chilling time: 1 hour
makes: 18 bonbons

There are two kinds of people in this world: those who *could exist* without chocolate and those who would drop dead without chocolate.

I'm the drop-dead type. (Obviously.)

Who are these nonchocolate lovers anyway? We shouldn't trust them.

Every two weeks or so I find myself in the RHR Kitchen staring down a big bowl of chocolate, trying to come up with a new, exciting way to get my fix. These Cookie Dough Bonbons may be the most exciting chocolate recipe yet. It's one of those you-just-have-to-try-it desserts, so next time that you're in charge of bringing something sweet somewhere or next time you just have to get your chocolate on, give this recipe a whirl. You can thank me later.

Ingredients

¹/₂ cup creamy peanut butter or almond butter (look for a version with nuts and salt as the only listed ingredients, no sugar or corn syrup)

¹/₄ cup raw honey

1 teaspoon vanilla extract

¹/₄ teaspoon sea salt

1¹/₂ cups unsweetened, shredded coconut

¹/₂ cup mini stevia-sweetened dark chocolate chips

4 ounces bittersweet chocolate, bar or pieces

4 ounces dark chocolate (73% cacao content)

2 tablespoons coconut oil

1 tablespoon coarse pink Himalayan salt

Steps

1. In a double boiler over medium heat (or a lazy man's double boiler; see tip), melt the peanut butter and honey together until smooth. Remove from the heat and mix in the vanilla and salt.

2. Grind the shredded coconut in a food processor until a fine powder forms. Add the peanut butter mixture and blend until fully combined. Transfer the cookie dough to a large bowl and fold in the chocolate chips. Cover the bowl with plastic wrap and chill in the freezer for 30 minutes.

3. Find a baking sheet that fits in your freezer and cover it with foil. Place a wire cooling rack on top of the foil. Remove the cookie dough from the freezer and form it into 18 balls. Arrange the balls on the rack and transfer the tray back to the freezer for 15 minutes, while you melt the chocolate.

4. Combine the chocolate (both types) and coconut oil in a double boiler over medium heat and mix until fully melted and smooth. Remove from the heat.

5. Balance a frozen cookie dough ball on a large fork, and submerge it in the melted chocolate. Lift it out of the chocolate and allow any excess to drip through the fork. Place the chocolate-coated bonbon back on the rack and repeat with the remaining dough balls. Use a small spoon to drizzle the remaining chocolate over each bonbon in a pretty zigzag and sprinkle with a pinch of the coarse pink Himalayan salt immediately, while the chocolate is still wet. Place the bonbons back in the freezer for at least 30 minutes before serving. Store in an airtight container in the freezer for up to 2 months.

(Per bonbon) Calories: 215 | Fat: 16g | Sodium: 116mg | Carbs: 17g | Fiber: 3g | Sugar: 11g | Protein: 5g

QUICK TIP

Lazy Man's Double Boiler: OK, I actually made this term up! This is a quick technique that I use to melt chocolate, raw honey, and coconut oil. Simply place a skillet over medium heat and fill it partially with water, then place a saucepan containing the ingredients you want to melt directly into the skillet. With this technique the intensity of the heat is reduced, so you're far less likely to burn the melting ingredients. Still, do pay fairly close attention to it while melting and stir often.

GLAZED ALMOND BARK

prep time: 20 minutes ● *chilling time:* 20 minutes ● *serves:* 30

Why should you make this Glazed Almond Bark? Let's count the reasons . . .

1. It calls for Marcona almonds, not regular, run-of-the-mill almonds. Marcona almonds are rounder and plumper with a texture that's closer to a macadamia nut. They're deliciously soft and buttery.
2. The almonds are glazed with liquefied coconut palm sugar. So basically we take a delicious exotic nut and coat it with sweet love.
3. The chocolate is super-dark and flavorful. It's not overly sweet, like milk chocolate, but rich and almost a little bitter. It balances perfectly with the sweetened almonds.
4. It's topped off with a sprinkling of coarse sea salt. Have you ever wondered why salty and sweet taste so good together? Just the right amount of sea salt actually intensifies the sweetness that our taste buds experience. Crazy, but true!

Best. Dessert. Ever.

Ingredients

- ¹/₂ **cup coconut palm sugar**
- **1 tablespoon water**
- **1 tablespoon coconut oil**
- **1¹/₂ cups Marcona almonds, roasted**
- **3 cups (about 1 pound) dark chocolate pieces (73% cacao content)**
- **coarse sea salt**

Steps

1. Line a rimmed baking sheet that will fit into your freezer with parchment paper and set aside.

2. In a small skillet, combine the coconut palm sugar and water. Bring to a boil over low heat, stirring often, and cook for about 5 minutes. Remove from the heat and mix in the coconut oil.

3. Put the almonds in a large bowl. Pour the sugar mixture over the almonds and mix until well coated. Spread the almonds over the prepared baking sheet and set aside to cool while you prepare the chocolate.

4. In a double boiler (or a lazy man's double boiler; see page 221), melt the chocolate over low heat, mixing until very smooth. Remove from the heat.

5. Remove one-fourth of the almonds from the baking sheet and set aside, then pour the melted chocolate and the remaining almonds into a large bowl and mix well. (Save that parchment-lined baking sheet!) Once fully combined, spread the chocolate-almond mixture evenly over the lined baking sheet. Sprinkle the reserved almonds over the top along with some salt.

6. Place the tray in the freezer for 20 minutes before breaking the bark into pieces and serving.

(Per piece) Calories: 141 | Fat: 9g | Sodium: 76mg
Carbs: 14g | Fiber: 2g | Sugar: 12g | Protein: 3g

QUICK TIP

Store your Glazed Almond Bark in the freezer. This is handy for two reasons: First, you'll love how fresh and flavorful it stays, and second, it's much easier to hide stuff in the freezer (under a bag of peas or behind a foil-wrapped casserole) than it is to hide in the pantry (where your kids, spouse, friends, visitors, and so on are bound to paw through for snacks). See, I've got you covered.

CHOCOLATE TRUFFLES

prep time: 15 minutes ● *chilling time:* 15 minutes ● *makes:* 30 truffles

I grew up eating See's Candies from the big white boxes. All those different flavors and fillings were so exciting! And then there was that annoying sugar crash that ensued.

Here's a candy recipe that you can really get excited about. Made with ground pecans, soaked dates, unsweetened cocoa powder, and a touch of honey, this is one candy that's packed with real, usable calories. Keep 'em in the freezer and pull 'em out when company comes over. Or just keep 'em in the freezer and pull 'em out whenever you want.

Ingredients

FOR THE TRUFFLES:

2 cups pecans

1 cup dates, pitted and soaked in hot water for 10 minutes

$^1/_2$ cup unsweetened cocoa powder

$^1/_2$ teaspoon sea salt

1 teaspoon raw honey, melted

FOR THE TOPPINGS:

dark chocolate (73% cacao content), melted

$^1/_4$ cup unsweetened, shredded coconut flakes

$^1/_4$ cup unsweetened cocoa powder

$^1/_4$ cup minced dark chocolate (73% cacao content)

$^1/_4$ cup finely chopped pistachios

$^1/_4$ cup finely chopped almonds

Steps

FOR THE TRUFFLES:

1. Line a rimmed baking sheet that will fit into your freezer with parchment paper and set aside.

2. Toast the pecans in a dry skillet over medium heat, stirring often, until fragrant and golden. Set aside to cool.

3. Drain the dates, discarding the soaking liquid, and transfer to a food processor with the toasted pecans, cocoa powder, salt, and honey. Pulse until coarse and crumbly. Form the dough into 30 balls.

FOR THE TOPPINGS:

Roll the balls in the toppings of your choice. Place the truffles on the prepared pan and freeze for 15 minutes.

(Per truffle) Calories: 76 | Fat: 6g | Sodium: 1mg
Carbs: 6g | Fiber: 2g | Sugar: 4g | Protein: 3g

QUICK TIP

Have fun with the toppings for these tasty little truffles. Try mixing it up with chopped nuts, shredded coconut, dark chocolate powder, or even the **RAINBOW COCONUT SPRINKLES** on page 240. And how cool would it be to give these to your sweetie on Valentine's Day in a pretty little white box with a red bow?

HOMEMADE PEANUT BUTTER CUPS

prep time: 15 minutes ● *chilling time:* 25 minutes ● *makes:* 40 peanut butter cups

If you checked my freezer right now, you'd find a big ol' bag of these insanely awesome peanut butter cups. I simply love having one of these as a treat after a day well lived.

You'll notice that the sweetness factor of these peanut butter cups is pretty low, as I used stevia and unsweetened chocolate with just a touch of raw honey. As your palate changes from not eating as much refined sugar, you'll learn to really appreciate the bittersweet quality of this treat.

Ingredients

FOR THE CHOCOLATE COATING:

$2^1/_2$ **cups unsweetened chocolate pieces, chopped**

3 tablespoons raw honey

1 tablespoon coconut oil

20 drops liquid stevia

FOR THE PEANUT BUTTER FILLING:

1 cup all-natural peanut or almond butter (look for a version with nuts and salt as the only listed ingredients, no sugar or corn syrup)

1 tablespoon raw honey

1 tablespoon coconut oil

pinch of sea salt

Steps

FOR THE CHOCOLATE COATING:

1. Combine the chocolate coating ingredients in a lazy man's double boiler (see page 221) over medium heat. Stir until melted and smooth. Remove from the heat.

2. Line 40 mini muffin cups with paper liners. Fill each liner with 1 tablespoon of the chocolate sauce. Chill in the freezer for 10 minutes.

FOR THE PEANUT BUTTER FILLING:

1. Meanwhile, combine the peanut butter filling ingredients in a food processor. Pulse until creamy and smooth.

2. Remove the muffin tins from the freezer and add a tablespoon of peanut butter filling to each. Cover with another tablespoon of the chocolate sauce and return the peanut butter cups to the freezer for 15 minutes, or until completely set.

(Per peanut butter cup) Calories: 97 | Fat: 5g | Sodium: 24mg
Carbs: 7g | Fiber: 1g | Sugar: 2g | Protein: 3g

HEALTHY EATING TIP

You don't need willpower to succeed. All you need is to tap into your inborn ability to create new habits. Put new daily habits in place that support your diet changes and be consistent until the new habits take hold. You know you're capable of forming habits—you once utilized habits to establish an unhealthy diet—so now put those habit-forming skills to work in your favor.

REAL HEALTHY SNICKERS BARS

prep time: 45 minutes
cooking time: 30 minutes
chilling time: 25 minutes
makes: 24 bars

Who doesn't love Snickers bars? The chocolate, the nuts, the caramel. It's a tantalizing combination, to say the least. Yet, while it's a candy bar that proclaims it will satisfy your hunger, I'd like to suggest that my wholesome version will do the job even better.

Why?

Well, for starters, my recipe uses very dark chocolate, which is lower in sugar than milk chocolate. My caramel is made with coconut palm sugar, which won't set you up for a sugar rush and energy crash. And my cookie layer is made with toasted ground nuts, which provide real, usable energy. And instead of peanuts I use dry-roasted macadamia nuts, just to change things up.

I simply love the challenge of taking an existing, unwholesome item and creating it anew with really nutritious ingredients.

The best part is when my taste testers tell me that my healthier version tastes even better than the original—whoop whoop!

Ingredients

FOR THE CHOCOLATE LAYER:

2 cups (12 ounces) dark chocolate pieces (73% cacao content or higher)

3 tablespoons coconut oil

FOR THE COOKIE LAYER:

$2^1/_2$ cups raw pecans

8 dates, pitted and soaked in hot water for 10 minutes, drained

2 tablespoons blanched almond flour

1 teaspoon coconut flour

$^1/_4$ teaspoon sea salt

$^1/_4$ cup coconut palm sugar

3 tablespoons coconut oil, melted

FOR THE CARAMEL LAYER:

1 cup coconut palm sugar

$^1/_4$ cup canned full-fat coconut milk

2 tablespoons coconut oil

pinch of sea salt

1 tablespoon vanilla extract

$^1/_2$ teaspoon baking soda

$^1/_2$ cup dry-roasted macadamia nuts, chopped

Steps

FOR THE CHOCOLATE LAYER:

Use a lazy man's double boiler (see page 221) to melt the chocolate and coconut oil. Stir until the mixture is smooth, then remove from the heat.

FOR THE COOKIE LAYER:

1. Preheat the oven to 350°F. Spread the pecans on a large rimmed baking sheet and bake for 8–10 minutes, until toasted.

2. Transfer the toasted pecans to a food processor and pulse until fine. Add the remaining cookie layer ingredients. Pulse until a dough forms.

FOR THE CARAMEL LAYER:

1. In a skillet over medium heat, combine the coconut palm sugar, coconut milk, coconut oil, salt, and vanilla. Once the mixture begins to boil, decrease the heat to low and continue to cook, stirring often, for 5 minutes.

2. Remove the skillet from the heat and whisk in the baking soda. The mixture will turn a lighter color and become creamy. Return the pan to low heat and cook, stirring often, for 2 minutes.

3. Remove the caramel from the heat and allow it to cool and thicken for 5 minutes.

ASSEMBLE YOUR SNICKERS BARS:

1. Line the bottom and sides of an 8 × 8-inch baking pan with parchment paper, so that the parchment paper hangs over the sides. (These will be your handles to easily pull the snickers bars from the pan once they're done.) Lightly rub the parchment paper with coconut oil.

2. Pour half of the chocolate layer into the bottom of the pan. Place in the freezer for 10 minutes.

3. Sprinkle the cookie layer over the hardened chocolate layer. Press down to create an even layer of dough. Place in the freezer for 5 minutes to harden.

4. Pour the caramel layer over the cookie layer and spread to evenly coat. Sprinkle the caramel with the chopped macadamia nuts, then pour the remaining chocolate over the top of the nuts and carefully spread to evenly cover. Place in the freezer for 10 minutes, until the top chocolate layer sets.

5. Use the parchment paper "handles" to ease the set mixture out of the pan. Transfer it to a cutting board and slice it into 24 bite-size bars.

(Per bar) Calories: 269 | Fat: 19g | Sodium: 110mg | Carbs: 25g | Fiber: 3g | Sugar: 20g | Protein: 3g

LEMON BARS

prep time: 20 minutes ● *cooking time:* 35 minutes ● *makes:* 30 bars

My entire life is patched together by a series of lists.

There's the work to-do lists that litter my desk in piles; the ongoing grocery list in my iPhone notes; my recipe ingredient lists filling notebooks that clutter the counters of the kitchen, within arm's reach for when inspiration strikes and marked with spills and stains of every assortment; and then there's the secret list of things that I imagine accomplishing one day. Dreams that refuse to leave me alone, no matter how hard I try to ignore them.

These lists keep my hours productive and my life on track, and for that I'm grateful.

There are times, however, when I'd like to gather all my lists into a great big pile and drop a fiery match onto it in order to relive the carefree oblivion of my youth.

Biting into a Lemon Bar is like turning back the hands of time to revisit what it felt like to not care about how productive a day would be, simply enjoying the moment instead. It's one of the first desserts that I attempted to make free of grains, gluten, dairy, and cane sugar back in 2009, so it holds a special place in my heart. Even now, when I take one bite and I can feel a whole new world of delicious, wholesome possibilities open up before me.

With no refined sugar or flour, you can enjoy this delicately sweet treat without worrying about adding an extra workout to your list.

Just close your eyes, take a bite, and allow time to stand still.

Ingredients

FOR THE CRUST:

3 cups blanched almond flour

1 teaspoon sea salt

1/4 cup coconut oil, melted over low heat

2 tablespoons raw honey

1 tablespoon vanilla extract

1/2 teaspoon almond extract

1 teaspoon lemon zest

FOR THE LEMON LAYER:

1/2 cup coconut oil, melted over low heat

1/2 cup raw honey

6 eggs

2/3 cup lemon juice

2 tablespoons lemon zest

2 tablespoons coconut flour

Steps

FOR THE CRUST:

1. Preheat the oven to 350°F. Generously grease a 9 × 13-inch baking pan with coconut oil and lightly dust with coconut flour. Set aside.

2. In a medium bowl, combine the almond flour and salt. In a large bowl, combine the coconut oil, honey, vanilla and almond extracts, and lemon zest. Add the dry ingredients to the wet and stir until well combined. Press the dough into the bottom of the prepared pan and bake for 15 minutes, or until golden.

FOR THE LEMON LAYER:

Combine all of the lemon layer ingredients in a blender and blend on high speed until smooth. Pour the filling over the baked crust and bake for another 15–20 minutes, or until just beginning to brown on top. Allow to cool for 30 minutes, then refrigerate for 2 hours until set. Cut into 30 bars and serve.

(Per bar) Calories: 121 | Fat: 9g | Sodium: 74mg
Carbs: 8g | Fiber: 1g | Sugar: 5g | Protein: 4g

QUICK TIP

Feel free to play around with the amount of honey in this recipe. It's meant to be tart, which is perfect if your palate has been off refined sugar for 30 days or more. If you're new to wholesome desserts, though, just add a little more honey or supplement with stevia to ease the transition.

MINI CHOCOLATE LAYER CAKES

prep time: 30 minutes ● *cooking time:* 10 minutes ● *makes:* 24 mini cakes

I'd like to introduce you to the sneakiest little layer cake you'll ever meet. Don't let its innocent look fool you—this bugger is hiding not one but *two* secret wholesome ingredients.

First secret ingredient: beets. That's right, there are beets hidden in the chocolate cake layers, adding subtle sweetness and a boost of nutrients.

Second secret ingredient: fresh, young coconut meat. This helps give the filling that extra bit of creaminess. Talk about nutritious and delicious! And sneaky. You can find young coconuts at most health food markets—it's the white coconut with the pointy top.

Ingredients

FOR THE CHOCOLATE CAKE:

1 cup (6 ounces) dark chocolate (73% cacao content) pieces

$1/4$ cup coconut oil

$1/3$ cup raw honey

2 eggs

2 teaspoons vanilla extract

$1/4$ teaspoon almond extract

1 (15-ounce) can beets, drained

1 cup blanched almond flour

2 tablespoons coconut flour

$1/4$ cup unsweetened cocoa powder

2 teaspoons baking soda

$1/4$ teaspoon sea salt

FOR THE CREAM FILLING:

2 cups young coconut meat

2 tablespoons raw honey

1 teaspoon vanilla extract

2 tablespoons lemon juice

2 tablespoons coconut oil, melted

$1/4$ teaspoon sea salt

Fresh raspberries (for topping)

Steps

FOR THE CHOCOLATE CAKE:

1. Preheat the oven to 350°F. Lightly grease 2 mini whoopie pie pans with coconut oil (or do two rotations if you only have one pan) for a total of 48 whoopie pies.

2. Combine the dark chocolate, coconut oil, and honey in a lazy man's double boiler (see page 221). Stir often until the chocolate melts and the mixture becomes smooth.

3. Combine the melted chocolate mixture, eggs, vanilla and almond extracts, and beets in a food processor. Pulse until smooth.

4. Combine the almond flour, coconut flour, cocoa powder, baking soda, and salt in a medium bowl. Add the flour mixture to the food processor along with the chocolate mixture and pulse until smooth.

5. Fill each whoopie pie cup with batter. Bake for 9–11 minutes, or until baked through.

FOR THE CREAM FILLING:

1. Blend the coconut meat, honey, vanilla, lemon juice, coconut oil, and salt in a food processor until very smooth and creamy. This may take 5 minutes or longer, so be patient and have faith that the coconut will become creamy! Chill for 20 minutes.

2. Assemble each mini cake with a bottom layer of cake, a shmear of the filling, another cake on top, more filling, and some raspberries. Use toothpicks to hold the cakes in place if need be.

(Per mini cake) Calories: 133 | Fat: 9g | Sodium: 147mg
Carbs: 12g | Fiber: 3g | Sugar: 8g | Protein: 3g

QUICK TIP

Store these cakes in the freezer to prevent them from falling apart. You could also hold them together with toothpicks before freezing, and remove them before serving. Hey, real food dishes are never going to be as cookie-cutter perfect as processed foods; embrace the mess because that's where the power of real foods lies.

MINI CHEESECAKES WITH CHOCOLATE CRUST

prep time: 25 minutes ● *makes:* 24 mini cheesecakes

Everything will be okay in the end. If it's not okay, it's not the end.

I didn't come up with this one . . . that was John Lennon. But I do whisper this sentiment to myself whenever things are looking particularly grim.

And then I reach into my freezer for one of these delightful Mini Cheesecakes with Chocolate Crust, and it becomes infinitely clear that everything really *will* be okay.

Ingredients

FOR THE CHEESECAKE FILLING:

2 cups (12 ounces) raw cashews, soaked in hot water for 2 hours, drained, and rinsed

$^1/_4$ cup raw honey

10 drops liquid stevia

$^1/_2$ cup coconut oil

1 teaspoon vanilla extract

$^1/_2$ teaspoon lemon juice

$^1/_2$ teaspoon sea salt

FOR THE CHOCOLATE CRUST:

1 cup pecans

$^1/_2$ cup dates, pitted and soaked in hot water for 10 minutes

$^1/_4$ cup unsweetened cocoa powder

$^1/_4$ teaspoon sea salt

1 teaspoon raw honey, melted

$^1/_4$ cup dark chocolate shavings (73% cacao content), for garnish

Steps

FOR THE CHEESECAKE FILLING:

Combine all of the cheesecake filling ingredients in a food processor, pulsing until creamy. Fill a piping bag with the cheesecake mixture and place it in the fridge to chill while you prepare the crust. Wipe out the food processor.

FOR THE CHOCOLATE CRUST:

1. Toast the pecans in a dry skillet over medium heat, stirring often, until golden. Set aside to cool.

2. Drain the dates, discarding the soaking water, and place them and the toasted pecans in the food processor. Add the cocoa powder, salt, and honey, and pulse until coarse and crumbly.

3. Line 24 mini muffin cups with paper liners. Divide the crust among the cups and press it firmly down. Pipe the cheesecake filling evenly on top of the crusts. Garnish with the chocolate shavings and chill for 15 minutes before serving.

(Per mini cheesecake) Calories: 141 | Fat: 10g | Sodium: 71mg
Carbs: 8g | Fiber: 2g | Sugar: 6g | Protein: 3g

QUICK TIP

Take this recipe for dairy-free cheesecake and go crazy with personal customizations. Add berries on top, serve it with berry sauce, serve it with chocolate sauce, or remove the cocoa powder from the crust for a more traditional take on the classic . . . just go nuts!

RUSTIC PUMPKIN PIE

prep time: 40 minutes
cooking time: 2 hours
chilling time: 1 hour
serves: 16

Your holidays just got a lot more wholesomely sweet. This Rustic Pumpkin Pie recipe literally starts with a whole pumpkin, rather than a can opener, which makes a huge difference in both nutrients and flavor. Both B and Andrew said that this was the best pumpkin pie they'd ever eaten. (Yes, an eleven-year-old said that!)

I mention in the ingredients below that adding a touch of pure maple syrup is optional. If you are serving this to kids, then I'd recommend adding that maple syrup to ensure that it's sweet enough. However, if you're serving to adults or you're really watching your sugar intake, the molasses does add enough sweetness so that you don't really need the maple syrup, or you can supplement the sweetness with a few drops of liquid stevia.

Ingredients

FOR THE PUMPKIN FILLING:

1 medium sugar pumpkin

1 (13.7-ounce) can full-fat coconut milk

2 tablespoons arrowroot starch

2 tablespoons molasses

2 tablespoons coconut oil

1 tablespoon pumpkin pie spice

$1/4$ teaspoon sea salt

3 eggs

3 tablespoons pure maple syrup (optional)

FOR THE CRUST:

3 cups raw pecans

$1/2$ teaspoon sea salt

$1 1/2$ cups dates, pitted

$1/4$ cup plus 2 tablespoons coconut oil, melted

Steps

FOR THE PUMPKIN FILLING:

1. Preheat the oven to 375°F. Line a large rimmed baking sheet with parchment paper and set aside.

2. Remove the stem from your pumpkin, cut the pumpkin in half vertically, and scrape out the seeds. (Save the seeds for roasting! They make a delicious snack; see page 154.) Place the pumpkin halves, cut side down, on the parchment paper and rub the skin with coconut oil. Roast for 1 hour, until tender. Remove the pumpkin from the oven and decrease the temperature to 325°F.

3. Once the pumpkin has cooled, discard the skin and transfer the soft pumpkin meat to a food processor. Add the remaining filling ingredients and blend until smooth.

FOR THE CRUST:

1. Combine all of the crust ingredients in a food processor. Blend until all of the ingredients are evenly incorporated. Lightly grease a 9-inch pie pan and press the crust firmly and evenly onto the bottom and sides of the pan. Set aside.

2. Pour the filling into the prepared pie crust. Bake for 45–60 minutes, until cooked through and set. To test, shake the pan—if it wiggles in the middle, then it's not quite done. Let the pie cool slightly, then chill in the fridge for 1 hour before serving.

(Per serving) Calories: 354 | Fat: 28g | Sodium: 128mg | Carbs: 21g | Fiber: 4g | Sugar: 14g | Protein: 6g

QUICK TIP

What's a slice of pumpkin pie without a little whipped cream? In our case, to avoid dairy and refined sugar, whip up this tasty Coconut Whipped Cream.

> 2 (13.7-ounce) cans full-fat coconut milk, chilled overnight
> 1/4 cup raw honey
> 1 tablespoon vanilla extract
> 1/2 teaspoon almond extract
> 1 tablespoon coconut oil, melted
> Pinch of sea salt

Carefully turn the cans over and open from the bottom. Drain out the liquid and scoop the white cream into a mixing bowl or stand mixer fitted with the whisk attachment. (Save the coconut water for a smoothie.) Add the remaining ingredients and beat for a few minutes, until creamy. If necessary, chill the cream in the fridge to thicken. Use a piping bag to add dollops of whipped cream to each slice of pie. Garnish with a sprinkle of cinnamon, nutmeg, or pumpkin pie spice.

BROWNIE PIE

prep time: 15 minutes ● *cooking time:* 35 minutes ● *serves:* 30

There was no way that I was going to complete this cookbook without adding at least one brownie recipe. No. Stinkin'. Way.

My love for brownies goes way back to adolescence, when I first learned how to make brownies from boxed mixes. When I discovered baking, a whole new creative world opened up. At the time, I paid no heed to the ingredients, the nutrition, or the impact that all the baked goodies were having on my body. It was all about taste and the joy of sharing the freshly baked sweet treats with others.

This recipe for Brownie Pie is made with wholesome ingredients that are going to love your body back. That said, it's still a treat, and even wholesome sugars need to be eaten in moderation.

Ingredients

FOR THE BROWNIE:

$2^1/_2$ cups coconut palm sugar

1 cup coconut oil

4 eggs

1 tablespoon vanilla extract

$1^1/_2$ cups blanched almond flour

$1^1/_2$ cups unsweetened cocoa powder

1 teaspoon baking powder

1 teaspoon sea salt

1 teaspoon instant espresso powder

$1^1/_2$ cups stevia-sweetened dark chocolate chips

FOR THE CHOCOLATE FROSTING:

1 cup dark chocolate pieces (73% cacao content)

$^1/_4$ cup full-fat coconut milk

$^1/_4$ cup coconut oil

$^1/_4$ cup palm shortening

$^1/_4$ cup raw honey

RAINBOW COCONUT SPRINKLES (page 240), for decorating

Steps

FOR THE BROWNIE:

1. Preheat the oven to 350°F. Line the bottom of a 9-inch pie pan with parchment paper and lightly grease the paper with coconut oil.

2. In a large mixing bowl, whisk together the coconut palm sugar, coconut oil, eggs, and vanilla extract.

3. In another medium bowl, combine the almond flour, cocoa powder, baking powder, salt, and espresso powder. Mix well.

4. Add the sugar mixture to the flour mixture and mix until fully combined. Stir in the chocolate chips.

5. Pour the batter into the prepared pie pan and bake for 30–35 minutes, until small cracks appear on the top and the middle of the pie doesn't jiggle when you shake the pan. Set on the counter to cool.

FOR THE CHOCOLATE FROSTING:

1. Melt all of the ingredients together in a lazy man's double boiler (see page 221), mixing until smooth. Place the melted chocolate in the freezer for 10 minutes. Remove from the freezer and beat, then return to the freezer for 10 more minutes. Repeat this process until the frosting has reached a creamy, spreadable consistency.

2. Once the pie is fully cooled, pipe the frosting around the edge and decorate with Rainbow Coconut Sprinkles. Slice and serve.

(Per serving) Calories: 112 | Fat: 9g | Sodium: 134mg
Carbs: 16g | Fiber: 3g | Sugar: 16g | Protein: 5g

QUICK TIP

Last week a friend of mine texted that she would be stopping by in an hour and that she hoped I would have some kind of healthy dessert ready—hint hint. I immediately thought of this recipe for Brownie Pie, but in the time crunch I decided to spread the batter over a parchment paper-lined rimmed baking sheet and baked for only 15–20 minutes in one big piece. It turned out perfect and was coming out of the oven just as she walked in. So if you're having a #ChocolateEmergency, and don't care if the brownie isn't in a pretty pie shape, give this brownie express method a try!

RAINBOW COCONUT SPRINKLES

prep time: 20 minutes ● *dehydrating time:* 6 hours ● *makes:* 1 cup

Did ya know that it's possible to create beautifully colorful sprinkles with 100 percent natural ingredients? My daughter, Chloe, loves using sprinkles to decorate homemade treats, which has been a point of contention for us because I know how toxic and harmful the ingredients in store-bought sprinkles are.

Now, using these Rainbow Coconut Sprinkles, Chloe is able to sprinkle her little heart out, and I rest easy knowing she's not taking in any harmful dyes or artificial ingredients.

I like to make a big batch of these sprinkles to store in the freezer in a zip-top bag. That way, whenever there's an opportunity to add a sprinkle of color to something, it's as easy as reaching into the freezer.

Ingredients

1 cup unsweetened, shredded coconut, divided

1½ teaspoons powdered stevia, divided

2 teaspoons beet juice

2 teaspoons carrot juice

⅛ teaspoon ground turmeric

2 teaspoons spinach juice

4 teaspoons red cabbage juice, divided

¼ teaspoon baking soda

Steps

1. In 6 small bowls, combine the following:

   - • • Red: 2 tablespoons shredded coconut + ¼ teaspoon powdered stevia + the beet juice

   - • • Orange: 2 tablespoons shredded coconut + ¼ teaspoon powdered stevia + the carrot juice

   - • • Yellow: 2 tablespoons shredded coconut + ¼ teaspoon powdered stevia + the ground turmeric

   - • • Green: 2 tablespoons shredded coconut + ¼ teaspoon powdered stevia + the spinach juice

   - • • Blue: 2 tablespoons shredded coconut + ¼ teaspoon powdered stevia + 2 teaspoons red cabbage juice + ¼ teaspoon baking soda

   - • • Purple: 2 tablespoons shredded coconut + ¼ teaspoon powdered stevia + 2 teaspoons red cabbage juice

2. Line 2 or 3 dehydrator trays with parchment paper and spread out the colored coconut, keeping the colors separate, and the remaining uncolored coconut. Dehydrate at 95°F for about 6 hours, until fully dried. Store in a zip-top bag in the freezer.

(Per 1 tablespoon) Calories: 13 | Fat: 1g | Sodium: 16mg
Carbs: 1g | Fiber: 0g | Sugar: 0g | Protein: 0g

QUICK TIP

These Rainbow Coconut Sprinkles can be made in either a dehydrator or the oven. I wrote the recipe for a dehydrator, simply because I have a large one that holds eight large trays, so it's convenient for me to use this rather than tying up my oven. But don't go out and purchase a dehydrator if you don't already have one. Simply put your oven on the very lowest setting and decrease the dehydration time. Watch the coconut sprinkles closely to ensure that they don't become toasted—the golden tinting from toasting diminishes the bright colors that make these sprinkles fun.

CANDIED PECANS

prep time: 5 minutes ● *cooking time:* 7 minutes
makes: 1 cup

What's life without the occasional handful of salty, sweet Candied Pecans?

Throw a handful into your salad, chop them and sprinkle over **COCONUT MILK ICE CREAM** (page 207), or eat them by the handful . . .

Ingredients

1 tablespoon coconut oil

1 cup roughly chopped pecans

¼ cup coconut palm sugar

⅛ teaspoon sea salt

Steps

In a small skillet, melt the coconut oil over low heat. Add the pecans and cook, stirring constantly, for 3 minutes. Add the coconut palm sugar and continue to cook, stirring constantly, for about 4 minutes, until the coconut palm sugar has melted and the pecans are golden. Remove from the heat and sprinkle with the salt. Store leftovers in an airtight container in the fridge for up to 2 weeks.

(Per 2 tablespoons) Calories: 128 | Fat: 11g | Sodium: 44mg
Carbs: 7g | Fiber: 1g | Sugar: 5g | Protein: 2g

QUICK TIP

Don't be alarmed when some of the melted coconut palm sugar clumps up, but be sure to quickly remove the pan from the heat when this happens. Just chop the clumps up with the pecans—they're like candy!

CINNAMON AND SUGAR ALMONDS

prep time: 5 minutes ● *cooking time:* 10 minutes
makes: 4 cups

One of my goals when giving up refined sugar was to create a cane sugar–free recipe for each and every sweet treat that I missed.

At the top of the list were toffee almonds—you know, the ones with the crunchy toffee shell on the nuts? I used to looooove those, and I knew there had to be a way to create that same sinfully sweet and crunchy snacking experience using coconut palm sugar.

And I was right! These Cinnamon and Sugar Almonds are so incredibly easy to make (they don't even require an oven) that they may just be the perfect snack. I also love packaging these up as a gift. Use a decorative bag tied with a ribbon or fill a cute jar and add a fancy label. They travel well, keep for a long time, and are always warmly received.

 Ingredients

**1 cup coconut palm
   sugar**

¹/₂ cup water

4 cups raw almonds

**1 tablespoon ground
   cinnamon**

1 teaspoon sea salt

Steps

1. Line a large rimmed baking sheet with wax paper and set aside.

2. In a large skillet, combine the coconut sugar and water over medium heat. Bring to a boil, add the almonds, and continue to cook, stirring often, until the liquid has completely evaporated, about 5 minutes.

3. Stir in the cinnamon and salt, evenly coating the almonds. Spread the almonds over the prepared baking sheet and allow to dry for 30 minutes. Store in an airtight container in the fridge for up to 2 weeks.

(Per ½ cup) Calories: 302 | Fat: 20g | Sodium: 235mg
Carbs: 25g | Fiber: 6g | Sugar: 17g | Protein: 9g

HEALTHY EATING TIP

You're not perfect, none of us is, so build some flexibility into your new diet. Rather than getting caught in a game of all-or-nothing, allow yourself some wiggle room. If you eat wholesome 80 percent of the time, then you'll lose weight and will make great strides toward the goals that you've set for yourself.

VANILLA PUDDING

prep time: 15 minutes ● *chilling time:* 2 hours ● *serves:* 4

Here's a simple pudding recipe you're bound to love. It's creamy and comforting and the perfect replacement for traditional pudding made with dairy and refined sugar. The first spoonful will have you smiling.

I could eat a huge bowl of this sweet vanilla pudding. (Notice the spoon in the photo? That's me about to take a bite . . .) Seriously, hold me back!

Ingredients

1 (13.7-ounce) can full-fat coconut milk

3 tablespoons raw honey

10 drops liquid stevia

pinch of sea salt

¼ teaspoon lemon juice

2 teaspoons vanilla extract

2 teaspoons gelatin powder

4 teaspoons dark chocolate shavings, for garnish

Steps

1. In a saucepan, combine the coconut milk, honey, stevia, salt, lemon juice, and vanilla over medium-low heat. Whisk continuously as the mixture warms, keeping it from boiling.

2. After 10 minutes, sprinkle the gelatin over the heated mixture so it can bloom and soften, about 5 minutes. Whisk the gelatin into the pudding and continue whisking over medium-low heat for 5 minutes, being careful not to let the mixture boil.

3. Divide the pudding among 4 bowls and place in the fridge to chill for 2 hours before serving. Garnish with the chocolate shavings.

(Per serving) Calories: 204 | Fat: 13g | Sodium: 98mg
Carbs: 17g | Fiber: 3g | Sugar: 15g | Protein: 3g

HEALTHY EATING TIP

Do you have dreams of one day being fit and healthy? Or do you have goals? There's a big difference between a goal and a dream. A dream is a hope and a wish. A goal is a specific, measurable promise with a deadline. Which do you think is more powerful?

SALTED PUDDING POPS

prep time: 10 minutes ● *chilling time:* 1 hour 30 minutes ● *makes:* 8 pops

I made these Salted Pudding Pops, gave one to each of my kids, and played a fun little game. It was called "Guess What Fruit or Veggie Is in the Pudding Pop." Maybe you've heard of it? No? Well, it's a good one.

They each wrote down their ideas of what was in this tasty pop, all the while licking and nibbling away. Their ideas were: banana, dates, zucchini (spelled "zukeeni"), and squash. But they were pretty much grasping at straws because all these cold treats taste like . . . pudding pops. With no trace of fruits or veggies.

When I told them what the ingredient was (AVOCADO!), they were blown away. And then they asked for another pop.

If you don't have eight ice pop molds, you'll need eight 4-ounce wax paper cups and eight flat Popsicle sticks.

Ingredients

FOR THE PUDDING:

12 dates, pitted and soaked in hot water for 15 minutes

3 avocados

$^1/_2$ cup unsweetened cocoa powder

2 tablespoons raw honey, melted

1 teaspoon vanilla extract

FOR THE CHOCOLATE SHELL:

$^3/_4$ cup unsweetened chocolate pieces

20 drops liquid stevia

2 tablespoons raw honey

1 tablespoon coconut oil

coarse sea salt, for garnish

Steps

FOR THE PUDDING:

1. Drain the dates, discarding the soaking liquid, and peel the thick date skins—they should flake off easily.

2. In a food processor, combine the dates, avocado flesh, cocoa powder, honey, and vanilla. Process until very smooth, wiping down the sides of the food processor every few minutes. This can take up to 10 minutes, so be patient.

3. Divide the pudding mixture among 8 ice pop molds or wax paper cups. Insert a Popsicle stick into each pudding cup and place them in the freezer for an hour.

FOR THE CHOCOLATE SHELL:

In the meantime, melt the chocolate shell ingredients, except the salt, in a lazy man's double boiler (see page 221), mixing until smooth. Remove the frozen pudding pops from their molds. Dip the pops into the melted chocolate mixture until fully coated. Sprinkle with salt and return to the freezer for 30 minutes, until frozen through.

(Per pop) Calories: 280 | Fat: 10g | Sodium: 87mg
Carbs: 31g | Fiber: 10g | Sugar: 15g | Protein: 9g

HEALTHY EATING TIP

Today, avocados are widely recognized as a superfood, which is a big change from the bad rap that avocados had back in the 90s when we were all afraid of fat. The monounsaturated fatty acid found in avocados is heart-healthy and beneficial. There's also more potassium in a serving of avocado than in bananas! So pass the avocado . . .

KAHLÚA SHAKE

prep time: 3 weeks + 10 minutes ● *serves:* 2

We started this book with a tall glass of green juice—as I like to start my day—and we shall end with a tall glass of Kahlúa Shake—which is how I choose to end my day, if I'm lucky enough.

What makes this shake a healthier alternative to a good old-fashioned Mud Slide at your local diner?

First, it's completely dairy-free. Instead of ice cream, heavy cream, and whipped cream, we are using coconut water and some **COCONUT WHIPPED CREAM** (page 237) made from coconut milk.

Second, while our Kahlúa Shake is creamy and dreamy and sweet, it's also hiding two full scoops of egg white protein, which means that you're fueling up on high-quality protein while you indulge.

Third, traditional Kahlúa contains corn syrup (EWWWWW!), and you know how I feel about corn syrup. Our Kahlúa is made with coconut palm sugar, so that even our indulgence is 100 percent wholesome and nutritious!

When you stop eating junk, you stop craving junk. When you stop drinking Oreo Cookie Shakes from the Jack in the Box drive-thru, you stop craving Oreo Cookie Shakes from the Jack in the Box drive-thru. When you start drinking this Kahlúa Shake for dessert, you start craving this Kahlúa Shake for dessert.

Ingredients

FOR THE KAHLÚA:

3 cups grain-free vodka

1¼ cups dark rum

1½ cups coconut palm sugar

¾ cup whole coffee beans

1 vanilla bean

1 tablespoon cocoa nibs

FOR THE KAHLÚA SHAKE:

1 frozen banana

1 cup ice cubes

1 cup coconut water or coconut milk

¼ cup Kahlúa (see above)

2 scoops high-quality chocolate egg white protein

dark chocolate (73% cacao content), melted

COCONUT WHIPPED CREAM **(page 237)**

Steps

FOR THE KAHLÚA:

Combine all of the ingredients in a jar with a secure lid. Place in a dark spot where it won't be disturbed for 3 weeks.

FOR THE KAHLÚA SHAKE:

1. Combine the banana, ice cubes, coconut water, and Kahlúa in a high-speed blender. Blend on high until creamy and smooth.

2. Top with melted dark chocolate and Coconut Whipped Cream. Throw in a fun straw, sit back, take a sip, and enjoy!

(Per serving) Calories: 235 | Fat: 12g | Sodium: 121mg
Carbs: 24g | Fiber: 4g | Sugar: 11g | Protein: 25g

QUICK TIP

It's always a good idea to keep bananas in the freezer for wholesome shakes such as this. I usually have a bunch or two out on the counter, and as soon as I see any getting soft and brown, I freeze them. When you want to make this shake or any blended drink, simply run the banana under warm water for a few seconds, then carefully use a sharp knife to remove the frozen banana peel. Break the banana in half and throw it into the blender.

CONCLUSION:
I HAVE A DREAM

I have a dream that one day we will rise up and live out the true meaning of a nutritious, life-promoting diet.

I have a dream that one day obesity and weight-related disease will become an anomaly and no longer the norm.

I have a dream that one day the toxic, processed foods that rob our bodies of health will be replaced with real, wholesome, synergistic foods that fill us with vitality and life.

I have a dream that my future grandchildren will one day live in a world where childhood obesity does not threaten to stifle the length and quality of their lives, but rather where good nutrition is plentiful and young bodies are vibrantly strong.

I have a dream today!

I have a dream that one day, we will regularly sit down together in our homes to enjoy lovingly prepared, nutritiously dense, generously flavored meals, in lieu of nutritionally bankrupt fast-food takeout.

I have a dream that one day menu planning will be simply automatic, done-for-us, and never again will we be caught off-guard by that inevitable question, "What's for dinner?"

I have a dream that one day weekly grocery lists will be generated in one click and never again will we resort to scribbled lists and forgotten ingredients.

I have a dream that one day our palates will be tickled and excited by a plethora of new flavorful recipes and never again will we resort to boring, tasteless, and repeated meals.

I have a dream that one day we will have a place to call home in our healthy eating journey, a place to be supported, inspired, encouraged, and equipped to succeed in not only restoring our health, our weight, and our energy, but also in motivating us to reach higher, to live fuller, and to dream bigger.

Come visit me at RealHealthyRecipes.com to see how I'm realizing this dream . . .

INDEX

Orange Marmalade, in Broccoli and
Almond Cauliflower Rice, 170–171
Oranges, in Your Daily Green Juice,
18–19
Oregano
in Best French Fries, 68
in Butternut Squash Spaghetti, 118–119
in Crispy Fish, 137
in Faux Fried Cauliflower, 70–71
in Garlic Herb Chicken Tenders, 94–95
in Quinoa Walnut Balls, 74–75
in Winter Quinoa Salad with Pomegranate
Dressing, 176–177
Oven-Steamed Beets, 193

P
Pancetta, in Stuffed Cabbage, 114–115
Paprika
in Bean-Less Pork Sausage Chili On Purple
Sweet Potato, 128–129
in Best French Fries, 68
in Butternut Squash Spaghetti, 118–119
in Cheesy Sauce, 200
in Fancy Cheese Ball, 64–65
in Faux Fried Cauliflower, 70–71
in Hamburger Casserole, 120–121
in Pizza-Stuffed Chicken, 98–99
Parsley
in Balsamic Mushrooms, 166–167
in Breakfast Pizza, 32–33
in Cauliflower Couscous, 168–169
in Cauliflower Steaks with Pickle Pesto,
90–91
in Chicken Soup with Quinoa and Roasted
Red Peppers, 162–163
in Crab Cake Eggs Benedict, 26–27
in Garlic Herb Chicken Tenders, 94–95
in Hamburger Casserole, 120–121
in Quinoa Egg Muffins, 34–35
in Roasted Carrots, 190–191
in Stuffed Cabbage, 114–115
in Stuffed Pitas with Tahini Sauce, 88–89
in Stuffed Zucchini, 110–111
in Winter Quinoa Salad with Pomegranate
Dressing, 176–177
in Your Daily Green Juice, 18–19
Parsnips
in Bacon Brussels Sprout Hash with Fried
Egg, 25
in Best French Fries, 68
in Maple Apple Brisket with Garlic Mashed
Root Veggies, 124–125
in Roasted Veggie Pockets, 86–87
in Stuffed Pitas with Tahini Sauce, 88–89
Pasta Sauce, in Pizza Casserole, 122–123
Peanut Butter
in Chocolate Peanut Butter Cookies, 214–215
in Cookie Dough Bonbons, 220–221
in Homemade Peanut Butter Cups, 226–227
in Monster Cookies, 218–219
Peanuts, in Chocolate Peanut Butter
Cookies, 214–215
Pear Cobbler with Balsamic Syrup,
206–207
Pears
in Field Greens and Pear Salad with Balsamic
Dressing, 184–185
in Pear Cobbler with Balsamic Syrup,
206–207
in Thanksgiving Fruit Salad, 208–209
Peas, in Veggie Stir-Fried Rice, 172
Pecan-Crusted Sea Bass, 138–139

Pecans
in Apple Spice Muffins, 40–41
in Candied Pecans, 242
in Chocolate Kale Chips, 152–153
in Chocolate Truffles, 224–225
in Field Greens and Pear Salad with
Balsamic Dressing, 184–185
in Gingersnaps, 216–217
in Harvest Nut Pancakes, 54–55
in Mini Cheesecakes with Chocolate Crust,
234–235
in Pecan-Crusted Sea Bass, 138–139
in Real Healthy Snickers Bars, 228–229
in Rosemary Pistachio Crisps, 66–67
in Rustic Pumpkin Pie, 236–237
in Stuffed Cabbage, 114–115
in Zucchini Muffins, 36–37
Pepitas
in Pumpkin Bread, 44–45
in Roasted Carrots, 190–191
in Rosemary Pistachio Crisps, 66–67
Pepperoni
in Pizza Casserole, 122–123
in Pizza-Stuffed Chicken, 98–99
Persimmons, in Thanksgiving Fruit
Salad, 208–209
Pickled Deviled Eggs, 80–81
Pickled Eggs, Beet Salad with, 182–183
Pickled Sweet Cherry Peppers, in
Broccoli and Almond Cauliflower
Rice, 170–171
Pickled Vegetables
in Faux Fried Cauliflower, 70–71
in Stuffed Pitas with Tahini Sauce, 88–89
Pickles
in Cauliflower Steaks with Pickle Pesto,
90–91
in Hamburger Casserole, 120–121
Pine Nuts, in BLT Pasta Salad, 186–187
Pineapple
in Aloha Meatballs with Pineapple, 78–79
in Thanksgiving Fruit Salad, 208–209
Pistachios
in Beet Salad with Pickled Eggs, 182–183
in Chocolate Truffles, 224–225
in Roasted Carrots, 190–191
in Rosemary Pistachio Crisps, 66–67
Pizza Casserole, 122–123
Pizza Kale Chips, 150–151
Pizza Sauce, in Pizza-Stuffed
Chicken, 98–99
Pizza-Stuffed Chicken, 98–99
Plantain Chips, 160
Pomegranates
in Stuffed Pitas with Tahini Sauce, 88–89
in Thanksgiving Fruit Salad, 208–209
in Winter Quinoa Salad with Pomegranate
Dressing, 176–177
Poppy Seeds
in Everything Crackers, 146–147
in Kale Salad with Poppy Seed Dressing,
180–181
Pork, Ground, in Chinese Noodle Bowl,
130–131
Pork Loin, Apple and Ginger–Glazed,
126–127
Pork Sausage
in Aloha Meatballs with Pineapple, 78–79
in Bean-Less Pork Sausage Chili On Purple
Sweet Potato, 128–129
in Butternut Squash Spaghetti, 118–119
in Pizza Casserole, 122–123

Pumpkin, in Rustic Pumpkin Pie,
236–237
Pumpkin Bread, 44–45
Pumpkin Pie Spice, in Rustic
Pumpkin Pie, 236–237
Pumpkin Puree, in Pumpkin Bread,
44–45
Pumpkin Seeds, in Cajun-Roasted
Pumpkin Seeds, 154–155
Purple Sweet Potatoes, Bean-Less Pork
Sausage Chili On, 128–129

Q
Quinoa
in Chicken Soup with Quinoa and Roasted
Red Peppers, 162–163
in Chorizo-Stuffed Peppers, 132–133
in Inside-Out Stuffed Cabbage, 112–113
in Quinoa Egg Muffins, 34–35
in Quinoa Energy Bars, 46–47
in Quinoa Walnut Balls, 74–75
in Stuffed Zucchini, 110–111
in Summer Quinoa Salad, 174–175
in Winter Quinoa Salad with Pomegranate
Dressing, 176–177
Quinoa Egg Muffins, 34–35
Quinoa Energy Bars, 46–47
Quinoa Walnut Balls, 74–75

R
Rainbow Coconut Sprinkles, 240–241
in Brownie Pie, 238–239
in Chocolate-Glazed Doughnuts, 50–51
Raisins
in Inside-Out Stuffed Cabbage, 112–113
in Quinoa Energy Bars, 46–47
in Roasted Carrots, 190–191
in Rosemary Pistachio Crisps, 66–67
in Stuffed Cabbage, 114–115
in Stuffed Zucchini, 110–111
in Walnut Raisin Rolls, 158–159
in Zucchini Muffins, 36–37
Raspberries, in Mini Chocolate
Layer Cakes, 232–233
Real Healthy Snickers Bars, 228–229
Red Cabbage Juice, in Rainbow
Coconut Sprinkles, 240–241
Red Chiles
in Chorizo-Stuffed Peppers, 132–133
in Spicy Coconut Curry Soup, 161
Red Curry Paste, in Moroccan Turkey
Burgers with Carrot Slaw, 108–109
Red Pepper Flakes, in Pizza Kale Chips,
150–151
Roasted Carrots, 190–191
Roasted Garlic White Bean Hummus,
62–63
in Chicken Soup with Quinoa and Roasted
Red Peppers, 162–163
Roasted Veggie Pockets, 86–87
Rose Apple Pastries, 212–213
Rosemary
in Best French Fries, 68
in Easy Spaghetti, 116–117
in Maple Apple Brisket with Garlic Mashed
Root Veggies, 124–125
in Moroccan-Spiced Butternut Squash,
198–199
in Roasted Veggie Pockets, 86–87
in Rosemary Pistachio Crisps, 66–67
Rosemary Pistachio Crisps, 66–67
Rum, in Kahlúa Shake, 248–249